DIAGHILEV AND FRIENDS

DIAGHILEV AND FRIENDS

HAUS PUBLISHING
LONDON

Copyright © Joy Melville 2009

First published in Great Britain in 2009 by
Haus Publishing, 70 Cadogan Place, London SW1X AH

The moral rights of the author have been asserted

A CIP catalogues record for this book is available from the British Library

ISBN 978-1905791-91-0

Typeset by MacGuru Ltd
info@macguru.org.uk

Printed in China by SC (Sang Choy) International Ltd.

Contents

Introduction

'**A**stonish me' Diaghilev famously told the French poet and playwright Jean Cocteau when Cocteau asked him what kind of work he wanted from him. But it was to be Diaghilev who astonished the world with his vision.

Many books have been written about Diaghilev and the Ballets Russes: about the variety of ballets he staged, the techniques of his choreographers and dancers, his innovative and unerring selection of painters and composers. My intention is to look at Diaghilev the man: what moulded him, motivated him, amused him, angered him, inspired him? I have also explored the flamboyant, talented and creative people in his circle, who coloured his life as he coloured theirs.

I have concentrated on certain aspects of Diaghilev's life, like the attitudes towards homosexuality which he, as a young homosexual, encountered first in Russia in the 19th century and then later in Europe where his entourage was mainly homosexual; and the aftermath of the first world war, when Diaghilev was struggling to re-establish his ballet company in a Europe decimated first by the war then by Spanish flu. I have also laid importance on Diaghilev's relationship with Nijinsky and Nijinsky's sad decline into schizophrenia. Finally, there is the gaiety of Paris after the first world war, when Diaghilev was a focal, charismatic character and the city was the artistic hub of Europe.

According to the dancer Serge Lifar, Diaghilev told him 'I, personally, can be of no interest to anyone: it is not my life that is interesting, but my work.' And indeed Diaghilev was the dominant father figure of the Ballets Russes from its inception in 1909 until his death in 1929 – admired, feared, loved, hated. He was jealous and possessive, full of Russian temperament – thrashing the furniture with his stick if he found his lovers unfaithful. Yet he could show touching tenderness. In the last year of his life, when he was ill, delibitated and walking with difficulty, he went to watch the ballerina Tamara Karsavina, with whom he had worked for many years, and told her he had left his bed to see her: 'Judge of my love.'

The King of Spain once laughingly asked Diaghilev, 'What is it then that you do in this troupe? You don't direct, you don't dance, you don't play the piano, what is it you do?' Diaghilev replied: 'Your Majesty, I am like you. I don't work, I don't do anything, but I am indispensable.'

1

The Boy from Perm

'At first we found his presence only just tolerable and nobody took any notice of his opinions ... He showed himself incapable of following our lectures closely or taking part in any aesthetic, philosophical or religious discussions, and showed it so obviously, yawning unrestrainedly, to make clear how remote and boring it all was that at times we became very angry. I used to shout and stamp at him, accusing him of being a thick-skinned Philistine ... Diaghilev took all this abuse very meekly, without any protest, and would even try to reform himself ... but all useless.'[1]

How did the Sergei Pavlovitch Diaghilev of later years, the knowledgeable, sophisticated and brilliant impresario, emerge from the chrysalis of this eighteen-year-old Philistine? This view of him was by Alexandre Benois, a visionary art student, who headed an artistic circle of students at St Petersburg University in 1889, the year Diaghilev enrolled there to study music. The young man from Perm hoped to become a composer, though – in Benois' opinion – his musical views were muddled and inconsistent.

Benois was passionate about music and

Diaghilev at eighteen, in his school uniform. He matriculated that year and left Perm to study in St Petersburg

the theatre. Gentle, quiet and rather short, he sported a pince nez. He was the son of the court architect and portrait painter Nikolai Benois and his mother, Camille, was the daughter of Alverto Cavos, the architect of the Marinsky Theatre in St Petersburg.

Diaghilev may have looked a provincial, lacking the young-man-about-town polish of some of his fellow students, but he came from a highly cultured, intensely musical background. He was born on March 19th 1872, in the province of Novgorod, where his father, a witty and handsome young officer and accomplished musician, was stationed with his regiment in the Selistchev barracks.

Diaghilev was fortunate in his stepmother a kind and cultured woman who recognised his early musical ability

His mother, Evgenia Nikolaevna, died giving birth to him – according to Diaghilev because of his large head – and two years later his father, now Squadron Commander of the Imperial Guards in St Petersburg, married again.

His second wife was Elena Valerianovna Panaeva and Diaghilev was to say that he never met another woman like her. Her brother was a well-known singer and her father bankrupted himself building a theatre for private opera. A kind and cultured woman, Elena recognised her stepson's musical ability and encouraged him to take piano lessons.

He was ten when the family moved to the provincial town of Perm, a czarist administrative centre on the borderlands of Siberia. The reason for the move was his father's mounting debts. His grandfather on his father's side was descended from ancient Russian nobility and only agreed to settle his son's debts if he and his wife and children returned to the family home in Perm.

His father and stepmother loved music and both had excellent singing voices. They held regular musical evenings at which they both sang – his father knowing whole operas by heart – and also hosted literary evenings. Indeed, the house was a cultural centre for the whole district and was nicknamed Perm's Athens. It was surrounded by rivers, forests and vast plains, leaving Diaghilev with a love of his country which vitally influenced his later artistic life.

As a boy he went to the 'Gymnasium' at Perm, where one of his classmates remembered his large head and expressive face. 'In talking, he would

Diaghilev (right) with his two step-brothers, father and stepmother. The latter two were accomplished singers and performed at the weekly concerts they held at home

frequently give an abrupt shake to his hand, and end with a snap of the fingers.'[2] Diaghilev had no particular academic success, but his home background ensured he grew up imbued with classical music. He sight-read easily and music had an emotional effect on him. Inevitably he chose it as his career, intending to become a composer.

In the summer of 1890, having passed his matriculation, the 18 year old Diaghilev left for university at St Petersburg – a tall, bulky young man, with his family characteristics of a protruding jaw and thick underlip.

His childhood had ended the previous year, when his father urged him to get some sexual experience. It was with a prostitute and a resounding failure, giving him 'a horror almost amounting to a phobia, and to the end of his life he mentioned it with extreme disgust.'[3] This was probably because he contracted an infection which, though quickly cured, revolted Diaghilev who had a lifelong fear of illness.

He had corresponded over the years with his cousin, the cultured Dima (Dimitri) Filosofov, who was the same age as Diaghilev and lived with his wealthy family in an apartment in St Petersburg. Filosofov had gone to the expensive May's private school in St Petersburg, rather than to a government school. His intimate circle of friends there included Alexandre Benois, Valechka (Walter) Nouvel, Kostia Somov, Nikolai Skalon and Gregor Kalin.

Diaghilev's intention was to study music at the university and he was invited to stay with the Filosofovs, joining them at their country estate in the summer of 1890. Diaghilev and Filosofov then left on a short European tour before the university term began, visiting (as cheaply as possible) Warsaw, Berlin, Paris, Venice, Florence, Rome, Geneva and Vienna and going to theatres, operas, museums and art galleries. Diaghilev heard *Lohengrin* for the first time and became besotted by Wagner, then in turn besotted by the art in Florence. The two tall, well-built young men formed what Benois called a 'heartfelt friendship', one of Diaghilev's most prized possessions after their trip being a photograph of the two of them reclining in a Venetian gondola.

Their love affair was to last years and they parted amicably enough until in 1905 Diaghilev suspected that Filosofov had designs on his current lover, a Polish student called Vicki. Learning that Filosofov was dining out, he went to the restaurant and caused a terrible scene. It was the end of their friendship.

Diaghilev, regarded as an artistically sophisticated figure at school, had to work hard to establish his artistic credentials in St Petersburg. Without Filosofov's guiding hand he might well not have been accepted by Filosofov's urbane, cultivated group. Thickset, plump, with sensuous red lips and perfect white teeth, Diaghilev looked a sturdy provincial and shocked many of the group with his uncouth manners and primitive views. However, he was tolerated as Filosofov's cousin and by degrees was accepted into the group.

For Russian schoolboys at the end of the 19th century, sport was frowned on and emphasis laid on intellectual ability. Instead of playing a game of football, young students would form discussion groups and argue heatedly about art and music. The group around Filosofov remained friends on leaving school and lightheartedly called themselves 'The Society for Self Improvement'. High-spirited and witty, they formed an artistic circle and met several times a week at Benois' house, as his father had an excellent library.

There was no laid-down doctrine: the aims were aesthetic and artistic rather than moral. Benois, the president, was the central figure of the group and from school his passions had lain in art, Nouvel's in music and Filosofov's in literature. Next to Benois, Filosofov was one of the most active members of

the group. Later he became involved in religious mysticism and faded from the circle.

Benois met the 24 year old painter Levushka Rosenberg (Leon Bakst) in the spring of 1890 and invited him to join the circle. Bakst was studying at the Academy of Art and earning a little money: he was the only professional in the circle. A remarkably good-humoured young man, he was clean-shaven and wiry, with carefully coiffed auburn hair and moustache, a lively expression and very short-sighted bright blue eyes, covered by gold-rimmed spectacles. He used perfume and was teased by the group about his liking for elegant clothes.

Diaghilev remained greatly under the influence of his cousin, behaving modestly enough, but over the next few years he began to flex his muscles and antagonised many of the group by his scarcely masked arrogance and air of grandeur. Nevertheless, from the start of his involvement with the St Petersburg group, Diaghilev listened and learned. Before travelling in Europe

Alexandre Benois, in a portrait by Bakst, was one of Diaghilev's inner circle of friends

he had rarely entered a museum or art exhibition, but now his artistic and musical knowledge started to become prodigious.

Gradually, the cultured Filosofov family had an effect on Diaghilev and he became more sophisticated. Surprisingly, neither he nor his cousin were interested in current politics in Russia despite the underlying revolutionary fervour.

He also had little interest in ballet. He had never seen a ballet before arriving in St Petersburg and dismissed it as a rather alien, unworthy art. Although he enjoyed opera, in the 1890s this was often thinly attended. The Russian actor and producer Stanislavsky (the stage name for Konstantin Sergeivitch Alexeyev) remembered the way men 'would play cards all evening while the performance was in progress and come to the theatre for the sole purpose of hearing some renowned tenor's C-sharp.' Until they turned up, the front rows of the stalls were half empty, but 'shortly before the famous note was due, noises would erupt accompanied by the sound of voices and the creaking of furniture.' After the singer achieved the note, he was applauded and then the noises were repeated as the clubmen went off to finish their game of cards.'[4]

The art of ballet was exported from Italy during the rule of Catherine de Medici (1519–89) to the French court, where under Louis XIV (1638–1715) it became a major art form. Ballet was first seen in Russia under Peter the Great (1672–1725) but it was in the 19th century that Tchaikovsky's music for *Swan Lake* (1876) and *The Nutcracker* (1892) laid the foundation for Russia's stunning supremacy in this art.

Until the late 19th century ballet followers were often dismissed as cranks. And as ballet dresses were at the time worn to the ground, the idea of scant ballet costumes was not approved. Diaghilev was not alone in disliking the sight of women's thighs in short classical tutus and only when fashions changed in the 1920s and women's figures became more boyish did he sanction the wearing of tights.

Bakst's portrait of Dima Filosofov, Diaghilev's cousin in St Petersburg. The two young men had what was delicately called 'a heartfelt relationship'

On the 3rd January 1890 there was a revival of the ballet *La Belle au Bois Dormant (The Sleeping Beauty)*, with music by Tchaikovsky. Benois liked ballet and persuaded Nouvel to attend it with him. They were wildly enthusiastic about it, saw it six times in a week, and when the eighteen-year-old Diaghilev spent the summer that year with his cousin Dima, he heard endless descriptions of it and it roused his interest. The germ of the Ballets Russes might have formed then, as the group's interest in theatrical performance ultimately extended to producing ballets.

Diaghilev was proud of his ancestry, often claiming that he was descended

on the wrong side of the blanket from Peter the Great. The two shared certain characteristics: they were both born leaders; had a love of power and an ability to detect people's weaknesses and play on these. The ballet critic Cyril Beaumont said that when Diaghilev was annoyed 'and his nostrils dilated and quivered, and his lips curved in a hard bitter line, he had – if you imagine his head crowned with a wig – a striking resemblance to Rastrelli's bust of Czar Peter the Great.'[5] Beaumont also made the point that both men could be obstinate and ruthless.

Diaghilev certainly aspired to be part of the social elite and Benois recalled his anxiety to be thought sophisticated. He dressed far more carefully than the rest of the group, but his society manners irritated them, as did his habit of making innumerable social calls and leaving cards everywhere. The group considered him a terrible fop and found it hard to take him seriously. Despite Diaghilev's social ambitions, Benois believed he was never really accepted by the St Petersburg society.

St Petersburg was a heady city for a provincial boy from Perm. Its beauty was mirrored in the low-banked, broad Neva river, the myriad small rivers and canals criss-crossing the city and the elegant colonnades, towers, turrets and cupolas: a far cry from the marshland on which thousands of workers, on the command of Peter the Great (1672–1725), first constructed the city. Its concept was based on the western architecture of that time. It was a fast growing city, swallowing up acres of desolate countryside. Extreme wealth and extreme poverty went hand in hand and this conflict produced a flood of diverse and vibrant art, fiction and music.

The wealthier citizenry copied European dress, but there the European look ended. In the winter, sleighs predominated; in the summer bearded coachmen with colourful head-gear drove droshkies. Summer also saw drivers in their bright red shirts walking alongside their carts – changing to sheepskin coats in winter.

The most spectacular sights in St Petersburg then were its brilliantly colourful marches. Everybody marched. There were the black and white plumed infantry, with their red-breasted uniforms on their way to change guard at the Winter Palace; there were bands with drum majors twirling their golden batons; and there were the spectacular funeral processions with their rows of black torch bearers, followed by a choir in gold-braided cassocks and the long-bearded clergy.

If the deceased was of Orthodox faith, a dray would be covered with a golden brocade canopy with ostrich feathers on the corners and in the centre a golden crown.

The hearse would be of shining gilt – as opposed to being completely black if another faith was involved. Finally, there were those who marched alongside the 'chariots of infamy' containing condemned criminals on their way to the pillory before their exile to Siberia.

There were also two giant and colourful fairs a year, where vast crowds thronged the dauntingly large ice switchbacks and clambered into equally giant swing boats. They were entertained by men with long flowing false beards and pale sheepskin coats. Benois said he drew on these visual impressions all his life and surely they must have had an effect on Diaghilev.

As well as the magnificent Winter and Summer Palaces, the three Imperial Theatres were also architecturally striking. The interiors of them were brilliantly decorated in white and gold and each had walls of brocade – blue for the Maryinsky, deep yellow for the Alexandrinsky and red for the Michailovsky. In each there was a blaze of lamps and chandeliers and every box had a small salon behind it for entertaining friends along with velvet ledges for ladies' fans, boxes of chocolates and marzipan. There was also a state opera house, Narodny Dom [The House of the People], but although an excellent company performed there, it was not considered smart.

Diaghilev came of age in 1890 and inherited £6,000 from his late mother, which allowed him to buy a small flat. He filled this with ornate, imposing furniture and paintings but no family photographs. The flat was near to the Faculty of Law at the university, where most of the group had enrolled.

As well as studying at the Faculty of Law, Diaghilev also attended the Conservatory of Music to learn musical theory. He showed some of his compositions to Rimsky-Korsakov, but the maestro was less than encouraging, telling him they were absurd. Diaghilev took immediate exception to this judgement, announcing in his own arrogant way that he believed he was gifted and that Rimsky-Korsakov would one day be ashamed of his opinions. In later years, Diaghilev must have taken a certain pleasure in ordering Rimsky-Korsakov to cut his own score for the ballet *Scheherazade*.

Diaghilev's baritone voice was being trained by a singer from an Italian opera company. He had no intention of making law his career, but meant to concentrate on his main interests: music, theatre and art. He had no artistic ambitions himself as he could neither paint nor sculpt, but he taught himself to appreciate the arts. He impressed the group by his speed in acquiring knowledge, particularly in becoming a connoisseur of Russian 18th century painters.

In 1892 he and his cousin went to Moscow for two weeks, visiting museums, art galleries and the theatre. They went to see Tolstoy and

Diaghilev started corresponding with the writer. Over the next few years he met Brahms and Verdi, Zola and the French composer, Chabrier.

The group found it convenient to congregate at Diaghilev's flat, near the university, for its weekly Monday meetings. They were now inured to Diaghilev's bravado and autocratic manner. Through a mutual love of music, Diaghilev and Walter Nouvel, another member of the group and the son of a rich merchant in St Petersburg, had become close friends, playing duets on the grand Bluthner piano sent from Diaghilev's home in Perm and giving impromptu concerts.

Nouvel was a clever, cheerful young man ('he makes one think of champagne'), who was highly opinionated and knew everyone in the musical world. He was a great connoisseur of music and could read a score with ease. He remained Diaghilev's lifelong friend and collaborator. Although not involved in the ballets, he saw to a great deal of correspondence and was nicknamed 'Foreign Minister' by Diaghilev.

Benois was none too enthusiastic about these concerts as he disliked Diaghilev's voice, complaining that it had 'an intense and piercing quality which might have done for the theatre but was intolerable in a room.' The group was indifferent to politics and careless of social conventions. Diaghilev's 'society manners' annoyed them. He made constant social calls, leaving his card, and in the theatre he would walk through the stalls 'with his enormous head thrown back in a lofty way,' only smiling charmingly or warmly greeting those who held potentially useful positions in society or in the Civil Service.

This combination of arrogance and charm served Diaghilev well both then and in the future as he pursued possible patrons. Throughout his life, his productions were always extremely expensive and he disregarded his budget. This meant that wealthy and sympathetic patrons were essential.

The young musician Nicolas Nabokov who was distantly related to Diaghilev (his stepfather's first cousin married Diaghilev's half brother) recalled seeing a photo of Diaghilev in the uniform of the university of St Petersburg. 'It showed a pale and slightly puffy face, but its traits were so well designed (especially the high arches of the eyebrows) that it looked delicate and surprisingly tender. It had two striking features: slightly protruding and sensuous lips and a large head totally out of proportion to the rest of the body.'[6]

Bronislava Nijinska, elder sister to the fabled dancer Vaslav Nijinsky, also recalled Diaghilev's 'big, almost square head, slightly flabby cheeks, and a full lower lip. In his big black eyes there was always a look of sadness, even when he smiled. The expression on his face was at once menacing and attractive – like a bulldog's.'[7]

Walter Nouvel remained Diaghilev's lifelong friend and collaborator

Diaghilev and Dima Filosofov went off to Europe again at the end of 1893 and stayed till early the next year. It was while travelling through southern Italy that the 22 year old Diaghilev became particularly interested in collecting 15th and 16th century furniture and he bought some Savonarola stools, a magnificent long table and some bronze vases and statuettes. His friends were greatly impressed when these arrived in St Petersburg.

Wanting to leave behind the last vestige of 'the boy from Perm', the 23 year old Diaghilev again set off to Europe in 1895 on what was virtually a 'grand tour'. He was intent on further educating himself artistically.

He wrote enthusiastically to his friends in St Petersburg from Antwerp in the June of that year about the literary, artistic and musical life he was leading, saying he had visited 24 museums and called on 14 painters in their studios. He impressed locals by emerging from the best hotels with his top hat, tailored clothes and eye glass. He went to Dieppe and acted the wealthy young Russian about town by wining and dining the literary and artistic set. It was paid for by the remains of his legacy.

Dieppe was becoming a highly fashionable bathing resort, with its gaming-tables, dancing-halls, vast flower gardens and concert hall. The surrounding bazaars had oriental domes, with colourful flags topping the pinnacles. During the season, from June to October, visitors added to the scene of gaiety. Jacques Emile Blanche, painter and young-man-about-town, whose villa in Dieppe acted as an artistic centre, entertained Sarah Bernhardt and Benoit Coquelin, the French actors, and the sculptor Auguste Rodin. He introduced Diaghilev to Charles Conder, the English-born Australian painter and lithographer, who worked in delicate water-colours on silk, and to the artist Aubrey Beardsley.

Diaghilev was particularly interested in Beardsley's *Masquerade* drawings, which encapsulated the artist's morbid and elusive spirit. Blanche believed these influenced Diaghilev, fanning his interest in anything fantastic and unorthodox. Matthew Sturgis, Beardsley's biographer, also thought that Beardsley's influence 'percolated Diaghilev's activities and flavoured some of Leon Bakst's early designs for the Ballets Russes, a telling link between Beardsley and the emerging modernist tradition.'[8]

Blanche did not think Diaghilev had any intention of being an impresario. He was just a young man of the world, an amateur of art. However, the trip crucially enabled Diaghilev to meet influential people in the world of the musical, literary and visual arts. He had a mania for making personal contact. Although when he was formulating his early ideas, he wrote to his friends about them, and also sent a multitude of cables or dropped reminder notes, he still preferred personal contact. Often rather than write to a colleague or friend he would make a lengthy journey to them in order to have an agreeable talk. His interest and emphasis was on meeting people and discussing ideas.

The letters he did write, however, were lively, expressive, full of projects and piercingly self-aware. He wrote to Alexandre Benois in 1897 to say, 'All my life, from age sixteen onward, I have done everything in defiance of everyone else ... society began to attack my vacuous outward appearance, my bombast, and my foppishness' and now 'everyone regards me as a scoundrel, a debauchee, a salesman – in brief, hell knows what.' He went on to say lightheartedly, 'I possess a certain boldness of spirit and the habit of spitting people in the eye' before admitting there were certain people, like Benois himself, whose judgement he accepted.

Such letters, along with a collection of other Russian writings by Diaghilev, impressed John E. Bowlt, a professor of Russian art and literature, who considers they 'reveal a perspicacious mind, a sophisticated wit [and] cultural concerns that encompassed literature, painting, industrial design, and museology, as well as opera and the ballet.'[9]

Although some friends put Diaghilev's gregariousness, love of meeting people and insatiable appetite for extending his circle of friends, down to his snobbish wish to meet celebrities, his social activities were the breath of life to Diaghilev. Throughout his life he was delightedly welcomed by unending new acquaintances. As Benois said of him, he 'was a great enchanter, a real *charmeur*. If he wanted something, for instance, it was almost impossible to resist the pressure he exerted, often very endearingly.'[10] Another friend, Prince Peter Lieven, agreed with this, believing 'his powers of persuasion arose from his intuitive understanding of people, from his grasp not only of their external character but of their innermost depths.[11]

When Diaghilev returned to St Petersburg late in 1895, he surprised his friends by being very smartly dressed, wearing a new and fashionable perfume, and presenting himself as a connoisseur of art. Writing from Europe about the paintings and other treasures he was bringing back, he suggested, only half jokingly, that a curator be appointed fo these new curiosities. His flat now stood out as a mecca of culture.

Benois thought that it looked as if he had at last begun to believe in his vocation. That year, Diaghilev assessed himself disparagingly, if lightheart-edly, in a letter to his stepmother:

'I am firstly a great charlatan, though with *brio*; secondly a great *charmeur*; thirdly, I have any amount of cheek; fourthly, I am a man with a great quantity of logic, but with very few principles; fifthly, I think I have no real gifts. All the same, I think I have just found my true vocation – being a Maecenas [a patron of literature or art]. I have all that is necessary save the money – *mais ca viendra*.'[12]

The university group continued to meet after graduation. Members came and went, but the nucleus remained the original four schoolfellows, Filosofov, Benois, Nouvel and Samov, along with Diaghilev and Bakst. The Frenchman Charles Birie and the half-English Nourok were now also members. Diaghilev had jettisoned his provincialism for a western gloss and was now one of the most forceful members of the group.

Art and westernisation bound the circle together. The twenty-four-year-old Diaghilev developed ambitions to be an art critic and some of his early articles surprised the group by their erudition, fervour and ruthlessness. Benois believed that Diaghilev's writings laid the foundation of his desire to educate public taste. Some of his art criticism appeared in the paper, *Novosti*, in 1896.

While at university, other members of the group had pursued their particular interests: Bakst produced a play and Benois and Nouvel together composed a musical drama. The whole group created a pantomime based on the story of *Daphnis and Chloe* – a spirited venture which contrasted with the despair of the author Anton Chekhov who, in 1896, rushed from the State Theatre of St Petersburg to walk the streets until the early hours after the disastrous first night of *The Seagull*, when the actors failed to understand its originality.

Diaghilev was now increasingly sure of his own judgement. In Europe he had discarded the last traces of provincialism, his visual memory was outstanding and he was constantly called on to attribute paintings. He now set about organising an exhibition in St Petersburg which celebrated British and German painters.

Opening in 1897 in the recently completed Baron Stieglitz's Museum, the intention was to show that the Russians had a cosmopolitan outlook and emphasise the close association between European and Russian art. The German painters included the group's favourites like Max Liebermann, with his scenes of working life. Diaghilev had visited London during his travels and been particularly impressed by the colourful Glasgow School of Painting. The British painters therefore included two of the 'Glasgow boys,' the portrait painters James Guthrie and James Lavery, who worked in Glasgow, though born in Belfast.

Diaghilev was now beginning to exhibit his entrepreneurial skills and brought his tremendous enthusiasm and extraordinary energy into organising a further exhibition, this time of past and present Russian and Finnish art. It opened at the Stieglitz Museum in 1897. His skilled touch was immediately evident. He had placed hothouse flowers throughout the museum and had invited most of the members of the Imperial family to the opening – an orchestra striking up on their entrance.

The exhibition successfully drew attention to the young Russian painters like Benois and Bakst. It included paintings by Valentin Serov, who was some seven years older than the rest of the group, and already had a reputation as an artist. His work enhanced the exhibition and the show was a magnificent success.

The four young men – Diaghilev, Filosofov, Benois and Nouvel – spent the summers of the late 1890s at the estate of Filosofov's aunt, Anna Pavlovna. She fiercely promoted women's liberation and was also a literary hostess whose salon in St Petersburg was visited by Dostoevsky and Turgenev. Revolution and populism were in the air and the group, although barely interested in politics, were alive with artistic ideas. Intent on spreading these they organised exhibitions and lectures.

The possibility of a magazine propagating their ideas and championing 'pure art', was discussed among the group, with the English art magazine *Studio* acting as a model. But although all the members were keenly interested, it was Diaghilev's enthusiasm which brought it to life. He had written to Benois in 1897 to say: 'I am full of projects – each more grandiose than the last. At present I am planning a magazine which would embrace all our artistic life – drawings and paintings would be shown in the illustrations. The articles would be outspoken and, finally, it would be linked with the new brand of industrial art which is developing in Moscow and in Finland.'[13].

In the autumn of 1898 this ambition became reality. The young men concerned were daring and arrogant and, intent on charting a new course, uninhibitedly launched their new publication, *Mir Iskussiva* (*World of Art*). The magazine was backed financially by two patrons who had been impressed by Diaghilev's organising abilities: the artist and collector, Princess Tenischeva (who was the publisher) and Savva Mamontov, a wealthy railway magnate who provided the financial backing. Mamontov also had a private opera company in Moscow, featuring Russian composers like Rimsky-Korsakov, Mussorgsky and Borodin. It was he who first suggested the idea of Russian seasons abroad, which Diaghilev later put into action.

One of Diaghilev's first acts was to commission D.S. MacColl, the Scottish painter and art historian, to write an article on Aubrey Beardsley, whose work was linked with the emerging European modernist movement.

For six years (1898–1904) the magazine was a beacon, an absolute necessity to painters, musicians and writers as it allowed them to read about, or write about, new ideas. It covered art, music, literature, drama, opera and ballet. Its slogan was 'art, pure and unfettered' and Diaghilev edited it in close collaboration with Filosofov, Benois, Bakst, Nouvel and Nourok. However it was Diaghilev's administrative, creative and entrepreneurial skill that moulded this talented but originally rather directionless group together.

Instead of just discussing ideas, Diaghilev got the group to work on solid projects as a team: 'Whilst Bakst drew a vignette, Diaghilev cut out photographs for the printing block, Filosofov acted as printer's devil, Benois corrected proofs, and somewhere in a corner Serov or Nourok wrote a trenchant article.'[14]

The group shared the same ideas as many of their fellows in Europe who followed the aesthetic belief, publicised in particular by Oscar Wilde, of 'art for art's sake.' But they thought ideas should be integrated into works of art. In *Natasha's Dance*, Orlando Figes stresses that the *Mir Iskussiva* group were dedicated to restoring an earlier ideal of beauty, making 'a cult of 18th century Petersburg. It was practically defined by nostalgia for a civilisation which they sensed was about to pass away.'[15]

Diaghilev turned his flat, which was on the top floor of a large house on the corner of Liteiny Prospekt and Simeonovskaia Street, into his editorial office. Liteiny Prospekt was one of the oldest streets in the city. The drawing room of the flat became Diaghilev's study and there he sat in an imposing armchair upholstered in velvet, with his black antique Italian table acting as his editorial desk. A large velvet Ottoman and gilded velvet armchairs, along with the Bluthner piano, Renaissance bronzes and autographed photographs of artists and musicians, completed the picture of a cosmopolitan savant. Indeed the whole group identified with the artistic ideas of the aristocracy.

The first issue of *Mir Iskussiva* was in full colour, with elegant print and elaborate woodcuts, and looked attractive and professional. The tone, as promised by Diaghilev, was challenging and included some vicious lampoons. It criticised the established artists of the day and the poor taste of the press and the public. The overall theme was Russian Art and the History of Russian Culture and it brought together many of Russia's contentious writers, poets, painters and musicians.

Mir Iskussiva was the first high quality art magazine in Russia and its appearance sparked off a whole series of art books with exceptional illustrations.

Diaghilev kept a firm hand on the tiller and although he consulted other members of the group, he never altered his decisions. Not unnaturally he had stopped singing and composing music as he hardly had time for either. As Benois recalled, 'the inspiration and fire which we professional artists expressed in our work was displayed by Diaghilev in the organising of everything in which we were associated ... He published books, edited the magazine ... the sphere of advertising and publicity was alien to us, whereas Diaghilev was marvellous in it ... '[16]

He had immense magnetism, zeal and bouts of craziness and gave the group working under him a great sense of adventure. He excelled in getting his own way, reproaching, pressurising or appealing to the conscience of

anyone not following the party line. He also had a highly developed sense for detecting new developments in the arts.

The daily editorial meetings were held from 4 pm to 7 pm. Diaghilev's old grey-haired nanny, Dunia, of whom he was extremely fond, was a key presence, presiding in her black lace cap over the hissing samovar. Jam, Russian sweets and *soushki* (biscuits in the shape of rings) contributed to the informality. Should ladies be present, the menu was extended to minced salt beef sandwiches. Diaghilev rarely entertained at home, preferring to take his friends out to lunch or dinner.

Leon Bakst, who painted the well-known portrait of Diaghilev with Dunia, complained that Diaghilev had posed 'disgustingly' for him that day, mincing around and pestering Bakst to make him look more refined and handsome. Bakst admitted to nearly attacking him with his brushes.

Yet it is Dunia, sitting quietly in peasant garb in the background, who catches the eye. She was a freed serf from his mother's family estate and from his birth had looked after the motherless Diaghilev. Because of his strong attachment to her, she accompanied him to St Petersburg where her duty was to prepare the afternoon and evening tea and look after the jam, that crucial part of Russian tea.

It was she who passed on to Diaghilev her strong peasant superstitions, which remained with him all his life. He was terrified of death, for instance, and no one dared even mention the word to him. He couldn't bear to be photographed and was horrified if someone left a hat on the table, which he thought would result in a loss of money, or on the bed, which he believed forecast ill-health.

He was phobic about illness and death and the ballerina Tamara Karsavina, who had known Diaghilev since she was a fifteen-year-old dancer in the Imperial Ballet, recalled him refusing to travel in an open carriage in summer time in case he caught glanders (infectious swelling of the glands) from the horses. If he saw a cat – even a black one which usually means good fortune – he quickly retraced his steps to avoid crossing its path; and he manifested obsessive traits in the way he scrubbed his hands with a handkerchief after opening a door, in order to avoid germs.

He also discriminated between 'bad' and 'good' days of the week and once, when Karsavina pointed out a print of Napoleon at Waterloo in the room, Diaghilev was visibly perturbed, considering it a bad omen. Hearing funeral music also made him feel anxious.

Notable funeral processions were, in general, more likely to inspire awe. Sometimes the dead were carried on shoulders in an open coffin with great

Diaghilev and his beloved nanny Dunia by Bakst

pomp; sometimes rows of black-suited torch bearers marched on either side of the street carrying burning lanterns. In the case of the penurious, the black-suited gentlemen were replaced by drunken, bedraggled tramps wearing shabby crepe.

Another member of Diaghilev's household was his manservant, Vassili Zulkov, who was responsible for the household duties. Benois remembered him being independent, but devoted to Diaghilev – so much so that when Diaghilev started his ballet company, Zulkov acted as costumier and assistant director, despite being unable to speak any language but Russian.

Diaghilev constantly emphasised the importance of beauty and he and other members of the group used the magazine to spread their ideas. However, the critics disliked the idea of art for art's sake, dismissed the magazine as foolishness and the group was promptly, if unfairly, labelled 'The Decadents'. It was a parallel to the public reaction to Oscar Wilde as 'decadent' and to his perceived homosexual traits.

Much of the hostility caused by the magazine was directed at Diaghilev himself and visitors to the Russian art exhibition, initially such a great success, began to react more critically. A cartoon of Diaghilev's patron Princess Tenischeva appeared showing her as a cow milked dry. Diaghilev was very tactful in his requests to her for money, in one case reminding her of his needs apparently casually, in a postacript to his letter.

He continued to propagate his views through the magazine. Having noticed in Europe the growing interest in primitive and 'exotic' art and the influence of African art, he decided to promote folk art in Russia.

Two arts and crafts cottage industries, one outside Moscow and one near Smolensk, were set up by the same two patrons who had funded *Mir Iskussiva* and artists came to work and study there. There were workshops on cottage industries like wood-carving, pottery and embroidery and those involved had their work displayed in the exhibition of Russian artists.

In the spring of 1898 the twenty-six-year-old Diaghilev travelled to Berlin, London and Paris. He had to organise the engraving of plates for his magazine (there were no fine-printing facilities in Russia then) and he also wanted to borrow paintings for the international exhibition he was now organising for the following year in St Petersburg.

He met Oscar Wilde in Paris that summer and Wilde wrote to his publisher, Leonard Smithers, about a drawing by Aubrey Beardsley of Mlle de Maupin, saying 'There is a young Russian here who is a great amateur [sic] of Aubrey's art, who would love to have one. He is a great collector and rich ...'[17] Diaghilev may have been rich ln Wilde's eyes, but he only had a moderate amount of family money. However, he certainly gave an excellent impression of the young man about town.

Diaghilev was a passionate admirer of European art and was invariably seen clutching a copy of Baedeker's *Guide*. He successfully borrowed the paintings he wanted and in January 1899, after returning from Europe, he launched his international exhibition in St Petersburg with great panache and publicity. The best of Russian contemporary art was presented side by side with European paintings by artists like Whistler, Renoir and Degas.

The exhibition represented Russian and European artistic development. Members of the Czar's family visited it, including the Grand Duke Vladimir Alexandrovitch, President of the Academy of Fine Arts, brother to Alexander III and uncle of Nicholas II. He alone of the Imperial Family was enthusiastic enough to support Diaghilev's enterprises in Europe. Reaction to the exhibition, sponsored by the *World of Art*'s patrons, was two-fold: sympathisers of the magazine admired it, but the press were antagonistic, accusing the magazine of 'corrupting youth, breeding ugliness, morbidity, and depraved tastes.'[18] Diaghilev, unmoved, threw off the criticism.

2

'Gentlemen's Mischief'

In Czarist Russia, serfs referred to sexual encounters with their masters as 'Gentlemen's Mischief.' Russian manhood, according to a study by Dan Healey, was an 'active' resource, 'to be tapped by Czars and commissars' and subordinate men and boys were viewed as 'sexually accessible'.[1] It was an accepted part of private life in Russia, despite sodomy having been legally banned in 1832.

Although no brothels for homosexuals existed, sexual relations between men for gain usually happened informally in upper or middle class households, or at night in boulevards and parks. The motive according to Healey was 'bettering one's material circumstances and deference to patriarchal authority.' It took place between masters and apprentices, householders and servants, clerics and male novices and bath-house attendants and customers – whose backs they had just scrubbed. Bath-houses were a focal point for male prostitutes and were run on a business footing. Private rooms ensured privacy and the work team shared out the money made from sex – after the manager had taken his cut.

Repressive and authoritarian Czar Alexander III's reign saw a reversal of all his father's liberalising rules

Homosexuality in St Petersburg was originally part of a patriarchal society, but by the late 19th and early 20th centuries, a new breed of male homosexuals whose 'vice' was the result of 'luxurious boredom' was seen on the streets. They became known as *tetki* (aunties). Invariably effeminate-looking, they used to congregate in certain places looking for custom. However, because these meeting points became well known, they attracted loitering, potential blackmailers. In the winter on Sundays the *tetki* would stroll around known

meeting places, 'where cadets and schoolboys came in the morning; and at six in the evening, soldiers and apprentice boys appear.'[2]

Soldiers would also head for the zoological gardens, hoping to earn a little money without much effort: the *tekli* would take them into toilets, inspect them, and pay the chosen ones some three to five roubles for anal intercourse. Upper class *tetki* also congregated at the Maryinsky Theatre during ballet performances. There would be occasional police raids on restaurant-based clubs or so-called 'dens' of pederasts.

Rumours of Diaghilev's homosexuality remained rumours, which was a wise precaution on his part. Historically, although foreign visitors to Russia in the 16th and 17th centuries were astonished at the open homosexual affection displayed among all classes of men, this did not last. Laws against homosexuality were introduced by Peter the Great in the 18th century. These initially just applied to the military, but in 1832 Article 995 in the criminal code made *muzhelozhstvo* (men lying with men, interpreted by the courts as anal intercourse) a criminal act. Those who violated the law lost all their rights and were exiled to Siberia for up to five years.

The Czarist regime and the Russian Orthodox Church combined to suppress any liberal tendencies. During the reign of Czar Alexander III (who died in 1894), men in higher positions than Diaghilev had been ruined by accusations of homosexuality. Such tendencies had to be very carefully concealed and resulted in a number of men committing suicide.

In the 19th century, for example, the fate of two brilliant men stands out. The first example is the novelist and dramatist Nickolai Gogol, who refers in his book *Dead Souls* to the passions that were born with him, which he had no power to reject. Gogol's most passionate relationship was with Josif Vielhorsky, whom he met in Rome in 1837, and lived with and nursed until Vielhorsky's death a few years later. A hoped-for relationship with the heterosexual Nikolai Yazykov failed to materialise, though loving letters survive.

Novelist and In 1852, at the age of 43, Gogol starved himself to death. On a copy of
dramatist *Dead Souls*, he wrote '... Inborn passions are an evil and every effort of man's
Nikolai Gogol rational will should be directed toward their eradication.'
kept his sexual
Simon Karlinsky wrote his book, *The Sexual Labyrinth of Nikolai Gogol*,
orientation because earlier biographies of Gogol had never clearly stated that the writer
secret, but after was homosexual because this had been kept hidden.
a 'confession' he
Karlinsky believes that in 1852 Gogol confessed his leanings to a hellfire-
was encouraged and-brimstone priest, Father Matthew Konstantinovsky, hoping to 'eradicate
to starve his inborn passions.' Father Matthew prescribed 'a fast that was actually a
himself to starvation diet, abstinence from sleep, and constant prayer.'[3]
death

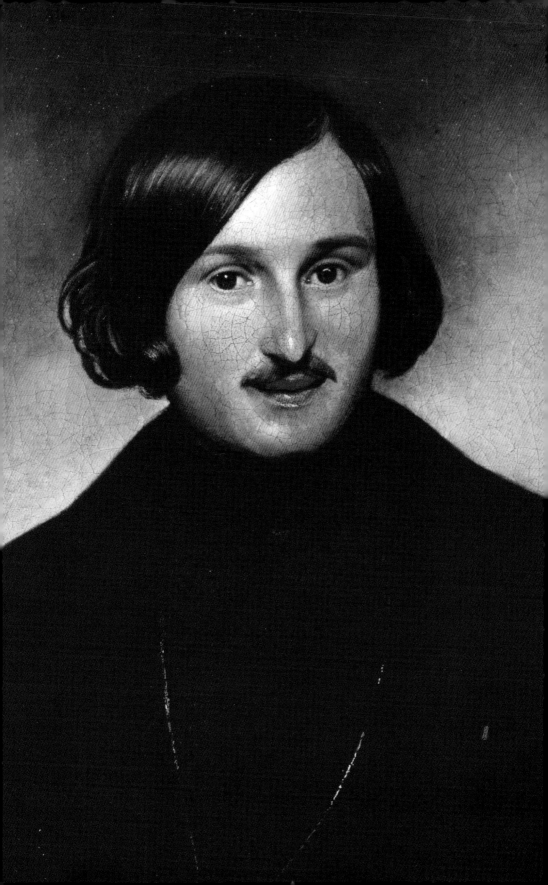

Gogol, under his influence, burnt the sequel to *Dead Souls* on which he had been working, cut down his food to a mouthful or two of soup or brine and spent his nights in prayer, sleeping merely two or three hours. Becoming ill, doctors bled him repeatedly, plunged him into icy baths and attached live leeches to his nose and mouth. Karlinsky considers his death, in such circumstances, 'was not only a suicide, it was also a ritual murder.'[4]

Another example was the introspective and melancholy homosexual, Piotr Tchaikovsky, remembered in particular for his passionate and lyrical music for *Swan Lake* and *The Sleeping Beauty*. Tchaikovsky had once before attempted suicide after being forced into a marriage in 1877. This had lasted only a month and left him in a state of nervous collapse.

His death at the age of 53 in 1893, three weeks after the premiere of his Sixth Symphony, was generally attributed to cholera, rampant at the time, which he allegedly contracted after drinking a glass of unboiled water. However, his body was not put in a closed casket, normal practice when someone died from a highly contagious disease, and the borrowed sheets in which he had lain were returned unwashed.

The other suggestion is that Tchaikovsky was 'ordered' to commit suicide because he had made sexual advances to a nephew of Duke Stenbok-Fermor and the Duke had threatened to complain to the Czar.

This resulted in a court of honour being convened consisting of eight fellows of the School of Jurisprudence in St Petersburg (which Tchaikovsky had attended and which feared his homosexual behaviour would blacken the law school).

The composer was present during the five hour meeting and allegedly told that if he did not commit suicide, 'the alternative would be family disgrace, exile in Siberia and the revelation of his indiscretion to the Czar himself.' Although he feared death, Tchaikovsky was also desperate to conceal his homosexuality. The next day, according to this account (by the wife of the man who had convened the court), a former classmate went to Tchaikovsky's house and handed him a phial of arsenic, which he took. This would have produced symptoms similar to cholera. It is claimed his doctor and his brother Modeste – also a homosexual – then covered up the manner of his death.[5]

Tchaikovsky the introspective homosexual composer was driven to suicide in order to escape a scandal

Speculation continues as to what actually happened. One lurid account was that 'Tchaikovsky was so large, he tore a sailor, who had to be treated and died. Tchaikovsky, out of conscience, committed suicide.'[6]

It has also been suggested that he died 24 hours before his death was officially announced, and that he did indeed have cholera, 'caught' from his

sexual partners in St Petersburg (despite cholera being transmitted through infected food or water).

It is said that Diaghilev told the story that Czar Alexander III (1845–1894) on hearing of Tchaikovsky's death, said 'Such a pity. I have so many sailors, but only one Tchaikovsky.'[7]

There was still a punitive attitude towards homosexuals in Czarist Russia, although attempts to reform the law were being urged by the turn of the century. Certainly homosexuality had become openly apparent by then in artistic and aristocratic circles and at least seven Grand Dukes made no secret of their predilections. One of these, Grand Duke Sergei Alexandrovich, an uncle of Czar Nicholas II (1868–1918), was openly seen at the theatre and elsewhere with his male lover.

Nevertheless, those outside the immediate court still had to be highly discreet. In the 1890s Diaghilev antagonised many officials with whom he came into contact and these knew that his vulnerable area was his homosexuality. According to Arnold Haskell, 'malevolent people now began to pay close attention to his morals and to talk scandal. The director [Prince Sergei Volkonsky, a homosexual himself] received visits and letters of complaint; Diaghilev himself received a powder-puff as an anonymous gift ...'[8]

As a result, Volkonsky sent for Diaghilev to tell him, with embarrassment, that his behaviour was causing comment and that he should be more discreet. Diaghilev was quick to deny the rumours and the accusations were not formally substantiated.

A distant relation of Diaghilev's recalled that when his name was mentioned at his cousins' home, it resulted in an odd mixture of pride and embarrassment: his princely splendour was admired, stories of his terrible irascibility, haughtiness and sexual irregularities were not. The family appeared unaware that Diaghilev and his cousin Dima had formed a passionate relationship.

When with his group of student friends, Diaghilev, along with the rest, boasted of female admirers. If the subject of homosexuality came up, he condemned it. Yet at the theatre, 'dressed in his smart, faultlessly fitting uniform, he had a way of walking through the stalls ... which made tongues wag and gossip about him – often unfounded – spread like wildfire throughout the town.'[9]

Arnold Haskell asserts that it was only after Diaghilev left Russia some years later that he admitted his homosexuality, though 'it had already become an open scandal that had even reached the columns of the less respectable boulevard papers.'[10]

In 1903 reduced penalties for sodomy were introduced. The sentence for homosexual acts between consenting adults was to be three months only, although if these acts took place with an 'innocent' youth, the sentence increased to three years. Under the Bolshevik regime, after 1917, the penalty for sex between consenting male adults was removed. Homosexuality was re-criminalised under Stalin in 1933–4 owing, it was said, to concern about young soldiers. Consenting male adults faced the harsh punishment of five years' hard labour.

Diaghilev spent the years between 1909 and 1929 in various European countries. Each had different attitudes and different laws about homosexuality: in each Diaghilev had to be circumspect and ensure his behaviour did not attract attention. He made no attempt to hide his orientation within his own circles, but it was not public knowledge.

Certain countries like England and Germany and the United States legally punished sexual acts between males. The last execution for sodomy in England was in 1836 but by the time Oscar Wilde was notoriously convicted in 1895, the maximum sentence was two years' hard labour.

Wilde was convicted under the Criminal Law Amendment Act of 1885 and a deep public revulsion in Britain against so-called sexual 'deviancy' remained strong for more than half a century. This witch-hunt attitude was heightened by the politically-backed British Social Purity and Hygiene Movement which attacked homosexuality as corrupting youth and weakening the moral fibre of the nation. The movement, which began in the late 19th century, became increasingly concerned in the early 1900s with the sexual morals of young people – organising night-time vigilante patrols to stop immoral behaviour in parks. Homosexuals were stigmatised as different and inferior to other men.

With homosexuals thus considered 'folk devils', many public libraries in Britain refused to display liberal books on the subject like those by the sexologist Havelock Ellis. His seven-volume *Studies in the Psychology of Sex* was published between 1897 and 1928. Some of the 'treatment' for homosexuals in the inter-war years and after was extremely repressive, confining suspects to mental hospitals where they were made guinea pigs for so-called remedies ranging from hypnotism to chemical experiments.

The first world war polarised attitudes towards homosexuality, which was openly criticised. Oscar Wilde's one-time lover, Lord Alfred Douglas, in an unashamed about-turn, warned that 'It is just as important to civilisation that Literary England should be cleansed of sex-mongers peddlers of the perverse, as that Flanders should be cleansed of Germans.'[11]

Two of the most memorable war poets, Seigfried Sassoon and Wilfred Owen were homosexual, and the novelist and playwright J.R. Ackerley first acknowledged his homosexuality during the war. Friendships naturally developed in the trenches, often revealed in the letters and poetry of the time, but under the military code sodomy was punished by imprisonment of ten years to life and gross indecency received two years.

In the twenties in England, attitudes relaxed but homosexuality remained illegal. In 1925, when the Ballets Russes was performing in London, there were some oblique references to decadence by the critics, who also suggested that 'young men in roll-top jumpers who stroll about at the back of the circle and talk and talk and talk should be thrown out.' This was a veiled allusion to the back of the circle and the gallery being well-known picking-up places for homosexuals.

Diaghilev, though an acclaimed visitor, would have known that homosexuals in Britain needed to be circumspect and secret. However, he met members of the Bloomsbury Group on many occasions. The group, an avant-garde colony centred around the Hogarth Press, which was run by Leonard and Virginia Woolf alongside artists like Duncan Grant and Vanessa Bell (Virginia's sister) and the economist, Maynard Keynes. Members were influential in the arts and homosexuality, such as Duncan Grant's passionate affair with Maynard Keynes, was of no more significance within the group than a heterosexual relationship.

After his success with the Ballets Russes in Paris in 1909, Diaghilev made his second home in that city. For some five years, the brilliant young dancer Vaslav Nijinsky was with him as his lover. France dropped sodomy from its statute books after its revolution, in 1791, and was less punitive about homosexuality – indeed, Oscar Wilde was urged to take refuge there before his last trial.

Yet even in Paris, in the early years of the 20th century, it was thought expedient not openly to admit to being homosexual. Salon society, however, condoned homosexuality: 'Men attended certain of these functions disguised by powder, rouge, wigs, and heavy cloaks'[12]

The young Jean Cocteau, a later friend of Diaghilev's, went to a ball with outrageously-dressed friends. He himself wore 'red curls, a tremendous tiara, a pearl-embroidered train, anklets, and painted nails.'[13] It was not a fancy-dress ball and guests were not amused. Sarah Bernhardt sent a message to Cocteau to say 'If I were your mother, I'd send you to bed.'

In Paris, Diaghilev invariably presented a dandified appearance, with his fur-lined coat and shirts made by Charvet, and made little attempt to conceal his preference for male company. Andre Gide, on the other hand, was diffident about publically admitting his homosexuality. Although homosexuality was attacked after the first world war for undermining France's ability to regenerate itself, in 1924 Gide published his essay *Corydon* 'in defense of pederesty'. He believed that 'tolerance of homosexuality was almost nonexistent outside of the capital and uncommon even within Paris.'[14]

Although the first French homosexual magazine, *Inversions*, was published in Paris in 1924, and some considered the twenties in that city a golden age for homosexuals, Gide's assessment was based on his experience.

Colette remembered being at one of the weekly salons given by Madame Arman de Caillavet when Marcel Proust with a male companion turned up. After they left, the hostess reacted furiously: 'Did you see them? Behaving like two doting twins! Billing like a pair of parakeets who can't be parted! That young man is really going too far! He's deliberately flaunting himself ... And even if he's determined to shock people, at least he needn't make himself ridiculous!'[15]

France's mainly liberal attitude towards homosexuality was shared by Spain and Italy: neither of these two countries punished sexual acts between consenting male adults. It was not 'excused' but regarded more as an illness than a 'vice'. Diaghilev spent a great deal of time in Spain with his company during the first world war and views there on homosexuality continued to remain liberal until the introduction in 1928 of the Penal Code.

Diaghilev delighted in Italy's art and so spent a great deal of time in that country, frequently taking his lovers and colleagues to look at artistic works. Venice particularly attracted him and it was a rare year when he failed to visit it. In Italy, like Spain, homosexual acts were not against the law. Indeed in 1908 Cocteau, no stranger to wearing rouge and lipstick, visited Venice as 'a concession to a certain kind of indiscretion that was just beginning to be smart' – in other words, he was with 'fashionably scandalous homosexual friends.'[16]

After the first world war, homosexuality in Italy was strongly criticised by the Catholic church – as it was in France – for undermining fertility and virility, both of which were needed to boost the birth rate and restore military might. Although fascist rule took over in the 1920s under Mussolini, his views were less extreme than Hitler's and homosexuals in Italy were never persecuted to the extent they were in Germany. When Italy's new Penal Code was introduced in 1930, it did not follow Spain's hard-line Penal Code against homosexuals but allowed them to go unpunished.

The liberal legislation of France, Spain and Italy differed radically from that of Germany where 'unnatural vice' between men was punishable with imprisonment for one to five years. The German Friedrich Engels (1820–95), founder of 'scientific socialism' and theorist on sexual matters, considered sodomy a 'gross unnatural vice' and was against a move to repeal Germany's sodomy law in the 1860s.

French writers had long associated homosexuality with Germany – it was often referred to as 'the German vice'. The writer Paul Gaultier recalled that Berlin had been 'the capital of vice' before 1914, pointing out that 'in addition to the prostitution that everyone admitted, one must also cite the ... unnatural prostitution that so ravaged Germany' before the war.[17]

A lively example was seen in 1907, when Germany rocked to a political scandal in Berlin called 'the Eulenburg Affair.' It involved a legal case which exposed a widespread homosexual network in the Kaiser's immediate entourage. At one stage, the chief of the Kaiser's military secretariat had dropped dead in the Kaiser's presence while dressed in a tutu in the middle of a drag act.

In 1923, the *Mercure de France*, a literary journal known for its hostility towards homosexuality, published an article called 'Organised Vice in Germany' which revealed in meticulous detail the homosexual subculture currently existing in Germany.

It is no wonder that homosexuals felt uneasy. In England it was claimed that on the evening of Oscar Wilde's arrest at the Cadogan Hotel in the May of 1895, some 2,000 anxious British homosexuals took the night train to Paris, terrified that they could be subject to mass arrests. It is an example of how homosexuals lived under the shadow of fear in Europe in the next decades.

Diaghilev in some ways resembled Oscar Wilde. Both could be annihilatingly witty, invariably at the expense of others, and uncaring of their victim's feelings. Both were sought after as celebrities and had a magnetic appeal; both were conscious of the clothes they wore, with Wilde presenting a careful artistic appearance and Diaghilev looking dandified in his fur-lined coat and hand-made shirts. Both believed in and promoted the aesthetic principle of art for art's sake.

It was said of Diaghilev that 'he was perhaps the first grand homosexual who asserted himself and was accepted as such by society.'[18] To an extent he created a homosexual mafia around him. But though homosexuals featured within his close group of friends, like his secretary Kochno, other members of his circle included heterosexuals like Alexandre Benois, George Balanchine and Bakst.

The talented men who attracted Diaghilev, whether homosexual, bisexual or heterosexual, were in no way effeminate. Nijinsky may have looked sexless, but he could create both a strong masculine image – take his mesmerisingly powerful leap in *Spectre de la Rose* – and also exert a strange erotic charisma, as he did in *L'Apres Midi d'un Faun*. He was short and thickset with very muscular thighs and calves, in contrast to his long neck and sloping shoulders. Overall, he had a quality of grace, a certain magic.

Homosexuality was not encouraged within the Ballets Russes. The image of the company and its dancers remained exotic, erotic and exciting. However, Diaghilev's own homosexuality and his love affair with Nijinsky left its stamp on ballet and created a lasting question about male dancers, whose public image has for years been unfairly regarded as homosexual.

Diaghilev was attracted by first-class creative artists, some of whom he loved. He loathed effeminacy and liked virile, masculine men. Unfortunately this meant that his search for a permanent companion invariably failed. It was a bitter blow to him when, for example, he lost Nijinsky and Leonid Massine to women – both men leaving Diaghilev to marry and have children. It left Diaghilev bereft, prey to rage, sadness and disappointment.

3

'Tactless but Talented'

In July 1899 the young and vigorous Prince Sergev Mikhailovich Volkonsky was appointed by the Czar to be the Director of the Imperial Theatres in St Petersburg. Volkonsky loved the theatre passionately and believed that Diaghilev's success with *Mir Iskusstva* made him the right man to inject life into the theatres. Volkonsky found him tactless but talented and said perceptively that Diaghilev 'was not yet by any means acknowledged as a great or an important man, but he had all the *allure* of one, and people resented it.'[1]

His relationship with Diaghilev ultimately proved a turning point in the latter's career. Initially, Volkonsky appointed Diaghilev, from September 1899, to be attached to the administration as Civil Servant with Special Duties. Diaghilev promptly put on airs, to the irritation of his friends who damped down his pretensions.

His first task was to compile the 1900 volume of the *Year Book of the Imperial Theatres*. It gave him his first practical contact with the theatre. Delighted, he set to work with immense enthusiasm, determined to make a success of it and further his career – hopefully impressing the Emperor and perhaps even becoming Volkonsky's chief assistant.

Succeed he undoubtedly did, totally transforming what had been a dull if informative volume into a luxurious affair. The striking cover was designed by Bakst, Somov contributed illustrations, Svetlov wrote 91 pages on classical choreography and Benois wrote equally learnedly on the architecture of the Alexandrovsky Theatre. Inevitably, Diaghilev exceeded his allowance for the volume.

Diaghilev aspired to be a young-man-about-town when he lived in St Petersburg in the 1890s

His appointment resulted in other members of the group getting prestigious commissions and becoming more involved with both the theatre and the *Year Book*. Diaghilev then began flexing his muscles, convinced he was set for glory. He made friends with the ballerina Mathilde Kschessinska, who had powerful contacts at court and who introduced him to the Grand Duke Sergei Mikhailovich.

The dancer was rather surprised at attracting Diaghilev, whose homosexual preferences were well-known. However, she was not displeased, as with his white streak of hair (resulting in him being called Chinchilla) and his arrogant type of good looks, he was an impressive escort. She found, though, that she could not pierce Diaghilev's 'elegant but cold amiability.' Diaghilev made a point of watching her dancing and the company, knowing his knowledgeable eye was on them, would quietly sing:

I've just heard
That 'Chinchilla' is in his box
And I'm terribly afraid
To make a mistake[2]

Everybody tended to keep an eye on everyone else. Theatrical life then was known for its strict morality and it was rare for an actress or dancer to be a kept mistress. One young actress was even thrown out of the Moscow Art Theatre for being seen in the street with a powdered nose. Only prostitutes powdered their noses.

It was that year, 1899, that the 15 year old ballerina Tamara Karsavina first caught sight of Diaghilev, after he had casually dropped into the rehearsal of *Casse Noisette*. She said she looked closely at his young, ageless face, seeing 'the fresh colour of youth, an insolent little moustache, eyes oddly drooping at the corners ... and a single grey lock cutting through the dark hair – mark of Ahasuerus [the name given to the Wandering Jew] or mark of genius?'[3]

Czar Nicholas II, the doomed and final Romanov Emperor of Russia, was delighted with Serov's portrait It was now two years since *Mir Iskusstva* was first published and Benois admitted that the public still regarded it as the fad of impertinent 'decadent' youngsters, challenging Russian society. Because of this attitude and money difficulties the patrons of the magazine withdrew their support. Friends and admirers came to the rescue and subsidised it for a further year to prevent it folding, and after Serov successfully painted Czar Nicholas II's portrait, the Czar, pleased with the result, gave the magazine 10,000 roubles, prolonging its life further. As Haskell pointed out, 'Diaghilev's whole career was marked by these last-minute rescues of his expensive enterprises.'[4]

The atmosphere at the magazine remained, as ever, volatile. Diaghilev took affront easily if his decisions were challenged, and on one occasion after the gentle Serov remonstrated at Diaghilev bodily throwing Bakst out of the room after an argument, Diaghilev nearly challenged him to a duel. However, Diaghilev rarely kept angry for long.

He flared up again, however, when without his permission some of the group set up concerts of chamber music. For the first time in Russia, audiences heard French and German composers like Claude Debussy, Maurice Ravel and Arnold Schoenberg. Young Russian composers like Igor Stravinsky and Sergei Prokofiev also auditioned.

Diaghilev was not invited to participate because, according to Nouvel: 'We were afraid of his dominating character, and we were quite certain that the modest scale on which we were operating would not interest him. He only cared for big enterprises.'[6]

The *Annual* was still greeted with great respect, praised by the Czar, and public opinion and the press at last began to applaud Diaghilev rather than insult him. In 1900 Russia scored a colourful success at the Paris Exhibition with its arts and crafts section and its reconstruction of a Russian village. It vindicated Diaghilev's enthusiasm for the arts and crafts movement.

Just as his career seemed to be entering on calmer waters, there was a catastrophic upset. Diaghilev was an admirer of Leo Delibes, the French composer, who had died in 1891. Wanting to commemorate him, he thought of staging *Sylvia,* a ballet in three acts and one of Delibes' works. Volkonsky agreed and in January 1901 Diaghilev started organising it, planning to make choreographic innovations and engaging members of the group like Benois and Bakst and Serov to design the décor and costumes. Bakst, the scenic inspiration of Russian ballet and opera, had very definite ideas about style, colour of the décor and its pictorial lines. He created the whole spirit of the production.

The group was enthusiastic, loving the music, and Diaghilev, deeply involved, insisted on taking total responsibility for the production – only to be told by Volkonsky that he was not officially entitled to take over its entire running. He wanted Diaghilev to produce it, but not to be the independent director.

Diaghilev, with the success of the *Annual* under his belt, flexed his muscles and declared high-handedly that if he could not produce *Sylvia* then he would refuse to edit the second volume of the *Annual* – even though this was already being prepared. Volkonsky commented that Diaghilev possessed the quality of making himself disliked wherever he went.

The row went as far as the Czar. As the Czar had already congratulated him on the *Annual*, Diaghilev was confident of the outcome. But in picking up the *Government Gazette* shortly after, he was mortified and horrified to read that 'S.P. Diaghilev is dismissed without pension according to Point 3.' It was public disgrace. Point 3 was only applied in extreme cases, such as improper conduct.

Diaghilev told Tamara Karsavina that he was sacked because he refused to be dictated to over the choice of repertoire and distribution of parts. She said that 'few people knew how hard the blow fell on Diaghilev. Fewer still realised his fortitude and his undaunted spirit.'[6]

Diaghilev fled abroad in the spring of 1901, remaining there until well into 1902. His interest in *Mir Iskusstva* was declining, though he sent in articles occasionally from abroad and remained the titular editor for another three years. He wrote a monograph on *Russian Painting of the 18th Century* and oversaw the group's exhibitions, but he had less influence and his heady confidence had taken a blow.

He was still the focus for criticism from reactionary forces like the Imperial Society for the Encouragement of Art, who considered he was a major influence in corrupting the taste of the younger generation.

The affair was an extraordinary turning point for Diaghilev: had he stayed at his job in St Petersburg, he might well have achieved a top artistic position and transformed the artistic or ballet scene in Russia. As it was, his dreams of such triumphant success and of receiving a title – one of his ambitions – vanished. He was forced to practise his entrepreneurial genius outside his mother country and so it was Europe, not Russia, which was the main beneficiary.

Sadly the Russians never saw the ballets created by their own countrymen: after Diaghilev left to re-create Russian ballet in Europe, taking with him over time much of the major balletic talent like Nijinsky, Bakst and Fokine, their work was never, or rarely, seen in their own country.

The artist Jacques Emile Blanche, commenting on Diaghilev, said that you couldn't tell in which direction his career would turn, 'unless it was this taste for what is new, this fickleness and this feverish impatience which made him discard very quickly the things he had once admired and pursue with equal zeal new objects for devotion ...'[7]

A few months after his enforced dismissal, it was formally announced that Diaghilev himself had made the decision to resign. He was then officially reinstated in another branch. However, this was merely a face-saver. He and the rest of the group were only too conscious of this and from that point onwards they began to look to the west for their future.

Prince Volkonsky lasted only a little longer than Diaghilev. He was sacked after fining the ballerina Mathilde Kschessinska who, as he should have remembered, was the mistress of the Czar, for refusing to wear a farthingale in the ballet *Kamargo*. She immediately persuaded the Czar to dismiss him.

Volkonsky was replaced by Teliakovsky, a man skilful in political intrigue. There was no love lost between him and Diaghilev as Teliakovsky regarded him enviously and was determined not to give him any more power. *Mir Iskusstva*, in return, attacked the ballet productions for which Teliakovsky was responsible, claiming justifiably that they lacked soul.

Diaghilev was still reviewing the art scene for *Mir Iskusstva*. While at the exhibition of Charles Rennie Mackintosh at the Moscow Society of Architects in 1902, he met the artist Mikhail Larionov. The two men 'talked about paintings, artists and the theatre: a close personal and creative relationship developed'[8]

It was nevertheless a frustrating time for Diaghilev, watching productions at the Imperial Theatres which he considered second class, yet was forced to stand and watch. Worse, Teliakovsky went outside the small official circle of painters normally responsible for the scenery and costumes, and in October 1902 poached Bakst to be the decorative artist for Euripides' *Hippoytus* at the Alexandrinsky Theatre.

Bakst was an enormous success and Teliakovsky asked him to create the décor for the ballet, *The Fairy Doll*. Tamara Karsavina, meeting Bakst for the first time at a dress rehearsal, thought he was 'a dandified young man in appearance, pernickady in his ways'.[9]

The same year, 1902, Prince Volkonsky commissioned a new ballet, *The Magic Mirror*. This was a failure, loathed by the conservative wing of the ballet because of its décor by the 'artist-decadent' painter Golovine and its equally 'decadent' music by Koreshchenko. Diaghilev wrote sharply to the editor of the *Petersburg Gazette* as a representative of 'that movement in art which is called decadent' giving his view that the real reason the ballet had failed was because it was 'utterly inartistic, unballetic, and chiefly, an infinitely boring spectacle.'[10]

The ructions within the artistic world were minor compared to Russia's current political upheavals. Nicholas II, the last Romanov Czar, who had acceded in 1894, was presiding over an increasingly volatile country. In 1903 *The Times*' correspondent ran an article on the new revolutionary parties in Russia and was promptly expelled. Between 1903 and 1906 there was a wave of massacres or pogroms (Russian for 'round-up' or 'lynching') against Jewish communities, with authorities dubbing them revolutionary troublemakers.

This unfinished potrait of Diaghilev by Serov captures his spirit far more closely than any contemporary photograph

The dancer Isadora Duncan, the pioneer of expressive movement, was a sensation when she danced in Russia in 1904. Her influence on the choreographer Michel Fokine was immense

The next series of pogroms, from 1917 to 1921, far outweighed previous atrocities and more than 60,000 Jews were killed.

The worlds of Russia and Britain remained far apart, socially, artistically and politically. Britain had been involved for three years in a war of attrition with the Boers, losing 5,774 men, and only in 1902 signing a peace treaty.

The end of the war boosted morale in Britain where the death of Queen Victoria was still felt and the country was acclimatising itself to its new King, Edward VII, and a new Conservative prime minister, A.J. Balfour. With so many of the personalities of the 1890s dead, like Oscar Wilde, Aubrey Beardsley and George du Maurier, the new century brought a new mood.

There was excitement about the burst of scientific discoveries: Marconi's first transatlantic message; the launch of Britain's first submarine; the Wright brothers flying the first powered aircraft. Emmeline Pankhurst founded the National Women's Social and Political Union, taxis appeared on the streets of London for the first time and a speed limit of 20 mph was fixed for cars.

Back In St Petersburg in 1904, the group reluctantly decided to close *Mir Iskusstva*. It had revolutionised artistic thought, but had now run out of steam and, more crucially, had run out of money.

The group's preoccupation with the theatre remained and in December 1904 they were all highly anxious to see the debut of the American-born dancer and choreographer, Isadora Duncan, the pioneer of expressive movement. There was such fascination with the American dancer that the leading lights of the artistic and intellectual society all turned up to see her perform. Diaghilev and the dancer and choreographer Michel Fokine were particularly interested. Years later, in 1926, Diaghilev wrote to W.A. Propert to say: 'I knew Isadora very well in St Petersburg and I was present with Fokine at her first performances. Fokine was mad about her, and the influence of Duncan on him was the foundation of all his creation.'[11]

Born in St Petersburg in 1880, Fokine trained at the Imperial Ballet and became an outstanding dancer and a bold and original choreographer. He jettisoned the rigorous academic technique of the Bolshoi ballet (such as women dancing *en pointe*) and, in a revolutionary move, substituted a natural, flowing series of movements – helped by his having the female dancers uncorseted. He excited dancers with his far-ranging ideas and a vivid, expressive approach. He also reformed ballet costume, ending the custom of the female dancers wearing tutus.

Rehearsals under him could be rather wild affairs as he had little control over his temper. The dancer Karsavina recalled chairs being hurled around, his walking out of rehearsals, and his voice shouting 'Putrid execution. Loose, untidy. I won't stand carelessness.'

Members of his company accepted his fury at rehearsals, his autocratic behaviour, his temper tantrums, his aloofness and intolerance and his quickness to quarrel. They remained devoted to him, deferring to his wishes because they knew he was a unique judge of their art and accepted that his fierce criticisms were because he cared passionately about perfection. His grasp of detail was phenomenal: he was an excellent critic, ferociously holding his opinions.

The Victorian actress, Ellen Terry, was a great admirer of Fokine, saying what surprised her about the Russian ballet was 'its *life*. This vitality came sweeping on to the stage with Russian *maitres de ballet* such as Fokine, who used tradition, used the technical perfection of classical dancing, but would not be a slave to them.'[12]

Diaghilev meanwhile had been preoccupied in preparing for the Historical Exhibition of Portraits, to be staged in St Petersburg in 1905. He had succeeded in getting the Grand Duke Nikolai Mikhailovitch to act as patron and the Czar also contributed a substantial subsidy.

The exhibition required an enormous amount of research and Diaghilev enthusiastically flung himself into a maelstrom of work, discovering and evaluating portraits across the country while researching in ancient books and periodicals. It meant travelling thousands of miles, often by peasant cart, as he set up the exhibition almost single-handedly. In looking at paintings – the exhibition was to range from 1705 to 1905 – he discovered some remarkable artists whose paintings had remained quite unknown.

This was because little interest was taken by Russians at the time in their privately owned works of art. Tamara Karsavina remembered three portraits of Russian theatrical history being kept in her father's old home and used as lids for water buckets. Understandably, the art exhibitions organised by Diaghilev and the group were thought of as a breath of fresh air in St Petersburg.

Diaghlev's stories of how he obtained many of the portraits read like a boy's own adventure story. He would read, for instance, in someone's memoirs or letters how the painter Borovikovsky – one of the best Russian portrait painters of the 18th century – spent a month at a certain Volga estate. That started him on what he called one of his hunting trips. 'First I would visit the direct heirs of the 18th century seigneur, who were so often half-witted in matters of art, and I would try to find out from them whether there was a Borovikovsky portrait in the family.' If no one could give him an answer, he would personally go to the Volga estate and turn the place upside down until he found what he was looking for.

He was often astonished by his own discoveries: 'Sometimes in an obscure and dilapidated country estate in a remote government beyond the Volga, I would be greeted by a whole row of superb portraits painted by some anonymous serf. They would be hanging, cracked, dirty, their varnish gone, in the drab office of the administration building. No one would know or care who painted the pictures, when they were painted, and whom they represented.'[13]

In his travels, Diaghilev was both surprised and shocked by the social situation in Russia. He had little interest in politics, but now for the first time he contrasted the appalling poverty and the virtually starving populace, compared to the wanton lavishness of the rich. It made him reassess the social and political situation of the time. He was to say, 'You can't imagine how many of these palatial estates, these jewels of 18th century architecture, were falling in ruins at that time. Their gardens were unkempt forests, the floors of their empty salons and ballrooms were littered with fallen plaster. The pigeons and swallows had made their nests in the galleries.

'Everything was death, decay, the collapse of a lost civilisation. It was there that I felt how inevitable the revolution was, how the pygmy heirs of a great period were not able to keep the past alive or cope with the ideas of the present, the new trends, the new desires and the new needs of our time.'[14]

Early in 1905 the Historical Portraits exhibition opened at the Tauride Palace – the first time that it had been used for such a purpose. Crystal chandeliers hung from the ceilings, luminous portraits shone out from the walls and large portraits of past Russian monarchs, enshrined under their canopies, took central place in the halls dedicated to their reigns.

Czar Nicholas II presided at the opening of the exhibition, though concealed his views about it. It was a grand social occasion, with the Grand Duke Nikolay Mikhailovich and Prince Dashkolv supporting the Czar. Diaghilev had proved that he was a man of extraordinary organising ability and phenomenal energy. Those who saw the exhibition were astonished at the riches of their own country, about which they had been totally ignorant.

Benois found the sight of the multi-coloured assembly of magnates in gold-embroidered coats, with their dressed-up ladies, oppressive. As well he might, given the background of the situation at the time – for Diaghilev's unease at the situation he found across Russia grimly foresaw the future.

On 22 January, 1905, only a day or so after the exhibition had opened, matters came to a head with an uprising. It was a forerunner for the later revolution of 1917, which finally overthrew the old order.

That day ('Bloody Sunday') the Benois children came home to report there was shooting in the streets. It happened after crowds of workers, singing the national anthem and holding holy icons, converged on the Winter Palace to petition the Czar. They wanted freedom of speech, freedom to hold meetings, industrial legislation, agrarian reform and, crucially, an elected national assembly. Although the marchers were peaceable and had no weapons, the troops on duty were ordered to fire and, as a result, killed several hundred people.

Such a shocking event naturally hardened people's attitudes and caused a series of riots, especially by industrial workers, along with a mutiny on the Battleship Potemkin. The riots spread to Moscow and other large towns. In October a general strike was called and a Workers' Council was set up in St Petersburg, headed by the young revolutionary, Leon Trotsky. The Russia of the Czars was disintegrating.

The volatile atmosphere broke up the group. Benois left for Paris and Filosofov followed shortly after. Diaghilev wrote to Benois in the October of that year to say how depressing the city now was: 'Everything's locked up, in total gloom, no pharmacies, streetcars, newspapers, telephones, or telegraphs – and machine guns any minute!'[15]

Outside Russia, it was a time of artistic and scientific experiment. Freud had published his theory of sexuality; Einstein formulated the Theory of Relativity; and the paintings in Paris by the Fauves had caused an uproar. The Parisian art and literary world was discovering Renoir and Bonnard, James Joyce and Marcel Proust.

Diaghilev had become close friends with the attractive, bisexual designer Sergei Sudeykin, but in 1905 he met the intelligent, good-looking Alexis Mavrine. They became lovers and early in 1906 left together for a long tour of Greece, Italy, France and Germany. Mavrine officially acted as his secretary.

Diaghilev was now anxious to reach a more sophisticated and knowledgeable audience. He also wanted to make his own decisions. Having been forcibly ejected from his job, he was enjoying the freedom it gave him. In speaking of his work in the Imperial Theatres, he recalled the stuffy, intrigue-ridden atmosphere of its management, saying it was like living in a morgue. With the success of the 1905 Historical Exhibition behind him, he decided that in 1906 he would launch a huge Russian exhibition in Paris.

4

Goodbye to St Petersburg

Diaghilev planned to include historical and contemporary Russian painting and sculpture in the exhibition, as well as ancient icons – which had mostly come, with the Czar's permission, from the Imperial Palaces. He also managed to persuade the Czar to back the project financially – no mean feat. The exhibition would be fresh and vital: Diaghilev's gift for organising and his creativity would be evident.

He had asked the Moscovite painter Mikhail Larionov to help and he and

The exhibition halls at the Russian Exhibition in Paris 1906

Diaghilev and Bakst joined Benois in Paris. The opening was to be 6 October 1906 and it would take over four large halls and several smaller ones at the Salon d'Automne in the Grand Palais.

It was an ambitious project. Diaghilev was then barely heard of in Parisian art circles and Russian art was almost entirely unknown in the west. Art connoisseurs in Paris, London and New York hardly recognised the name of a single Russian artist, yet Diaghilev organised the exhibition with such panache and enterprise that *tout Paris* flocked to it.

Bakst, whose painting *Terror Antiquus* dominated one entire wall, was busy decorating the galleries with paintings by other artists who would later be memorable for their settings for Diaghilev's ballets and operas. Serov, for instance, would design the curtain for the ballet *Scheherazade*; Roerich would be responsible for the décor for *Prince Igor* and *Le Sacre du Printemps*; and Alexandre Benois would design the décor for *Pavillon d'Armide* and *Petrushka*.

W.A. Propert, later author of *The Russian Ballet in Western Europe*, believed the 1906 Russian exhibition of painting and sculpture was only moderately successful, but that Diaghilev remained undismayed. He merely changed tactics and 'indefatigable as ever, began to organise that company which, through the association of the already accepted composers with the hitherto rejected painters, was destined to take the world by storm.'[1]

Diaghilev moved on. At the end of the Parisian art exhibition he decided to organise a 1907 Russian season of concerts at the Paris Opera: 'Russian Music Down the Ages.' The programme would include several operatic selections and Diaghilev asked Fedor Chaliapin – the brilliant, charismatic and attractive Russian singer who had been appearing in major European cities since 1901 – to sing excerpts from *Boris Gudonov*, composed by Mussorgsky, Diaghilev's then favourite composer. Chaliapin said of Diaghilev, 'There was almost more movement and life around him than on all the streets of Paris.'[2]

While in Paris for the Russian art exhibition, Diaghilev used his skills to meet and persuade influential contacts in French society to back him financially. One such contact was the Comtesse de Greffulhe who found him remarkably well-informed. When he told her he wanted to organise a festival of Russian music through the ages, and began to play examples of such music on her piano, she was impressed enough to tell him she would do everything she could to help him succeed.

Diaghilev never had any money and needed the rich and well-connected to sponsor his ideas. Over the next 20 years he took his begging bowl around Europe and had it not been for many generous sponsors, his name would not now be known.

Yet it was his enthusiasm which fuelled the new fascination for Russian art, opera, ballet and music which shortly swept through western countries. These arts revolutionised thought and fashion and influenced artistic creativity for decades to come.

The papers in Paris in 1906 mentioned the Russian art exhibition but were more occupied with the verdict of treason against Alfred Dreyfus, the French army officer, being overturned. World news concentrated on San Francisco's severe earthquake, followed by a fire, which killed hundreds of people.

Diaghilev's own attention at the time was wholly focused on his fear of

The designs by Alexandre Benois for the ballet Le Pavillon d'Armide were both sumptuous and elegant. In the story the hero falls in love with a beautiful woman who comes to life from a Gobelin tapestry

The programme for Boris Gudunov, *one of the operas included by Diaghilev in his season of concerts in Paris in 1907*

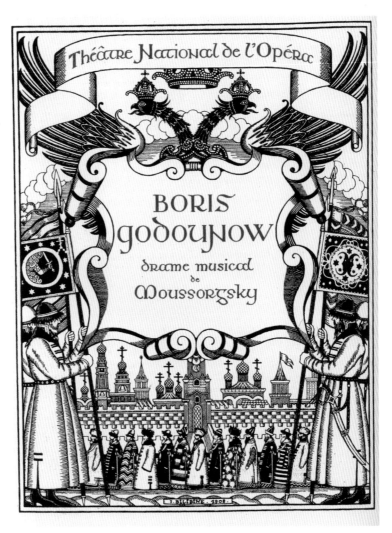

contracting scarlet fever from Benois' children. Although he needed to meet Benois to discuss the concerts, he only dared phone him from cafes and even then insisted that Benois held the phone at some distance from his mouth in case the fever was transmitted by wire.

More seriously (though not to Diaghilev), events in Europe foreshadowed political change. In 1907 Emilio Marinetti, the Italian writer and one of the founders of Futurism, published the Futurist manifesto in the newspaper, *Figaro*. In his tub-thumping lectures around Europe, he glorified war.

That year the stage designer (and son of the actress Ellen Terry) Edward

Gordon Craig, was working in Florence on a possible new ballet called *Psyche*. It was to have great hangings and 'wide spaces swept by changing light and shade, and human figures caught, as it were, in the stance of movement.'[3] Denis Babley, in *The Theatre of Edward Gordon Craig*, points out that though Diaghilev was shown Craig's spacious visions, he found them too daring, too different from the decorative ventures of the Russian ballet. Yet within half a dozen years Diaghilev was to shake all Paris with the ground-breaking ballet, *Rite of Spring*.

However, Diaghilev was interested when Gordon Craig published his revolutionary new theatrical magazine, *The Mask* – which lasted over 20 years. Craig aimed to simplify theatrical design and he used *The Mask* to portray and represent the theatre of the future.

Returning to St Petersburg in 1907, with the scarlet fever safely behind him, Diaghilev was delighted to see the new ballet, *Eunice*, based on the novel *Quo Vadis* and choreographed by the 27 year old Michel Fokine. Fokine dared break with tradition, replacing corseted tutus with flowing tunics. Dancers were not permitted to dance barefoot on the Maryinsky Theatre stage, so the look of ancient Greece was maintained by painting toenails on tights (done by Nijinsky's elder sister, Bronislava). Inevitably the old guard and the new took up entrenched positions regarding the move from tradition, with Diaghilev allying himself with the new guard.

Diaghilev was also impressed by the production that November by Benois of Nikolai Cherepnin's one-act ballet *Le Pavillon d'Armide* at the attractive Maryinsky Theatre, with its sky-blue and gold decorations. The idea was based on a story by Theophile Gautier in which the hero falls in love with a beautiful woman who comes to life from a Gobelin tapestry. Benois' designs were sumptuous and elegant and these, along with Fokine's modern choreography, again delighting Diaghilev even though the public remained lukewarm.

Backstage intrigues, however, were rife at the Imperial Theatres and at the last minute the dancer Mathilde Kschessinska withdrew from the main role, perhaps intending to sabotage it. Fokine, furious, called her a she-devil. The role was given to Anna Pavlova instead. Kschessinska, in a quick move to keep ahead of Pavlova, kept all eyes on her by elevating the brilliant young dancer Nijinsky to be her partner.

Nijinsky had graduated from the Imperial Theatre School In April 1907 and his brief appearance in *Le Pavillon d'Armide* was watched by Diaghilev. From the start Nijinsky was breathtaking on stage, but Diaghilev was not formally introduced to him until late in 1908. Nijinsky at the time was

involved with one of the ballet's patrons, Prince Pavel Dmitrievich Lvov. Like Diaghilev, he had a distaste for women after his one and only sexual encounter with a female prostitute.

Although Diaghilev at the time was having an affair with his secretary, Alexis Mavrine, over the following year, according to Benois, he 'quite openly deserted Mavrine, being more and more taken with Nijinsky'.[4]

After the success of the *Boris Gudonov* excerpts, Diaghilev decided to risk seeing how artistic Paris reacted to the first entire production of the opera. In 1908 he channelled his phenomenal energy into this project, wanting to show the world his fervour for the dramatic shape and splendour of Mussorgsky's composition.

Diaghilev's had rock-hard self-confidence in his own views whether they involved productions or people. Only occasionally, according to Benois, did he falter. One such time was the removal of an unsavoury inn scene in *Boris Gudunov*. 'This cut was the result of an attack of fear to which Sergei, for all his bravery in general, was occasionally prone. When he was in the grip of some fear, no argument could prevail upon it. It suddenly seemed to him *impossible* to show something so coarse and "dirty" to the elegant, fastidious Parisian public.'[5]

Modest Moussorgsky, the composer of *Boris Gudunov*, had died of chronic alcoholism in 1881 and his friend Rimsky-Korsakov acted as his musical executor, completing his unfinished works and rearranging some of his finished ones. Diaghilev made his cuts and alterations without consulting Rimsky-Korsakov, but the composer by now was too ill to stand up to the bullish Diaghilev, and died a month after the Paris premiere.

What Diaghilev brought to his debut in Paris in 1908 was an essentially Russian way of working. In Russia artists were given a great deal of responsibility in the staging of opera and ballets, designing décor and costumes. The prominence Diaghilev gave to painters and musicians in his productions and their innovative intertwining was an essential part of his success.

Money for these projects continued to be the problem. Diaghilev came to an agreement with the Imperial Theatres about borrowing production sets. He also managed to persuade the Grand Duke Vladimir to back *Boris Gudunov*, along with other imposing patrons like His Imperial Highness the Grand Duke Paul and, in Paris, the sewing machine heiress Princesse Edmond de Polignac. Colette remembered the Princesse turning up at weekly musical evenings, always in a high-necked dress and admired 'the indestructible character which was able to harmonise the definitive blue of her eyes with that conqueror's chin.' Her husband always wore a beige vicuna shawl, looking like 'a great ironic bird.'[6]

Despite these patrons, money was scarce and Diaghilev and Benois had to scour the markets, looking in all the Tartar and Jewish shops to get the genuine head-dresses and folklore costumes they needed for what was to be a ravishing production.

Their initial encounter with Parisian officialdom did not bode well. The head of the stagehands at the Opera, Petroman, seemed determined to slow

Anna Pavlova and Vaslav Nijinsky dancing together in the ballet Le Pavillon d'Armide *probably staged at the Maryinsky Theatre, St Petersburg*

down and wreck the production. His last-minute attempted sabotage, when he declared at the dress rehearsal that the décor did not fit, failed. Diaghilev calmly said in that case they would cancel the performance and Petroman, afraid of a gigantic row, reluctantly gave in.

Diaghilev held a council of war to canvass opinion as to whether the show should open the next day – a democratic move which was totally out of character. The vote was yes and the show was a triumph. The intensity of the music, Chaliapin's sublime singing and the sets painted by Golovin were a revelation and delighted the Parisians who stood on their seats, yelled and waved their handkerchiefs. The reception was uproarious and Chaliapin's personal success was tremendous.

The Russians went off to drink champagne at Le Café de la Paix until the small hours, at which point Benois and Diaghilev retired to their adjacent hotels where they shouted happily at each other from the windows. They had every right to be delighted as Diaghilev promptly received innumerable offers to make the concert an annual event. It was a magnificent foretaste of the talent to come: within a couple of years Russian composers, painters, singers and dancers would mesmerise Paris. Diaghilev believed that recognition and appreciation of the greatness and beauty of Russian music was long overdue in Europe.

Two of the sophisticated audience at the first night were Misia Edwards and her lover, later husband, the Spanish painter Jose-Maria Sert. Misia was a celebrity in Paris. One of the most liberated women of her day, she embodied the spirit of the city. Her salons were attended by everyone of note, she was a friend of Proust and painted by Renoir and Toulouse-Lautrec.

She was ecstatic about the opera, going to every single one of the remaining six performances and even buying up tickets for any empty seats, which she then sent to her friends.

While dining with Sert after the first night, Misia saw 'a rather effete gentleman' coming into the restaurant. 'Handsome and aloof, with a white streak like a swan's feather in his black hair, he was adjusting the black pearl in his tie with heavily ringed fingers.'[7] She recognised Diaghilev, having met him the previous year at his exhibition of Russian paintings in Paris, and Sert immediately invited him to join them. Misia ecstatically praised the production and talked excitedly to Diaghilev until five in the morning. They then agreed to have lunch in a few hours. 'Diaghilev's aloof expression had turned into a boyish grin.'

He remained strong friends with Misia all his life, valuing her opinion, telephoning daily when involved in a ballet in Paris to discuss details,

Fedor Chaliapin's role as Boris Gudunov was to become the triumph of his career

gossiping over friends, sharing a passion for music, quarrelling, making it up, whispering and laughing. He wrote to her once, after she had taken offence at one of his requests to her, to say 'I *love* you with all your faults ... Please remember that not so very long ago we came to the conclusion, in all serious-ness, that you were the one *woman* on earth that we loved.'[8]

Arthur Gold and Robert Fizdale, Misia Sert's biographers, point out that 'Neither Misia nor Diaghilev was particularly gifted sexually, and both found sublimation in controlling their friends and lovers by other means. Surpris-ingly infantile in handling their own love affairs, they were harsh and worldly in their judgement of other people's ... They lavished favours, money, and gifts on friends out of affection, and on enemies in the hope of disarming them.'[9]

The two had extraordinary parallel lives. Both were born in Russia in the March of 1872 and both lost their mothers at birth. Their stepmothers – as each father remarried within a few years – were artistic, intelligent women who not only encouraged them musically but helped open up the whole world of music to them. Both had been involved with innovative magazines, Diaghilev with *Mir Iskussiva* and Misia with the *La Revue Blanche*, a literary magazine funded mainly by the family of her first husband, Thadee Natanson.

When Misia Edwards first met Diaghilev at the start of her passionate liaison with Jose-Maria Sert she was feeling radiant. Her self-confidence had previously taken a blow when her second husband, Alfred Edwards, had left her early in 1908 for the spectacularly beautiful actress, Genevieve Lantelme.

Then she had met Jose-Maria Sert. He had the physical magnetism of many an ugly man – indeed, Salvador Dali claimed that his head looked like a potato though his tall, baroque figure and bushy moustache made him appear a Spanish grandee. He had an immense joy of life and he and the elegant, witty Misia shared the same friends. While holidaying with him in Rome she was captivated by his dominant views on art and artists. Misia divorced Edwards in 1909, the year that Diaghilev planned to bring over both the opera and the Imperial Ballet to Paris.

Writing years later of the start of the Ballets Russes, Diaghilev admitted that in St Petersburg he had noticed a slight reaction against the classical tradition in ballet by the younger members. 'I began wondering whether it would not be possible to create a number of short, new ballets, which besides being of artistic value would link the three main factors, music, decorative design, and choreography far more.'[10]

Diaghilev never lost sight of those three factors. The meticulous way in which he kept control of the whole operation is shown in how he regularly

Misia (later Sert), Diaghilev's closest woman friend, by Toulouse Lautrec

went to 'the scene-painting studios, the sewing-room, attend orchestral rehearsals, and every day visit the production studio to watch artists at work, from the stars to the boys in the *corps-de-ballet*, completing their training.'

This was how Diaghilev ran his empire over the next 20 years. It was an extraordinary joint enterprise. Composers, painters, ballet-masters, authors and some dancers all met to propose and discuss subjects, planning the work for the next months. All ideas were listened to: everyone felt involved. But Diaghilev had total belief in his own judgement and was inevitably proved right.

In January 1909, while in St Petersburg, Diaghilev heard the 27 year old Igor Stravinsky play his *Scherzo Fantastique* and then, later, at a private concert at St Petersburg Conservatory, a composition of his called *Fireworks*. Stravinsky's name was just starting to be known outside the capital and

Diaghilev in 1909, the year he founded the Ballets Russes which took Paris by storm

Diaghilev had an infallible instinct for quality and an unerring judgement in spotting potential. He sent in his card after *Fireworks*, asking Stravinsky to meet him the following day.

Stravinsky didn't hesitate: Diaghilev's name held a decided attraction. But he kept Stravinsky waiting for 20 minutes and the young man, impatient, had opened the door to leave when Diaghilev appeared. If Stravinsky had missed Diaghilev, the music for his great radical ballets, *The Firebird*, *Petrushka* and *The Rite of Spring* (*Le Sacre du Printemps*) that would shock Paris, and help establish Stravinsky as arguably the greatest composer of the 20th century, might never have been written.

Stravinsky himself said that Diaghilev 'was the first to single me out for encouragement, and he gave me real and valuable assistance. Not only did he like my music and believe in my development, but he did his utmost to make the public appreciate me.'[11] Stravinsky believed that Diaghilev enjoyed producing his music and liked forcing a rebellious audience to listen to such works as the revolutionary *Rite of Spring*. The two became lifelong friends.

Diaghilev showed great loyalty to Stravinsky over the years, as indeed did

Stravinsky in return, but it was a tumultuous friendship with breaks in the relationship, mostly due to quarrels over money. Diaghilev was invariably behind with payments for work he had commissioned from Stravinsky and Stravinsky also felt he cheated him over his rightful royalties. As a result, the two would break off communication, refusing to speak to each other for months, sometimes years. Nevertheless, their underlying mutual affection and respect remained until almost the end. On Diaghilev's death, Stravinsky's feelings about his were 'equivocal and complex. Gratitude, indebtedness, admiration, anger, guilt, hostility – they ran the gamut.'[12]

It was in 1909 that Diaghilev asked Michel Fokine, then employed by the Imperial Theatres in St Petersburg as dancer and ballet master, to resign and accompany him to Paris as choreographer and dancer. Fokine was a decided catch, if Diaghilev could snare him. He was highly acclaimed for his choreography for *Le Pavillon d'Armide* and his solo, *The Dying Swan*, for the dancer Anna Pavlova and was both popular and revered by the dancers at the Imperial Theatres.

Diaghilev worked out Fokine's normal income and offered him sufficient to tempt him to leave the Imperial Theatres and Russia. Fokine said later that whenever he negotiated contracts with Diaghilev, his left ear would become swollen after arguing on the phone for four hours. His lawyer would invariably have to stay overnight.

One reason why Diaghilev may have wanted to entice Fokine away from the Imperial Theatres was because of an unpleasant incident two years previously during a rehearsal of the new ballet, *Le Pavillon d'Armide* choreographed by Fokine, which still rankled. Diaghilev had been invited by Benois to watch the performance, but a policeman had approached him and 'invited' him to leave. To his embarrassment and chagrin, he was forced to do so.

No explanation was given, and it could have been because of his 'suspect' morals, but Benois thought it was because Fokine had taken sides with his comrades during the revolution of 1905 and had appeared before the Director as one of their delegates. The revolution over, hostility had reasserted itself. The 'subversive' Fokine was friendly with Benois, who was in turn friendly with Diaghilev. It would be a revenge on the Directorate if Diaghilev managed to tempt Fokine to leave the Imperial Theatres and work for him.

Fokine, like Chaliapin, was greatly impressed with Diaghilev. He accepted his offer because, 'I knew that whatever he undertook was rewarded with success... the foundation of our work for the first season was my implicit trust in and enthusiasm for the new undertaking.'[13]

After Fokine joined the Ballets Rusees in Paris in 1909 as choreographer, he allowed no one, not even Diaghilev, to interfere with his ideas. He occasionally received vague criticism by one or two watchers, like Benois. 'Then it dawned on me that it was Diaghilev who did not approve of my work and had delegated the unpleasantness of criticism to his friends without specifying just what displeased him in my composition.'[14] Fokine worked out exercises to make dancers twist their trunks and bend forwards from the waist, and introduced a variety of hand movements.

It was Fokine who introduced his friend Serge Grigoriev to Diaghilev. Grigoriev was dancing with the permanent company of the Maryinsky Theatre and had appeared in a ballet choreographed by Fokine, *Le Pavillon d'Armide*. He was 'tall, dark and spare, with pale features and sad eyes. His hair, thin on the crown, was brushed straight back'.[15]

On Fokine's recommendation Diaghilev asked Grigoriev to be his *regisseur*, a position which made him responsible for the efficient and smooth running of the performances. Grigoriev accepted with delight, recalling that Diaghilev then gave him 'a curious smile: his mouth alone smiled, the rest

of his face remaining entirely serious ... I often noticed this peculiar smile on Diaghilev's face, polite but cold, and reserved for people he knew but slightly.'[16]

Grigoriev was excellent at his job, which was an extremely onerous one. It was also crucial. Diaghilev could not be all things to all men. The amount of detail and decision in running a ballet company is immense. It was impossible for Diaghilev to control everything. He needed to focus his talents on commissioning new ballets and choosing new dancers and choreographers. He also needed to be aware of new developments in music and art and to meet and talk to those in the avant-garde of artistic thought. Someone meanwhile had to take care of the detail.

From 1909 to 1929, Grigoriev – whose name appeared on both the first programme of the Ballets Russes and the last – was to be Diaghilev's devoted and efficient manager. He watched all the rehearsals, immediately aware if a movement had been omitted or badly executed. 'He inspected the materials of which the costumes were made ... He knew the music cues for the curtain to rise and fall ... and the tempo at which the different numbers should be played. He knew how each costume had to be worn and the type of make-up required. He knew how each scene had to be set.'[17]

Grigoriev carried a pocket-book with him and, sitting in the prompt corner, took notes on every phase of the performance that had not been

Michel Fokine at a rehearsal, one of the few figures in the Ballets Russes who could set an independent path from Diaghilev

to his liking. He would call further rehearsals if any ballet scenes did not meet his own high standards of efficiency. When the season ended, he was responsible for making sure that the vast quantities of materials belonging to the company were packed and transported to the next venue, and that any costumes or décor not needed were put into storage.

Altbough Diaghilev had to leave much of the detail to him, the two nevertheless worked closely together, drawing up the advance programmes and deciding which members of the company were best suited to understudy particular roles.

Diaghilev, too, was a stickler for accuracy and detail, criticising colours or compositions, checking every phase of the lighting. He would not hesitate to spend half the night asking electricians to try out different colours, uncaring about rising costs of overtime or whether he or the stagehands had eaten. At their protests he would reluctantly grant them precisely ten or fifteen minutes of rest before restarting. There was a fair amount of under-breath swearing, but Diaghilev was obeyed.

He would also check costumes carefully against the original design, asking each individual dancer to come forward on stage for this purpose. He would then ask them to do some dance steps, to ensure they could move easily in the costume, sometimes reducing tailors to tears as he ordered that sleeves were altered, braid stripped off and coat skirts shortened.

His authority was absolute, awe-inspiring. He impressed, whethei on or off stage. When Bronislava Nijinska saw Diaghilev at a rehearsal of *Le Pavillon d'Armide* she thought him an imposing figure, impeccably dressed and holding his usual walking cane.

Bronislava Nijinska was three years older than her brilliant brother Vaslav Nijinsky. She had studied at the Imperial Ballet School in St Petersburg where she was taught by the classical ballet master, Cecchetti, and by Fokine. She was a most gifted dancer, showing grace and delicacy, and had graduated with distinction in 1908. She became a soloist with the Maryinsky company.

In 1909, although still employed by the Maryinsky Theatre, she came over to Paris to dance with Diaghilev's company in its early seasons. Although her dancing could never match that of her brother, she had much of his strength and elevation. The Parisian couturier Coco Chanel described her, unflatteringly, as 'small, muscular, and thick-ankled' and thought her face had 'a kind of Mongol flattening, heavy chin, fleshy lips, unattractive mouth and slanting eyes,' reminiscent of her brother.[18]

Bronislava Nijinska the elder sister of Vaslav Nijinsky went on to a long and highly-praised career in ballet

Headlines in 1909 were devoted to Louis Bleriot, the French airman, successfully crossing the English Channel in a small monoplane. Few realised what the future impact would be of Diaghilev, that year, bringing his company of Russian dancers over to Paris.

The birth of the Ballets Russes was haphazard. Diaghilev had been most impressed with the ballet *Le Pavillon d'Armide*, at the Maryinsky Theatre in 1907 and had enthusiastically decided it should be shown in Europe. Astute as ever, he realised 'there was money to be made from the export of more Russian ballets in this vein'.[19]

He and his circle planned a *saison Russes* in Paris. This would include, they decided, the ballet *Le Festin*, with its Ukrainian and Caucasian dances in national costumes; *Les Sylphides*; and also *Cleopatre* – featuring Bakst's colourful and imaginative costumes.

While Diaghilev was staging various painting exhibitions, concerts and opera, his main financial support came from Russian sources. Sometimes he was subsidised by Czar Nicholas II, but he could not rely on this.

His main patron, the Grand Duke Vladimir Alexandrovich Volkonsky, approved of the idea of including ballet in Diaghilev's 1909 season in Paris and helped him obtain 100,000 roubles from the Czar, borrow costumes and sets from the Maryinsky Theatre and use the Hermitage Theatre for rehearsals.

Because of the ballerina Kschessinska's influence with the Grand Duke, Diaghilev thought it prudent to include her in his company. Fokine was against this, regarding her dancing as old-fashioned. Finding she was only to be given one dancing role she pulled out and asked that 'her' request for a subsidy for the ballet be cancelled.

In the middle of all this, the Grand Duke died. Without his protection, Diaghilev's enemies immediately started a savage campaign against him, furious at his intention to replace classical ballets with more modern works. The company was denounced as revolutionary and decadent.

The number of machinations at court practically recalled Borgia times: so many wanted to revenge themselves on Diaghilev for perceived slights or reasons of jealousy.

Kschessinska, for example, managed to get the Czar to withdraw the promised subsidy along with the offer of rehearsal rooms and the loan of costumes and décor. Another of Diaghilev's enemies, the Grand Duke Sergei, suggested Kschessinska actually replace Diaghilev to lead the Paris company.

This spiteful suggestion came to nought, however, and Diaghilev survived whereas a less confident man might have folded. Coping with these interminable machinations and incessant moves against him strengthened him and when minor palace revolutions occurred in the future, he was experienced enough to handle them.

Nevertheless, the Parisian season juddered and could well have foundered without support from sources in that city. The end result was that without giving a single performance in Russia, the company turned their backs on that country and in the year 1909 looked to the west for their future.

5

Soaring Talent

At its start the company was called The Russian Ballet and Diaghilev's name as impresario was in small type. Gradually, his name on the programme became larger and finally topped the bill: by the end of 1909 the company was known as DIAGHILEV's Ballets Russes.

The company left St Petersburg for Paris at the end of April, 1909. Its members were young and excited and looked more like holiday-makers than a ballet company. Striped hampers and trunks were tossed on luggage racks and after arriving at the Gare du Nord in Paris everyone, chattering in Russian, went gaily off to various hotels on the Boulevard St Michel, singing and dancing in the hallways, calling out to each other from balcony to basement.

Excited rumours had been sweeping Paris about the Russians' forth-coming production at the Theatre du Chatelet. There was particular speculation about the leading dancer, 19 year old Vaslav Nijinsky who was born in Kiev, Poland, and was a graduate of the Imperial Ballet. Russia was still seen by many as a land of barbarians: they did not quite know what to expect and were certainly not prepared for the first night on 19 May 1909 to be such an overwhelming success.

Originally, Diaghilev intended the Paris season to consist of a broad operatic programme, including the successful *Boris Gudunov*. But after the death of his crucial backer, the Grand Duke, he reversed his plans and instead of having a season of expensive opera with a sprinkling of ballet, he put the emphasis on ballet with a sprinkling of opera.

Benois made the point that in his early years in St Petersburg, Diaghilev

SAISON RUSSE 1910 L'OPERA BALLETS

Bakst's programme cover for the 1910 Ballets Russes season

had 'looked upon the ballet as something alien and slightly unworthy.' Only gradually had he become interested in it and even then Benois thought that his interest in the ballet 'was of a definitely worldly and snobbishg kind. The joys and delight which the ballet aroused in his friends ... were unknown to him.'[1] Now his fervour for ballet was mounting.

Diaghilev created such a sensation with the Ballets Russes that fashionable and artistic Paris fought to see the ballets every evening. With an unexpectedly provocative programme, he made overnight celebrities of Nijinsky, Fokine, Bakst, Karsavina and Benois. Coco Chanel was to call one of her collections the 'Bakst style'.

Nevertheless, Diaghilev complained to Benois 'that his work had been narrowed down and reduced to some sort of ballet management by the vagaries of fate.' In future years he still tried at times to break free from ballet and widen his programme by including operas in his productions – staging an operatic production in Monte Carlo as late as 1924.[2]

Parisians had previously shown little interest in ballet or dancing, apart from praising Isadora Duncan. As Propert points out, 'There was the Opera House ballet with capable dancers spinning like tops ... and scores of strong young legs in pink tights doing the same things in the same little gauze skirts and smiling the same smile ... Or there were the intellectual amateurs, the solitary dancers, guileless of tights or technique, who trailed their yards of black tulle through the *Death of Asa,* or skipped like young lambs to the strains of Mendelssohn's *Spring Song*.'[3]

Now it had all changed. Diaghilev transformed ballet from a moribund art form into a marvellously effective vehicle for promoting avant garde ideas. The luminaries of the Ballets Russes were taken up by chic Paris, by the socialites, celebrities, writers, artists and déclassé aristocrats. The company was also the darling of the intellectuals who were anxious to be seen to be part of the avant garde movement. There were dinner parties, meetings at cafes, an endless round of entertainment.

The company adored being in Paris and were delighted by the Bohemian life they could lead in the city, dashing in and out of the sidewalk cafes and restaurants in the Latin Quarter, Montparnasse and the Bois de Boulogne, watching the student demonstrations, going to the museums, visiting the Eiffel Tower and the department stores. Bronislava Nijinska recalled how the Russian girls' lack of make-up and modest clothes made them very noticeable.

Jean Cocteau, a sufferer from the 'red and gold disease' [ie, theatre-mad] was exhilarated by his first sight of *Pavillon d'Armide*. He was a protégé of Misia Sert's and knew the only way into Diaghilev's magic circle – the new focus for his creative ambition – was through her. He was an assured 20 year old in 1909 and – so irritating to the less talented – became novelist, critic, artist, actor, director and scenario writer. Many of the painters he met 'disliked his air of fashionable wealth, his restless avidity for notice and his incessant flow of words, witty though they sometimes were.'[4]

Having successfully introduced himself to Diaghilev at Misia's home in the rue de Rivoli, Cocteau brazenly infiltrated the inner group. At the theatre he would sit in a box where, along with Misia, eye-catching with her head-dress of feathers, Diaghilev would watch his dancers through elegant mother of pearl opera glasses.

Cocteau recalled Diaghilev wearing a fitted fur coat with an opossum collar that he sometimes buttoned up with safety pins. 'His face was a bull dog's, his smile a very young crocodile's, one tooth on the edge. To grind this tooth was for him the sign of pleasure, or fear, or anger.' Another feature he recalled about Diaghilev was a wet eye which looked downwards with 'the curve of a Portuguese oyster'.[5] The thirty-seven-year-old Diaghilev, in turn, nicknamed him 'Jeanchic'.

Art in the last 30 years in France had exploded with talent, causing the era to be dubbed *La Belle Epoque.* It was an age of extremes, encompassing painting styles from Post Impressionism to Art Nouveau: painters as diverse as Monet and Picasso. They were all working feverishly, with immense excitement.

Diaghilev became the rallying point of radical European art: thousands who knew little of modern painting learned of the work of artists like Picasso, Matisse, Utrillo and Derain through the Ballets Russes. The same applied to Russian composers.

He attracted those with passion and clarity of vision, working through the minds of younger men, stimulating them and creating excitement: audacious ideas swirled around his inner circle. By its combination of artistry and talent, his company would dazzle the world.

Yet throughout his career, Diaghilev had no guaranteed, dependable source of money; there was no powerful creative group he could join; he did not even have a bank to extend him credit. He relied totally on wealthy patrons or, when in St Petersburg, 'cash for honours' deals – he once raised a crucial hundred thousand gold roubles by cajoling a grand duke to organise a patent of nobility for a manufacturer of galoshes. No personal gain was involved, it was all for the glory of Russian art abroad.

One financial backer was the wealthy aristocratic Russian, Baron Dimitri Gunzburg. Diaghilev would beg for help after purchasing some highly expensive item for a production, details of which he invariably jotted down on his shirt cuff. He would then despair when he would accidentally send the shirt and its crucial contents to the laundry.

When Diaghilev formed his ballet company, however, money became a much more serious concern. He spent lavishly on what he considered

The beautiful Countess Greffulhe was one of Diaghilev's earliest and most generous patrons in Paris

essentials. From 1909 to 1911 the budget of the Ballets Russes climbed to two million francs. Only his determination kept the entire wheel whirling an inch above the ground.

His extraordinary way of tossing off monetary disasters and his Micawber attitude that he and his company would somehow survive, carried him through two decades. He unashamedly networked. One woman he had charmed enough to sponsor him on his first foray in Paris was the beautiful Comtesse Greffulhe, famed society hostess and President of La Societe

Musicale, an organisation founded by the music publisher Gabriel Astruc to promote new music.

Astruc was a witty, lively and popular Parisian, invariably seen in a grey bowler or top hat, with a crimson carnation and rings on his fingers. Later employed by Diaghilev as manager, he was extremely capable and organised and despite frequently falling out with Diaghilev the Ballets Russes was lucky to have its affairs in his hands.

Diaghilev often appalled his sponsors by the casual liberties he took with money. After finding enough sponsors to back his Paris debut, he grandiosely went ahead and commissioned the entire redecoration of the Theatre du Chatelet. Workmen hammered and sawed non-stop. Diaghilev 'guaranteed money he did not have, then scurried about to raise the money he had guaranteed. The magician did it all with mirrors.'[6]

The pressure on Diaghilev was admittedly immense, artistically as well as financially. But without the finance the show could not go on. To realise his dream, Diaghilev 'bargained, lied, broke promises, stormed, bullied, cajoled, charmed and mesmerised.'[7] And invariably succeeded.

He also managed to calm the hysteria which sometimes threatened to overwhelm the rehearsals, full of fervour though they were. He was everywhere and nowhere, appearing and disappearing with the suddenness of the Cheshire cat in *Alice in Wonderland*. He soothed, encouraged, inspired. An equally memorable figure was Leon Bakst, about whom everyone was talking. Tamara Karsavina thought his 'sly, dandified primness, imperturbable good nature stood in sharp contrast to the stormy chaos of our rehearsals.'[8]

The programme for the first season included *Prince Igor* (which featured the agile, charismatic Russian dancer Adolph Bolm in the lightning-swift, rhythmic Polovtsian warrior dances from Borodin's opera); *Le Pavillon d'Armide*, with the bird-like grace of Karsavina in an 18th century guise partnered by Nijinsky; the romantic moonlit dances of *Les Sylphides* (as Diaghilev renamed Fokine's *Chopiniana*); the one-act drama of *Cleopatre* with Pavlova and Nijinsky; and a suite of dances under the name *Le Festin*. Diaghilev had also publicised a ballet called *The Firebird*, still to be composed: unperturbed, he presented instead the old Bluebird *pas de deux* from *The Sleeping Beauty*.

Although Anna Pavlova appeared with Nijinsky during this, her only season with the Ballets Russes in Paris, she clearly did not want to tie herself down to the company. She could see that its focus was on its artistic excellence as a whole, not a background for a specific ballerina. There was no star system in the Ballets Russes: every dancer had a chance of distinction. Even

The superb dancer Tamara Karsavina was for years the prima ballerina at the Ballets Russes. As the imprisoned Firebird, in the ballet of that name composed by Stravinsky

Nijinsky once claimed that he was only the centre piece of a great mosaic.

Later on Pavlova made several guest appearances for the company. Diaghilev had been one of the first to recognise her genius and was angry at what he considered was her desertion of the Ballets Russes after one season, choosing to take Michael Mordkin as a partner when she danced in London over the next couple of years. Mordkin set himself up as a rival to Diaghilev and in 1911 took a company to America he called the Imperial Russian Ballet.

Pavlova was as legendary a figure as Nijinsky. Born into a poor family in St Petersburg in 1882, she trained at the Imperial Ballet School there, achieving ballerina status in 1906, and the following year Fokine created *The Dying Swan* for her. Her magnetic appeal and superb technique brought in crowds to her performances and when she danced in Denmark and Sweden she was cheered in the streets as she sat in her carriage. Technically flawless, she shared with Nijinsky the ability of *becoming* a character, rather than just acting the part. She showed this clearly in her role in *The Dying Swan*.

She had bursts of generosity mixed with violent tantrums, and was annoyed when Diaghilev gave an interview comparing her with Spessivtseva and saying that though they were like two halves of a superb apple, it was the Spessivtseva half which had been ripened by the sun.

Karsavina, who was not only a brilliant dancer, but also a great artist and great beauty, was for years the prima ballerina with the Ballets Russes. She frequently partnered Nijinsky and recalled the audience's growing excitement that season when she performed a *pas de deux* with him in *Le Festin*. 'You would have thought their seats were on fire.' Nijinsky should have walked off the stage to reappear in a solo, but 'On that night he chose to leap off. He rose up, a few yards off the wings, described a parabola in the air, and disappeared from sight. No one of the audience could see him land; to all eyes he floated up and vanished. A storm of applause broke; the orchestra had to stop.'[9]

When Nijinsky was asked if he found it hard to stay in the air when jumping, he replied, 'No! No! not difficult. You have just to go up and then pause a little up there.' An earlier ballet master of his in Russia had irritably commented that Nijinsky was a little devil, and never came down with the music. But it was true that as soon as the audience saw Nijinsky spring out of the wings, with raised arms and feet hardly touching the ground, they knew they were seeing something fantastic, incredible. He did not just bound into the air, but once down and touching the ground, he used this action for a still higher flight.

Ellen Terry thought that Nijinsky projected an emotion which 'has in it all the force of spontaneity, but is at the same time conscious and considered.'[10]

To her, however, he never projected human experience or mankind's passions, but was always the dancer.

Karsavina also became a legendary dancer. Ethel Mannin thought that her personality was essentially of the theatre but that she was completely without affectation. Mannin recalled her intense appreciation of life and 'the authentic artist's lack of artistic self-consciousness … instead of reclining on silk cushions and recalling past glories she goes to a spirit stove and makes an omelette for luncheon.'[11]

What captivated the French audience that season was the barbaric splendour, frenzied movements and wild primitiveness of the dancers. They loved the brilliant costumes of the Polovtsian dancers, were sensationally aroused by Bolm's dancing as Chief Warrior in *Prince Igor*, and captivated by the blazing colour of the Georgian silks.

The wild enthusiasm among the audience matched that of Russian audiences. Fitzroy Maclean considered that 'as a form of artistic expression, the ballet appeals to something deep down in most Russians: to their feeling for colour, for the dramatic and the romantic, to their love of music and movement, to their explosive sense of rhythm.'[12]

One feature in the Ballets Russes put ballet on a higher artistic level than previously achieved. Male dancers in Russia had always been a marked feature, but from the first performances of the Ballets Russes in 1909 they were given an even stronger role. The male ballet dancer was normally subordinate to the female dancer, but in the Ballets Russes he had equal status. As Lynn Garafola says, in her definitive book, *The Ballets Russes and Its World*, Diaghilev 'adopted the one-act ballet as his company's basic format, emphasised dramatic and formal consistency, and focused attention on the male dancer.'[13]

Much of this focus on the male dancer was due to Fokine, as choreographer, for he realised that by using the male as a *dancer* rather than just as a 'lifter,' the male could give 'character, light and shade to a work and that, dramatically, the *pas de deux* is a love duet.'[14] Male solo dancers did not please everyone. One provincial theatre manager in America commented, 'I like the ballet very much, it's dainty, but what's that guy doing there all by himself? I'd get rid of him.'[15]

Nijinsky's brilliant dancing and the massive physical strength of the male Russian dancers electrified the Ballets Russes performances and gave the male dancer a new image. After Nijinsky's soaring talent, ballets were no longer staged just for ballerinas. From now on ballets like *Le Spectre de la Rose, Petrushka, Narcisse* and *Le Dieu Bleu* were created mainly for male dancers.

Ellen Terry once said that the word ballet was 'synonymous for vice' because it allowed women to attract admirers through their physical charm rather than their dancing. She thought a mixed ballet concentrated attention on the art of the dance rather than the attractions of the dancers. Karsavina too thought Diaghilev's vision of the future of the ballet could 'find better expression through the incisive, virile element than through that of feminine grace.' Diaghilev understandably wanted to enlarge the scope of a magnificent dancer like Nijinsky.

Those close to Diaghilev said his affair with Nijinsky began in the days when *Le Pavillon d'Armide* was staged in St Petersburg. Until then, Diaghilev had been involved with his secretary, Alex Mavrine. Yet that year, 1909, Mavrine had become highly attracted by the ballerina Olga Feodorova and eloped with her. Diaghilev was furious. He immediately dismissed Mavrine and had nothing further to do with him. This was classic Diaghilev behaviour: he was incredibly jealous when even discarded lovers deserted him, particularly if they did so for a woman.

Diaghilev was spellbound by Nijinsky, of whose dancing he said: 'the guise of a plain, unprepossessing boy fell off – a creature exotic, feline, elfin, completely eclipsed the respectable comeliness, the dignified commonplace of conventional virility.'[16]

Many physical descriptions of Nijinsky were unflattering – though Charlie Chaplin thought him beautiful, with high cheekbones and sad eyes. Nijinsky was quite short, with a very wide neck and slightly bulbous features. His fingers were exceptionally short and his heavy thigh and calf muscles stretched his trousers so tightly that it almost looked as if his legs curved backwards. One of his ballet masters in St Petersburg had called him the 'fly-swallower' as his mouth was sometimes open.

He appeared socially inept, frequently blushing and lacking enough confidence to speak. He was so nervous at parties that at one official reception he began to chew up his wine glass. On another occasion, at a public ball, his woman partner reportedly told him that he was a nice boy, but that he should really learn to dance.

Describing him, one dancer thought he looked like a faun, a trapped, ill-at-ease creature who 'turned his head furtively, looking as if he might suddenly butt you in the stomach. He moved on the balls of his feet, and his nervous energy found an outlet in fidgeting: when he sat down he twisted his fingers or played with his shoes. He hardly spoke to anyone, and seemed to exist on a different plane. Before dancing he was even more withdrawn, like a bewitched soul.'[17]

On stage, however, he was transformed, becoming a bewitching, erotic, breathtaking figure. As one observer said, 'On the stage his overdeveloped muscular system appeared supple. He grew taller (his heels never touched the ground), his hands became the foliage of his gestures and his face radiated light.'[18]

Diaghilev was unable to love anyone without trying to educate them in

Nijinsky in The Firebird. On stage 'his hands became he foliage of his gestures and his face radiated light'

the arts, his own lifeblood – a reminder of the ancient Greek love between teacher and disciple. He did all he could to tutor Nijinsky in art appreciation, but although Nijinsky attempted to give his views on what he had learned, his remarks were frequently confused. Diaghilev, always beside him, would tactfully correct him.

Diaghilev was delighted with the way the whole company was performing, calling out for Tamara Karsavina on one occasion so that he could embrace her. She recalled that from that day he had always called the company 'his children.' He had every right to be delighted, presiding as he was over the most extraordinary talent. At the time the company included the ballet dancers Nijinsky and Karsavina; the singer Chaliapin; the painters and set-designers Alexandre Benois and Leon Bakst. Bakst's dazzling designs increasingly came to be regarded as an essential part of the Ballets Russes productions: his costumes and scenery were unforgettable: opulent, exotic and colourful, full of oriental grandeur with a touch of the romanticism of the nineties.

Diaghilev's ability was to act as puppet master, controlling, cajoling, keeping an unwieldy caravan of diverse artistes on the road, inspiring them to even more extraordinary heights.

The ballets and the opera played on alternative nights, though much of the enthusiasm for the opera *Prince Igor* was due to its dancers. The last ballet of the 1909 Paris season, *Cleopatra*, proved the most successful of all. Bakst, who designed the costumes, shut himself up for several days in the Hermitage Museum making sketches, and wrapped Cleopatra in a long strip of linen, nearly the width of the stage, sumptuously designed with Egyptian hieroglyphs and motifs.

The title role of Cleopatra was sensationally played by Ida Rubinstein, who came from a wealthy, artistic family in St Petersburg. She had a strange beauty, with almond eyes, long dark hair and an androgynously slim figure. She was a mime rather than a trained dancer, but moved with a mesmerisingly attractive elegance. Frederick Ashton commented that in interviewing her, 'All Diaghilev had her do was lie on a couch and then she probably stood up and made a few gestures.' Nevertheless, the way she walked captivated all Paris and it was said that Pavlova was so irritated that she refused to take part in Diaghilev's next season.

Fokine, the young ballet master of the Ballets Russes, had choreographed the bacchanale and the watching Parisian audience had applauded so enthusiastically that the conductor had to stop the orchestra for several minutes.

The one serious worry for Diaghilev was his fear for Nijinsky, who was

Spectre de la Rose became notorious for Nijinsky's spectacular leap through a French window to land lightly besides the sleeping Karsavina

A portrait of the mime and dancer Ida Rubinstein by Bakst catches her strange beauty and androgynously slim figure

suddenly taken ill. Initially, it seemed to be just a bad sore throat. Nijinsky's sister, Bronislava, recalled that her brother laughingly told her how once when he was ill Diaghilev had immediately shied away from him, never once entering his room but talking to him from outside the door, which he made sure stayed only slightly ajar. Diaghilev now anxiously called in a doctor to diagnose what was wrong and was devastated to be told that Nijinsky had typhoid fever, possibly through drinking tap water.

The hotel where Nijinsky was staying was anxious that the fever did not spread to its other guests, so despite Diaghilev's strong fear of infection he rented a flat and nursed Nijinsky himself. According to Nijinsky's sister, Nijinska, it was here that Diaghilev suggested to Nijinsky that they should live together. The dancer agreed.

During the winding down of the season, the company was deflated by Diaghilev's virtual withdrawal from the scene. Anxious and weary, he was in no mood for celebration, but the company looked to him for approval or criticism and without it, the fun, the whole point of the hard work, simply disappeared. Despite his dictatorial demands, he inspired loyalty and devotion.

Although the enthusiasm of the audience and the critics implied a financial success, the second Paris season had proved very expensive. Astruc, Diaghilev's manager, had told him that receipts had fallen short of expenses by some 86,000 francs and the result could have been disastrous. However, Astruc took possession of the sets and costumes and raised a loan on these.

Nijinsky (left) accompanying Ravel on the piano 1912

Nijinsky told his sister about the difficulties Diaghilev had encountered in settling the accounts. 'Bill after bill kept coming. Bills from the theatre, the ateliers, from the advertisements, all rained in on him.'[19] Nijinsky himself received a stack of bills from doctors, nurses, hotel and restaurants. He never claimed his full, promised salary in order to help out Diaghilev, and in return Diaghilev made himself responsible for Nijinsky's bills. As Diaghilev also owed the hotel several thousand francs, Astruc formally made him bankrupt.

Extricated from creditors, Diaghilev and Nijinsky left for Carlsbad on 'honeymoon' (yet took Bakst with them) and then went on to Venice where Diaghilev delightedly showed Nijinsky his favourite artistic treasures and Bakst painted Nijinsky standing alone in the sea – without Diaghilev, who feared the sea. It was at a party given by Diaghilev that Nijinsky met Isadora

Duncan. She proposed marriage to him, saying that this would be a splendid union because their children would undoubtedly be dancing geniuses. Nijinsky told his family – though hopefully not Isadora – that he didn't want any children of his to dance like her.

Despite being without a penny to his name, Diaghilev was buoyed up by the success of the Paris season and was full of plans for the next. He commissioned *Daphnis and Chloe* from the composer Ravel and went to Paris to talk to Debussy about another ballet – which came to nothing. This antagonised Astruc, who as Diaghilev's manager expected to negotiate his contracts by entering into direct negotiations with the Paris *Opera* for a new season.

Diaghilev and Nijinsky then left for St Petersburg as Nijinsky was contracted to dance at the Maryinsky season on 1 September. Diaghilev, still planning, wrote to the composer Anatole Liadov to say that he knew Liadov needed a year's notice for music to be ordered, but, 'I need a *ballet* and a *Russian* one, since there is no such thing. There is Russian opera, Russian symphony, Russian song, Russian dance, Russian rhythm – but no Russian ballet. And that is precisely what I need – to perform in May of the coming year in the Paris Grand Opera and in the huge Royal Drury Lane Theatre in London. The ballet needn't be three-tiered. The libretto is ready. Fokine has it. It was dreamed up by us all collectively. It's *The Firebird* – a ballet in one act and perhaps two scenes.'[20]

Liadov was interested in the idea but, as Diaghilev knew, he could not be hurried. Asked several weeks later how he was getting on, he said very well indeed: he had already bought the music paper. Despairing, that December Diaghilev commissioned the 27 year old composer Igor Stravinsky to compose *The Firebird*.

Stravinsky was delighted as he had seen two productions by Fokine, *Prince Igor* and *Le Carnaval,* and had greatly admired them both. He worked closely with Diaghilev and Fokine during the winter of 1909. Bakst also contributed many ideas regarding the story and the group ended most days with a good dinner and equally good claret.

The hero of *The Firebird* is Ivan Czarevitch (danced initially by Fokine), who goes into the evil Kostchei's forbidden garden in search of the imprisoned firebird (who was to be danced with eastern languor by Tamara Karsavina).

The score was finished in the March of 1910: its most striking feature was Stravinsky's use of folk music. The composer was an educated, artistic man after Diaghilev's own heart, interested in painting, sculpture, folk lore and architecture. Diaghilev thought very highly of him and during the first rehearsal of the ballet he pointed him out to onlookers telling them to mark him well as he was a man on the eve of celebrity.

What Stravinsky most admired about Diaghilev was his intelligence and unrivalled gift for spotting the novelty and freshness of an idea. Less pleasing was the tenacity he displayed in getting his own way. Stravinsky found it

Ivan Bilibin's illustration from The Firebird*. The hero Ivan Csarevitch enters the forbidden garden in search of the imprisoned firebird*

almost impossible at times to work with him simply because any argument was so exhausting. And you always lost.

The dancer Serge Lifar in later years described how Stravinsky looked and worked when watching him rehearsing for the Ballets Russes: 'I was astonished by his appearance. He was thin and he stooped. His head was rather bald and his great forehead betokened intelligence. I wondered who such a monkey could be – he wriggled about, thumped the keys, panted, made up for missing chords by kicks on the pedal ... or to keep up the tempo he would bring his elbows crashing down on the piano.'[21]

However exhausted, Stravinsky attended all the rehearsals for *The Firebird*. Diaghilev did too and so did the gifted artist Golovine who designed some sets and costumes. The dancers complained that there was no closely-defined melody in Stravinsky's score – though Benois said it was impossible to imagine music which was more poetic, expressive, fantastic and beautiful.

Golovine designed some of The Firebird's sets and costumes, but Bakst designed the costumes for the principal roles. This is his design for The Firebird

6

Splashing all Paris with Colours

As the opera productions had proved too expensive, Diaghilev decided to concentrate on ballet for the new season in Paris in 1910. His interest in ballet had also intensified through his continued passionate involvement with Nijinsky and he wanted to make the ballet a catalyst for what was progressive, striking and exciting in the arts.

Money was still the stumbling block and it was often only his love for Nijinsky that prevented him from pulling out of a further season in Paris. A vast amount was needed as the productions had to be prepared in St Petersburg before they arrived in Paris. Despite the loss of his main financial and personal backer, the Grand Duke Vladimir, Diaghilev still hoped for sponsorship from Russia for the forthcoming Parisian season. His hopes ended when he found Astruc, to whom he owed money, had written a damning financial report on the last season to the Czar.

Astruc was a capable and efficient manager and fortunately for the future of the Ballets Russes Diaghilev's debt to him was paid by a sponsor and Astruc overcame his antagonism. The two men furiously fell out from time to time but invariably renewed their friendship and professional partnership.

The organisation needed for the next season at L'Opera in Paris was immense: indeed Benois said that, at one time, matters got so bad the company feared Diaghilev would have a breakdown. He had to pay off past debts but also raise enough for the new season; he was worried about only staging ballet without opera, as he considered opera had a higher intellectual appeal; and anxious though he was to promote Nijinsky, he needed new ballets to avoid repeating previous ones.

The new season opened on 4th June 1910 and all the tickets were sold out for the gala premiere of *Scheherazade*. The reviews even surpassed those of the first season and there was sometimes a fight for tickets.

Benois paid credit in the Russian newspaper *Rech* to Bakst's unique brilliance in designing the décor for *Scheherazade*, a ballet which virtually re-created *Arabian Nights*, 'a world of special sensations,' with its emerald awnings, hangings, walls and throne, the piles of embroidered cushions and mattresses. The designs stunned the audience and changed public fashion. Cocteau commented that the ballet 'splashed all Paris with colours' and Andre Varnod, a French critic, wrote that 'the fashion in everything was Ballets Russes. There was not a middle-class home without its green and orange cushions on a black carpet. Women dressed in the loudest colours, and the *bibelots* were all striped.'[1]

There was both sensuality and cruelty in *Scheherazade*. It was

Bakst's brilliantly designed set for Scheherazade *virtually recreated the* Arabian Nights

choreographed by Fokine, with sets and costumes designed by Bakst – full of riotous scarlets and golds apart from his castle, built for dreadful deeds. Nijinsky danced the part of the Negro slave, the Sultan's favourite, portraying the spirit of evil with menacing serpentine movements.

It had a dream-like quality, but Bronislava Nijinska recalled that Fokine wasn't at all happy with the production, 'yelling at everyone and being rude to the artists'.[2] She thought this was because he was highly sensitive about publicity and a crucial article had failed to mention him as either a *premier danseur* or the choreographer.

Benois was also angry, as the programme credits for the libretto of *Scheherazade* were attributed to Bakst. The ballet had been chosen by Diaghilev, based on Rimsky-Korsakov's symphonic poem. It was in homage to the composer who had died in 1908 and who had been Diaghilev's tutor at the Conservatory of Music in St Petersburg.

The design for the costumes and décor for the romantic ballet *Giselle*, which opened two weeks later, was by Benois. When Diaghilev planned it he wanted Anna Pavlova to dance the part of Giselle, together with Nijinsky. She agreed, but at the last minute backed out and Tamara Karsavina replaced her. Nevertheless, the reviews were ecstatic as were the reviews for the following production, Robert Schumann's *Le Carnaval*, in which Lydia Lopokova created the role of Columbine.

The premiere of *The Firebird* was on 25th June 1910 and it cemented the extraordinary success of the Ballets Russes. Inevitably there were problems, one of which was Stravinsky's music. Early rehearsals had proved difficult for the dancers: they were not used to music which they found discordant, with a melody they could not clearly define. *The Firebird* needed a number of quick changes of sets and masked figures stood in the wings, blocking the entrances and causing general confusion.

Nevertheless, success was assured from the start. After Diaghilev had envisaged Pavlova dancing the Firebird as well as Giselle, and she had informed him that she had commitments in London, Diaghilev prevailed upon Tamara Karsavina to take these title roles. Originally a dancer with the Imperial Ballet in St Petersburg, she had worked for Diaghilev since the previous year. She formally joined the Ballets Russes in 1911, the year Diaghilev established it as a permanent organisation.

Karsavina, a highly expressive and intelligent dancer, brilliantly interpreted Fokine's choreography in various ballets including *The Firebird*. With just a few words, Diaghilev helped her interpret her various parts. While she worked on her part as Echo in *Narcisse*, he stopped to say 'Don't trip lightly

A Bakst drawing of Nijinsky as the Negro Slave, the Sultan's favourite, in Scheherazade. Nijinsky portrayed the spirit of evil with menacing, serpent-like movement

as a graceful nymph; I see rather a monumental figure, a tragic mask, Niobe.' And when she despaired of dancing *Thamar* (the cruel and amorous Queen in the poem by the Russian Mikhail Lermontov), Diaghilev told her that omission was the essence of art, along with 'a livid face – eyebrows in a single line.' It was all Karsavina needed to interpret the character.

Both the dancing and the décor of *The Firebird* were acclaimed. Bakst had designed a dazzlingly original costume for Karsavina, showing a woman's head and shoulders above a bird-like body. On her head she wore a cap with curved feathers and the greenish material which covered her body was also trimmed with feathers, ending in swansdown. Her brilliant orange gauze trousers, flashing across the stage, added to the magical effect of the Firebird.

Despite the ups and downs, there was a great deal of happy socialising, with tea and pastries being served in the theatre's foyer while Diaghilev talked art and ballet with the artists and musicians. He wanted performers to meet well-known personalities in the audience and usually brought them backstage. The ideas for ballets were often created in evening sessions at the Café de Paris.

It had been while working exhaustively on *The Firebird*, that Stravinsky thought of the idea for *The Rite of Spring*. He imagined 'a solemn pagan rite: sage elders, seated in a circle, watched a young girl dance herself to death. They were sacrificing her to propitiate the god of spring.'[3] Stravinsky described the scene to his friend, the painter Nicholas Roerich, who specialised in pagan subjects. He was delighted with the idea and later collaborated on it with Stravinsky. Diaghilev too, when told about it, was immediately carried away by the prospect.

Although asked to give further performances at the Opera after the season ended, Diaghilev took the company off to Brussels. He wanted Karsavina to dance there even though she had, with Diaghilev's knowledge, agreed to dance that summer at the Coliseum in London. This did not stop Diaghilev from badgering her: 'Telegrams were served to me with every meal. Others met me at the theatre. Their dreaded yellow envelopes wickedly popped at me from the corners of my looking-glass; they jaundiced my very make-up.' However, when she finally managed to get leave and join Diaghilev in Brussels, he was so delighted that she forgave him.

Back in St Petersburg, all high society, including the Dowager Empress sitting resplendent in the Imperial box, attended a performance of *Giselle* danced by Nijinsky and Karsavina on 24th January 1911. Social rules prevailed. In pre-revolutionary Russia the men in the audience always stood in front of their seats facing the auditorium before the performance and

Bakst's dazzlingly original costume for Karsavina as The Firebird, which showed a woman's head above a bird-like body

during the interval. It breached etiquette for them to sit should any member of the Imperial family be unseated.

Nijinsky, though reaching inspired heights that evening, was guilty of a much greater breach. According to his sister, his costume designed by Benois was a short brown tunic over tights, rather than the usual trunks worn over tights. It revealed rather more than the imperial family usually saw. The next morning he was told that by the order of the Dowager Empress, 'You are to be immediately dismissed from the Imperial Theatres for appearing in the presence of her Imperial Highness Maria Fedorovna in the ballet *Giselle* in an indecent and improper costume.'[4]

There are various versions of what happened, including the Dowager Empress thinking it all a good joke. It is also quite possible that Diaghilev encouraged Nijinsky to wear the revealing costume, hoping this way he could lure him away from the Imperial Ballet to become the star of his own company.

It was suggested Nijinsky apologise and petition for reinstatement and that, if he did so, this would promptly be granted. Nijinsky, however, refused, considering that if there were to be any apologies, *he* should be the one to receive them. Diaghilev encouraged him to stand firm.

Nijinsky's departure from the Imperial Ballet marked a significant point in the history of the Ballets Russes. It meant that Nijinsky was now free to perform all the year around instead of when permitted to – such as only between his booked performances at the Imperial Theatres. It decided Diaghilev to establish Les Ballets Russes de Serge de Diaghilev as a permanent company.

He immediately signed various contracts with artists and theatres abroad. The schedule was non-stop and more performers from the Imperial Theatres, like the ballerina Lydia Lopokova and the dancer Adolph Bolm, left to join the Ballets Russes. Diaghilev was particularly pleased at having successfully approached the eminent Professor of Dance and Mime, the Italian Enrico Cecchetti. Cecchetti agreed to give lessons to the company and weld it into a whole.

The first season began in the spring of 1911 in Monte Carlo. Diaghilev loved being there and he was lucky that winter quarters were provided for his company by the Societe des Bains de Mer et de Monte Carlo, which ran the small, but highly attractive Opera House. This had been built by the same architect responsible for the Opera House in Paris, and was part of the Casino complex.

Michael Powell, the director of the film *Red Shoes* (in which the Ballets

Lermontov had slight similarities to the Ballets Russes) remembered often seeing Diaghilev at the Monte Carlo casino – though the impresario went there not to gamble but to look for potential backers for his ballets. Powell remembered his exquisite manners. 'He was always in control of himself, always the most important person in the room.'[5]

The 17th April saw the premiere of the ballet *Le Spectre de la Rose*, choreographed by Fokine and danced by Karsavina and Nijinsky. It was a sentimental langorous ballet about a young girl returning from a ball, sinking into a chair and cradling a rose in her hand as she slept. In her dreams, the rose comes to life. Everyone who saw it remembered Nijinsky's spectacular leap through an open French window to land with incredible lightness besides the sleeping Karsavina.

The physical effect on Nijinsky of his final leap from stage to off-stage was immense. He was caught like a boxer, according to Jean Cocteau, before being 'wrapped in hot towels, slapped and his valet Dmitri spat water in his face.' Cocteau said he would never forget the thunder of applause and would 'always see that young man smeared wth rouge, gasping, sweating, pressing one hand to his heart and holding onto a prop with the other, or even collapsed in a chair' before he returned to take a curtain call.[6]

Cocteau was fascinated by Nijinsky and Diaghilev watched carefully to make sure the fascination remained solely in the mind and that he took no part in the massaging or rubbing down of the star. Diaghilev may not have noticed that one of Cocteau's commissioned publicity posters for *Le Spectre de la Rose*, showed the dancer Karsavina dreaming of being kissed by Nijinsky but with a profile distinctly resembling that of Cocteau.

After leaving Monte Carlo the company went on to Rome in May, where they rehearsed the new ballet *Petrushka*. The idea had come to Stravinsky the previous year in Switzerland. It was the story of a puppet at a fair who, together with other puppets, comes to life. Petrushka is brutally manipulated by a conjuror and his love affair ends in tragedy with his death. When Stravinsky first played some of the music to Diaghilev, he was so delighted he persuaded Stravinsky to turn the idea into a full-length ballet.

In Paris in early June, the company continued rehearsing *Petrushka*. But when the costumes and décor designed by Benois arrived from St Petersburg they were in a very battered condition – particularly the portrait of the Conjuror, a vital reminder to Petrushka of his master's power. Bakst designed a substitute, which so annoyed Benois that he immediately resigned as Artistic Director.

Although Diaghilev, immaculately dressed as ever, appeared almost daily

Lady Ottoline
Morrell,
the English
aristocrat,
became one
of Diaghilev
and the Ballets
Russes' great
champions

at rehearsals, Benois saw that he looked very tired, conscious of the burden he had taken on himself. Diaghilev was only too aware that the coming summer season at the Theatre du Chatelet in Paris would need a strong input of his energy and strength.

One visitor to Paris that summer was Lady Ottoline Morrell. Daughter of the Duke of Portland, she was famed for wearing ridiculous feathered hats along with cascades of beads. At one point she dyed her hair bright orange. The Bloomsbury Group mocked her behind her back, and Virginia Woolf dismissively called her 'Lady Omega Muddle.' However, members of the

Group were not averse to accepting her hospitality at Garsington Manor, her 17th century mansion near Oxford.

In Paris Lady Ottoline saw a performance of *Le Spectre de la Rose* and Maynard Keynes, the economist and a member of the Bloomsbury Group, begged for her impressions of Nijinsky, his new idol. He was then irritated when she described him as 'rather spotty' and admitted not having taken a great deal of notice of him, having 'been too enthralled to find herself sitting next to Diaghilev to look at the stage.'[7]

Diaghilev's company was acting as a testing ground for new ideas, styles and techniques. The enthusiasm was tangible.

The impresario had had an extraordinary, bold success with his first season in Paris, captivating new audiences with all the magic of a conjuror. How had he done it, this boy from Perm?

His phenomenal energy and gift for organising gave him a head start. He first applied his abilities to the magazine *World of Art*, then to the Imperial Theatres *Annual*. The success of these boosted the innate confidence his artistic background had given him. Music was his mainspring, but his interests were incredibly wide and he enthusiastically applied his skills to everything: producing, directing, setting up exhibitions.

It was his work at the Imperial Theatres in St Petersburg that excited his interest in opera and ballet. His revival of ballet, for so long rather a static and overlooked art, gave him full scope for his powers. The major part of his success was because despite his already formidable knowledge of music, he never stopped listening and learning. This applied to all the arts: he would visit cities throughout the world to see composers, choreographers and artists.

He was interested and delighted by new styles and ideas – whether in music or art. He also had an unending appetite and enthusiasm for the work of young painters and composers, uncaring about their wider appeal. Diaghilev positively foisted innovatory work on the public, his success making him increasingly confident in his own judgement.

It was his constant fascination with new ideas and his willingness to try them out that kept the world's eyes on Diaghilev over the next 20 years. As Karsavina said, 'There is no toxin of sentimentality in Diaghilev. Not only does he not regret yesterday, but all his mental attitude tends towards tomorrow. He does not treasure relics, he does not turn back to look at the past. In this may lie the explanation of his untiring creative power.'[8]

Nevertheless, despite his undoubted creative success in Paris, Diaghilev was conscious of Napoleon's remark that 'It is not enough to take the Tuileries; the problem is to stay there.'

7

London: 'Exciting to be Alive'

The year 1911 was a heady time for the arts in London. In November 1910 Roger Fry, who had been working at the Metropolitan Museum of Art in New York, launched the exhibition 'Manet and the Post-Impressionists' at the Grafton Galleries in London. It included Cezanne's geometric landscapes and voluptuous Gauguins and the zenophobic British public laughed or raged at it. Critics poured scorn on the works, the *Morning Post* calling for all the paintings to be burned. There were few examples of post-Impressionism in England and virtually no interest.

Reactionaries, who considered the new art movement signified the end of civilisation as they knew it, pointed in delighted proof to the Post-Impressionist ball held in March 1911 – attended by many of the Bloomsbury Group – with 'the women scandalising the press and the other guests by appearing as Gauguin-like savages, draped in African cloth.'[1]

That same year, at Gatti's restaurant in Regent Street, various artists including Walter Sickert, Harold Gilman and Spencer Gore decided to set up the Camden Town Group. It consisted of 16 artists, all of whom lived and painted in the rather grubby surrounds of Camden Town, whose aim was to accustom the public to paintings of a 'modern character.'

However, as Virginia Nicholson points out in *Among the Bohemians*, England remained isolated from the cultural explosion on the Continent. 'French literature and art, Russian novels and drama, the works of Ibsen: all were regarded as depraved, insofar as they were regarded at all.'[2] The English critic Clement Scott made one of the milder comments on Ibsen when he called the characters in *A Doll's House* 'an unlovable, unlovely and detestable crew.'

Yet despite such reactions, the publisher and writer Leonard Woolf claimed that 'It was exciting to be alive in London in 1911,' and wondered whether human beings might really be on the brink of being civilised. There was certainly a feeling of stimulation, a buzz of energy, a sense of impending change: cars and aeroplanes were coming off the production line; Freud and Einstein's theories discussed; and Ibsen's plays were drawing attention to the position of women. Politically, there were constant suffragette protests and riots; the trade union movement was flexing its muscles amid industrial unrest: and the dockers, railwaymen and weavers went out on strike.

Socially, there were exuberant celebrations for the Coronation of George V on 22 June 1911. The excitement reached the same pitch as it had the previous year, when Crippen was executed for murdering his wife. And when in June 1911 the Ballets Russes burst on to the stage, people flocked in amazement to the performances. Diaghilev's company succeeded in revolutionising British lacklustre attitudes to dance, scenery and costume.

John Singer Sargent's drawing of Lady Ripon gives a glimpse of her fabled beauty

Diaghilev had originally planned his London season for 1910, but the death of King Edward VII in the May of that year had caused him to postpone his plans. It was not until the June of 1911 that he brought his company over to Covent Garden.

The season was sponsored by Lady Ripon who was a daughter of Sidney Herbert, Secretary for War during the Crimean War. Her second marriage was to Lord de Grey and on her father-in-law's death in 1909 she became the Marchioness of Ripon.

During the 1890s, she was a spectacular figure. The writer E.F. Benson remembered her dazzling beauty. Despite being six foot tall, she wore her hair piled high on her head, and had 'so matchless a grace that the effect was not that she looked tall, but that most other women looked squat.'[3]

There was little at the time to preoccupy bright women: she regarded politics with 'a sort of weary repulsion,' disliked cards and physical exercise and loathed the interminable round of trivial social engagements which allowed women to fritter away unwanted time by changing clothes five times

The daughter of Lady Ripon, Lady Juliet Duff, became a valued patron of the Ballets Russes, often given to writing hundreds of begging letters

Anna Pavlova and Mikhail Mordkin appeared as an alternative 'Russian Ballet' in London in 1911, causing Diaghilev no small irritation

a day. She was well-known for her numerous affairs. Occasionally she gave a 'Bohemia in tiaras' party, to one of which Oscar Wilde drifted along, saying to one of the guests 'Oh I'm so glad you've come. There are a hundred things I want not to say to you.'[4]

Of high social status, with ability and brains, Lady Ripon was at heart a rebel, who wanted a cause to occupy her, and she found it in opera. At the time opera at Covent Garden, a once great institution, was 'ill-rehearsed, ill-staged, and interpreted by a wretched orchestra and squalling singers to shabby and sparse houses.'[5] Although the then Lady de Grey knew little technically about music, she had the force and the skill to revitalise opera and

make it fashionable again by means of inviting friends like the outstanding singer Melba to make an appearance at Covent Garden.

Although her involvement waned over the years, her interest in Covent Garden revived sharply when Diaghilev brought his company there, as ballet excited her more than music had ever done. She became a crucial patron of the Ballets Russes and at the end of the first season gave Diaghilev a black pearl stud. He was always to wear it, except on those occasions when it graced a pawnbroker's.

Lady Ripon's daughter, Lady Juliet Duff, followed in her mother's footsteps and also became a crucial patron of the Ballets Russes. Lady Juliet was as tall as her mother, but lacked her outstanding beauty – indeed it was reputed that her mother had her highly educated to disguise her deficiencies.

Anna Pavlova irritated Diaghilev by appearing in that summer of 1911 as an alternative, possibly rival entertainment to the Ballets Russes. Along with her partner, the then unknown Mikhail Mordkin, she danced at the Palace Theatre in London. Although the ballet critic of *The Times* politely and coolly referred to them as 'This talented lady and gentleman,' their reception was wildly enthusiastic and the Palace Theatre had never had such a success on its hands.

A gala performance of the company at the Theatre Royal was scheduled for 26th June as part of the celebrations for the coronation. Diaghilev told the dancers they must look their best as the host of parties expected and indeed London was flying all its flags. Arches decorated with garlands lined the streets, buildings sported portraits of the King and Queen and roads melted in the heat.

The scene at the Theatre Royal was spectacular. Inside bouquets and garlands of flowers vied with the glittering jewels, tiaras and colourful decorations of the audience.

Diaghilev still stood out. In dark clothes during the day, he invariably wore dinner jacket or tails in the evenings, opera hat at a fashionable angle. His evening clothes sometimes looked a little worn, although his linen was always immaculate.

He had heavy-lidded eyes that drooped at the corners, a moustache in the shape of an inverted V, and a trick of 'plucking a handkerchief from his sleeve and extending one foot, which quivered distractingly.'[6] You could always tell when he was near as he perfumed his hair with an almond-blossom brilliantine.

His manners were impeccable and his great charm inspired devotion among his followers. The ballet critic Cyril Beaumont recalled his suave address and caressing voice. 'His *mon cher ami*, accompanied by an affectionate touch of his hand on your wrist or forearm, was irresistible. On the other hand, when cross, he could be brutally curt and arrogant, and no one could snub with more biting sarcasm.'[7] Physically he moved slowly, as if his body was heavy to support. One acquaintance said, disparagingly, that shaking hands with him was like clasping a ball of cotton wool.

The Theatre Royal was sold out, even requests for boxes at £500 being in vain, while the gallery was packed with those who were as interested in the audience as the production. When the performance ended, Diaghilev wondered at there being no applause from the stalls. Only gradually did he realise that the constant ssshhh sound was that of kid gloves, gently clapping.

This entire London season of the Ballets Russes was an exhilarating experience for the public. They were expecting Cossack dancing: instead they were captivated by sensational ballet dancers, exotic sets and spectacular new ballets like Carl Weber's *Le Spectre de la Rose* and Robert Schumann's *Le Carnaval*, both choreographed by Fokine.

The poet Rupert Brooke, who went in delight to several performances that summer, told the actress Cathleen Nesbitt one night that they had seen a miracle, as Nijinsky had actually stopped still in the air.

Watching *Le Carnaval*, Ellen Terry was amused by Bakst's designs for the corps de ballet, with their peg-top trousers and crinolined ladies, and said that for the first time she used the word 'acting' in connection with the ballet. She was also highly impressed with its 'true comic spirit' and admitted that until then she had not credited the Russians with humour. 'The story is interpreted more through genuine pantomime than through dancing, which perhaps accounts for the popularity of this particular ballet with us English.'[8]

Eugene Goossens, the brilliant young conductor and composer, who made his name conducting the London premiere of *Le Sacre du Printemps*, remembered watching the performers night after night, intoxicated by the sumptuous productions and the legendary, inimitable dancing of Nijinsky and Karsavina. Goossens' own compositions inspired Noel Coward to write the lighthearted lines 'My heart just loosens when I'm listening to Mr Goossens'.

The stage designs by Bakst had an immediate impact on audiences. Their colour and exotic appearance strongly influenced fashion and interior decoration in London. Through them Bakst changed a generation's taste in theatre and interior design. Some of the more avant garde and wealthy members of the audience were quick to imitate the colours and design of his productions.

Lady Cunard, then one of the best-known hostesses in London, totally

EMU.

redecorated her house at 20 Cavendish Square – which had been rented from the Asquiths after they moved to 10 Downing Street. She casually converted it to evoke the spirit of the Russian ballet:

'The dining room was hung with curtains of arsenic-green lamé. Against one wall stood a black lacquer screen of carved porcupines framed in the nimbus of their bronze quills ... The dining room table was a huge circle of lapis-lazuli, in the centre of which reflecting the candlelight stood a gilt-bronze *epergne* supported by naked figures of nymphs and naiads ... In the walls was a great Chinese incense-burner.'[9] She also had a cloth-hanging painting of dappled giraffes, acting as background to her delicate French furniture.

Diaghilev knew these luminaries of London's social life, Lady Ripon socially smoothing the way for him. As ever, Diaghilev took care to move in a circle where he could meet possible patrons. Two examples were Sir Joseph Beecham, the famous 'pill millionaire', and his son, Thomas Beecham, conductor and producer of opera, whose orchestra accompanied the Ballets Russes during its first London season.

Thomas Beecham was a great admirer of Diaghilev, claiming he was the greatest impresario he had ever met: 'There was nothing that he did not know about dancing; he had a sympathetic understanding of modern painting ... he was a musician of estimable parts.'[10] Beecham considered this combination of abilities made Diaghilev's company unrivalled. This scintillating group of the most gifted composers and scenic artists of the day lifted stage decoration out of its dull decline.

Diaghilev spoke only Russian and French, but he and Beecham managed to converse in a mixture of French and English. Diaghilev had a prodigious appetite and the writer and art critic Sacheverell Sitwell said he found it an inspiring moment when Diaghilev examined the menu through his eyeglass. When lunching with Diaghilev at Kettner's restaurant he got the impression that Diaghilev was allowed double helpings for the price of a single portion.

Diaghilev's love of food encouraged him to learn three words of English. It was at the Savoy – where he always stayed when he was in London – that Sacheverell's elder brother Osbert heard him ask one of the waiters, in a low voice, for 'more chocolate pudding.'

Diaghilev turned his room at the Savoy into a workroom with a piano, top-heavy with music scores, on which he would play Russian music. He always checked the designs for costumes and décor, though would discuss these over a meal downstairs.

To his company, Diaghilev was a highly visible icon. They were all very

A cartoon of the conductor Thomas Beecham, who considered Diaghilev the greatest impresario he had ever met

conscious of him calmly standing in the wings night after night, hands in pockets, distinguished, elegant, a dandy to his fingertips. Only when he saw that everyone was present did he give the signal to raise the curtain.

Fokine was a different character, far more worried and nervous than anyone else, while Bakst 'is to be seen everywhere, no matter where one looks. Now he is near the dressing table, explaining the makeup to one artist, now he is checking over another dancer's costume; he calls the dressmaker, the hairdresser, and shows them the changes he wants.'[11]

At the end of their season in London the company had two months' holiday before returning for a further six-week engagement. After their return that autumn, the corps de ballet complained that the company only gave them one pair of shoes which were expected to last for ten performances. The shoes had not lasted, had holes in them and it was too painful for them to dance. Informed of this, Diaghilev started to speak in a high-pitched voice, as he always did when he was angry, and shouted, 'I am not a shoemaker. I am not responsible for your shoes. That is not my profession.'[12]

During the break, Diaghilev left for St Petersburg to organise a company appearance in Paris and then a winter season in Russia. Nijinsky did not accompany him, to avoid the strong possibility of having to sign up for military service.

The educated avant-garde Russians at that time knew a considerable amount about western art. Many had travelled abroad or worked there and some currently based in Paris had influence in the art world. Diaghilev fitted into this world of Russian émigrés and from 1912 onwards he spent less and less time in St Petersburg. When he did so he made a hotel his headquarters.

He was now essentially a European, at home in most of the major cities in Europe, moving through countries at speed, recognised instantly wherever he was. Although he surrounded himself with Russian dancers, painters, choreographers and musicians, the country which had moulded him was now rarely to see him.

8

Crash, Crash, Cling, Clang, Bing Bang, Bing

The year 1912 saw the then largest steamship in the world, *The Titanic*, sink on the 15th April after striking an Atlantic iceberg on its maiden voyage and drowning 1,513 crew and passengers.

Greater tragedy apart, it must have horrified Diaghilev who had a traumatic fear of drowning ever since a fortune teller told him he would die on water. At the time, however, he was busy touring with his company. After seeing in the New Year in Paris, he took the Ballets Russes to Berlin for a month before going on to Dresden.

Although there was little interest in the ballet in this city, Diaghilev was anxious to meet again the Swiss composer Emile Jacques-Dalcroze, who had devised a method of dance called 'Eurhythmics.' This trained the body through exercise to move gracefully and harmoniously, usually to music.

Jacques-Dalcroze ran a school based on his doctrines and Diaghilev took Nijinsky with him on daily visits as he hoped to inspire Nijinsky choreographically, so that he could apply these ideas to the composition of a new ballet, *l'Apres-midi d'un Faune*. Diaghilev had the idea for this ballet after first meeting Jacques-Delcroze and had held a few secret rehearsals the previous spring in Monte Carlo with Nijinsky, Bakst and a few other dancers. The reason for the secrecy was to prevent Fokine from realising that Nijinsky was now being groomed to take over from him as choreographer. Adolph Bolm, who was not only an outstanding dancer but was interested in choreography and directing and stood in for Fokine when he was away, was also overshadowed by Nijinsky.

When the company rehearsed the steps for the first time, the dancers disliked the rhythms, found the ballet very difficult and complained that they couldn't force their bodies into such unusual positions. They showed their feelings clearly by yawning unreservedly.

The next stop was in Vienna where the Austrian poet and dramatist, Hugo von Hofmannsthal, met Diaghilev and Nijinsky, and was captivated. 'Since the evening of this Saturday I have actually only existed with no one else but Diaghilev and Nijinsky, evenings in the theatre, breakfasts with them, sitting and speaking from breakfast until the theatre again – nights either sleeping poorly or entranced, writing ballets for them of which two, a tragic, antique, and a macabre in the costume of Carpaccio now [have been] written, fixed, enriched and modified ...'[1]

The company was booked to dance *Petrushka* at the Opera in Vienna, but the orchestra there refused to play the accompanying music by Stravinsky. They considered each note conflicted with the laws of harmony and were insulted at the mere idea of being asked to perform.

Diaghilev was having none of this. Bronislava Nijinska remembered him standing behind the barrier of the orchestra with such a look of contempt on his face that it had an immediate effect on the musicians. The noise and bow-rapping stopped. He spoke decisively, saying he could hardly believe he was talking to the world-famous Viennese orchestral musicians and not to some shoemakers.

Fixing his monocle in his eye, he continued his tirade, saying that Stravinsky was a musical genius, admired throughout Europe, and they must all be lacking in culture if they couldn't understand his music. 'There was a time when Vienna accused Beethoven of violating the rules of harmony. Do not show yourselves to be as ignorant again.'[2]

After a dressing-down like this, the orchestra had little option but to start playing and at the end they gave Diaghilev an ovation, which he graciously acknowledged.

Diaghilev never hesitated to remove what he considered weaknesses in the original version of ballets, replacing dances he considered poor with others he liked, such as the *Dance of the Sugar Plum Fairy*. He would work on the literary structure of a ballet, even going so far as to change the century in which it was set. Before a ballet was presented, Diaghilev supervised every stage of its evolution. 'Les Ballets Russes, c'est moi,' he could well have said.

It was in 1912 that a 21 year old girl, who came from an aristocratic Polish family which had settled in Hungary, secured an introduction to the 22 year old Nijinsky. She had watched him dance before in Paris but on seeing him again wrote to friends ecstastically to say she was in the presence of genius. Attractive, fair-haired, with remarkable blue eyes, her name was Romola de Pulszky and within a year and a half she would be married to Nijinsky.

Her pursuit of him was carefully planned. Although she had taken dancing lessons in the past, she was by no means an accomplished dancer. Yet within a few months she had persuaded Diaghilev to allow her to take classes with his dancers – taking great care at her interview to disguise from him her interest in Nijinsky. In writing later about Nijinsky, she admitted she could scarcely believe she had managed to fool Diaghilev.

The company left Vienna to go to Budapest, but on arrival Diaghilev angrily discovered that Fokine (taking a leaf out of Diaghilev's own book) had been secretly rehearsing the company not for their next opening in Monte Carlo in April, or for the Paris season in May, but for a charity performance at the Maryinsky Theatre in St Petersburg. Fokine had initially been high in Diaghilev's estimation because of his creative ability and his daring inauguration of a new era in ballet by reforming the old classical school of dancing, but relations between the two men were clearly deteriorating.

Fokine was incredulous to find that Diaghilev, infatuated with Nijinsky and convinced of his powers, was thinking of him as the company's new choreographer. The change was backed by Stravinsky, composer of *Le Sacre du Printemps*, who wrote that month from Monte Carlo to Anna Stravinsky in Russia to complain that Fokine was likely to be the choreographer. Stravinsky considered him an exhausted artist who 'writes himself out with each new work.'

For four years Fokine's name had been identified with the Ballets Russes as choreographer. Conscious that Diaghilev was losing interest in his work, and puzzled by his indifference, he decided to leave the company at the expiry of his contract in June. Diaghilev received the news with apparent indifference.

Serge Grigoriev, Diaghilev's stage manager, aware of the situation, commented that Diaghilev 'valued his collaborators only as long as, in his view, they had something new to contribute. Once they ceased to fulfil this role he felt no regret in parting with them.'[3]

The Paris season opened at the Theatre du Chatelet on 13th May 1912. The one new ballet was Reynaldo Hahn's *Le Dieu Bleu*. Hahn, a French composer born in Venezuela, was a friend of Proust and a darling of the salons. Fokine had started working on the choreography of this new ballet in Berlin that year, inspired by some Siamese dancing he had seen, and the scenario was written by Jean Cocteau.

Its décor, created by Bakst, was memorable. Too memorable, perhaps. It featured a huge, bright orange rock with two poles protruding from it, both of which were holding up enormous lifeless pythons. The critic of *Le Figaro* praised the dancing of Karsavina and Nijinsky but the general reaction was reserved to the point of coolness. Even Diaghilev had doubts about it, especially the music.

The next ballet, *Thamar*, opening a week later, had a little more public success. Karsavina effortlessly evoked the avid, fatal heroine who makes death the penalty of an hour of her love. Bakst had contrived magnificent settings and the entrance of the lover and his companions, silent, black-coated and black-hatted men, with their faces muffled in scarves, was highly effective.

The third premiere, on 29 May, was *L'Apres-Midi d'un Faune*. The story was of nymphs coming to bathe in a spring and being spied on by a faun. Spotting him, the nymphs run off, but one drops her veil. It is picked up by the faun who takes it, leaps spectacularly to his lair, and lies caressingly on the veil.

It was the first ballet to be choreographed by Nijinsky and Fokine jealously commented on the unprecedented measures taken to ensure its success. On the day of the dress rehearsal 'a reception – champagne, caviar, and so on – was held for invited guests and critics, something that had never been done during the preceding four seasons.'[4]

The first night drew friends and supporters and from the start there was excitement and anticipation. Jean Cocteau reported that the 'spotted, skin-tight leotard that Bakst had designed for Nijinsky to make him look '*plus nu que nu*,' the swaying bunch of grapes attached over his genitals, and especially his copulatory movements, on opening night, as he lowered himself over the nymph's scarf, brought down the house and the wrath of virtuous editors.'[5]

According to a photograph in *Le Prelude a l'Apres Midi d'un Faune*, published in 1914, on the first night 'Nijinsky slid his hands *under* his body in such a way as to suggest masturbation.'[6] The audience reacted noisily – loud applause was mixed with equally loud boos.

Diaghilev appeared on the stage looking flushed and agitated, never having encountered such a turbulent reaction to one of his ballets. But in response to the applause, he promptly asked the cast to repeat the whole performance. Auguste Rodin stood up in his box, shouting 'Bravo, bravo.'

The critics mostly praised the production. The editor of *Le Figaro*, however, thundered against it. 'We are shown a lecherous faun, whose movements are filthy and bestial in their eroticism, and whose gestures are as crude as they are indecent ... And the over-explicit miming of this mis-shapen beast ... was greeted with the booing it deserved.'[7]

Bakst's costume for a temple dancer in Le Dieu Bleu, *a ballet with a Hindu theme*

The sculptor Auguste Rodin promptly wrote to the paper *Le Matin* applauding the ballet and defending Nijinsky. 'When the curtain rises to reveal him reclining on the ground, one knee raised, the pipe at his lips, you would think him a statue; and nothing could be more striking than the impulse with which, at the climax, he lies face down on the secreted veil, kissing it and hugging it to him with passionate abandon ... I wish that such a noble endeavour should be understood as a whole ...'

There was a further acrimonious correspondence between the editor of *Le Figaro* and Rodin, the public took sides and the police were ultimately called in to view a (sold-out) performance. However, they took no action.

Diaghilev was so pleased with Rodin's defence he carried the newspaper extract around with him for several days. Nijinsky had once posed for Rodin and on one occasion through tiredness had fallen asleep in Rodin's studio. Diaghilev had come in to find not just Nijinsky asleep on the couch, but the seventy-one-year-old sculptor also asleep with his head resting at Nijinsky's feet. Diaghilev forbade further sittings.

Diaghilev was delighted at the publicity surrounding *Apres-Midi d'un Faune*. He was still enthusiastic about Eurhythmics and that summer he and Stravinsky went to visit Benois in Lugano. There they listened to Stravinsky playing parts of the music he was composing for his new ballet *Le Sacre du Printemps (The Rite of Spring)*.

Stravinsky was enthusiastic about past and primitive history and intended his new ballet to evoke early barbarian rituals, including a ritualistic sacrificial dance as practised by the pagan Slavs. Stephen Walsh, Stravinsky's biographer, makes the point that in reading Russian folk poems, Stravinsky 'was probably more interested in the way the wrong accents could work against the right ones to make a highly subtle and complex rhythmic music.'[8]

Diaghilev shared Stravinsky's interest in folklore and primitive history and arts. When asked about the intellectual origins of the Ballets Russes, he said these were based on 'domestic implements in the country districts, in the painting on the sleighs, in the designs and colours of peasant dresses, or the carving around a window frame.'[9]

In the June of 1912 Lady Ottoline Morrell was joking with the writer Lytton Strachey about Nijinsky, in whom Lytton had a predatory interest. Lady Ottoline suggested that once Nijinsky arrived in London they 'throw the beautiful Henry [Lamb] to Diaghilev to keep him quiet', leaving Lytton free to court the Russian dancer.[10] She suspected that Lytton's enthusiasm for the Russians was directed more at the male performers' muscular beauty than their art.

Bakst's painting of Nijinsky in L'Apres Midi d'un Faune, which depicted a faun's erotic dreams. The performance caused a storm of protest

Irritated by the fervour of Lytton and his friends over Nijinsky, she was half prepared to be scornful. However, when she saw him perform in *Carnaval*, she too became one of his devoted fans, saying 'I was completely converted ... he seemed no longer to be Nijinsky, but became the *idea* which he was representing.'[11]

The Ballets Russes company was due in London later that month. Lady Ottoline, having met Nijinsky in Paris had grown 'very fond of the little figure with long, muscular neck and pale Kalmuk face, and the hands so expressive and nervous ... he was incessantly thinking out new ballets, new steps.' Off-stage he was both nervous and highly strung, and Lady Ottoline noted that 'his guardian and jailer, Diaghilev, did not allow him to go out into society as it tired and upset him, and I was one of the few people that he was allowed to come and see, as at my house he could be quiet and only meet other artists.'[11]

The return of the Ballets Russes to London that June was greeted with delight. The critic of the *Daily Mail* welcomed the company back and looked forward to spectacles 'of a complete and luxurious beauty.'

The forty-year-old Diaghilev opted for a calmer season in London after the turmoil in Paris, so decided not to stage *L'Apres-Midi d'un Faune*. Instead, as well as some known ballets he premiered three new ones for London, *The Firebird*, *Thamar* and the mythological poem *Narcisse*, all three featuring Nijinsky and Karsavina and all proving highly successful.

Karsavina was particularly acclaimed. *The Times* thought she surpassed herself in *The Firebird* 'in agility, grace and sensuous beauty' and the ballet critic Cyril Beaumont considered her *Thamar* splendid, 'a dangerous, feline creature, as she stretched langorously on her couch, her pale brooding features made sinister by the dark eyebrows ...'[12] Beaumont believed Nijinsky and Karsavina were the perfect partners. Diaghilev agreed and when Karsavina told him that her name on the billing had appeared below a minor member of the company, in a fury he half-strangled the man responsible.

In parallel with the Ballets Russes, Adeline Genee, the Danish ballet dancer famous for her interpretation of Swanilda in *Coppelia*, was at the Coliseum. Diaghilev went to see Genee that July and when she appeared he 'was as excited as a child, and superlative praises poured from his lips'.[13] Although anxious to have her in his company for his next season at Covent Garden, he was unsuccessful.

Nijinsky meanwhile was preoccupied with the idea of a new ballet called *Jeux*, about two women and a man engaging in provocative games. Jacques-Emile Blanche, one of Lady Ripon's lunch guests at the Savoy Hotel in the summer of 1912, received a note from Diaghilev asking him to come to the grill room to join him, Bakst and Nijinsky as Nijinsky wanted to talk to him about his idea.

Blanche recalled that Nijinsky 'was drawing on the table-cloth when I reached the grill-room. Diaghilev looked as if he were in one of his cross moods, he was biting his fingers; Bakst looked at the drawings on the cloth aghast – but Nijinsky understood only Russian, and it took me some time to find out what was in the wind. The "cubist" ballet – which became *Jeux* – was a game of tennis in the garden; but in no circumstances was it to have a romantic décor in the Bakst manner!'[14]

Sent the score by Blanche, Claude Debussy rejected it as 'idiotic and unmusical'. Nijinsky, furious, announced he would not dance in London any more. Debussy was offered twice the fee and accepted. It showed, however, that Nijinsky's creative ideas and those of Diaghilev were beginning to differ and a certain uneasiness prevailed between them. Once when Diaghilev was telling a long story at the lunch table at the Savoy, Nijinsky asserted his independence and announced at the end that it had been too long and boring.

Lady Juliet Duff, writing in her memoirs, considered Diaghilev 'an odd mixture of ruthlessness and vulnerability. He could make others cry, but he could cry himself, and I remember a day at my mother's house on Kingston Hill when he had had a disagreement with Nijinsky, who had refused to come, and he sat in the garden with tears dripping down his face and would not be comforted.'[15]

After London, Diaghilev unexpectedly took the company to perform at Deauville, the new fashionable bathing resort on the coast of Normandy. Gabriel Astruc who was in Deauville had just been appointed to the post of director of the new theatre in Paris, Theatre des Champs Elysees. Astruc was determined to engage the Ballets Russes to open in that theatre in the spring of 1913. Knowing L'Opera Theatre in Paris was equally intent on engaging them, he offered Diaghilev such an enormous sum that he accepted immediately.

Benois had been busy in Russia in 1912 and from now on he was hardly involved with the Ballets Russes. He and Diaghilev amiably drifted apart.

A winter tour of Germany and Austria was due to begin in Cologne in October. Diaghilev meanwhile went off to his beloved Venice for a holiday before visiting St Petersburg to negotiate with the Imperial Theatres for artists, sets and costumes for a planned Russian opera and ballet season in Paris and London the following summer. The programme would include *Boris Gudunov*, with Chaliapin as singer. Diaghilev arranged this mixture as, with the loss of Fokine, Nijinsky had now been elevated to the company's choreographer and Diaghilev still worried whether he would cope with the premiere of the new Stravinsky ballet.

Diaghilev arrived in Cologne just in time for the first performance, but he was lucky there was one at all. When the company arrived, no one was there to pay for the costumes and sets to be taken from the station to the theatre. Worse, there were notices up in the theatre to say that unless these were collected right away, they would all be sent back to Paris. Fortunately for Diaghilev, Bronislava Nijinska bailed them out and paid the requisite money for the costumes and sets to be released.

The company moved on to Berlin and one of the people Diaghilev met there was Baron Gunzburg, an impresario who suggested to Diaghilev that the company tour South America the following autumn. Diaghilev was not particularly interested in South America and decided not to go himself – his fear of drowning predominating over the wish to be with his company. Had he known the result of his absence, he might have changed his mind. However, Gunzburg remained useful to Diaghilev, backing many productions until his death in the civil war in Russia in 1919.

In November 1912, Stravinsky finished his score of *Le Sacre du Printemps*. At Christmas Diaghilev took on Miriam Ramberg (later known as Marie Rambert) who was one of Dalcroze's best pupils. He was aware that Stravinsky's score for his proposed new ballet, *The Rite of Spring*, was complex and knew the dancers would be struggling with the difficult rhythms of the ballet.

Ramberg was to help teach and explain Eurhythmics to them and naturally worked closely with Nijinsky. She noticed that when the two of them were rehearsing, Vassily, Diaghilev's old servant and now a general manager, was constantly coming in for some minor reason such as putting a cardigan around Nijinsky's shoulders. He was under instructions from Diaghilev to prevent any flirting between the two dancers – no one yet realising that the real threat came from Romola.

Over the next months Romola cultivated the friendship of Miriam Ramberg, who was half in love with Nijinsky herself. Through this deliberate friendship, Romola found out a great deal of information about Nijinsky: how he worked and thought, what he liked and what he didn't. It was to prove highly useful when she finally managed to be alone with Nijinsky.

Despite frequent rehearsals over the next few months, the dancers still found it hard to grasp the constantly changing rhythms for *The Rite of Spring*. The music was basically unsuitable for dancing, but the intention was to focus on a series of groups moving rhythmically.

Miriam Ramberg remembered Stravinsky turning up at a rehearsal, pushing aside the German pianist who was playing his score, and playing it twice as fast as the dancers could possibly dance. 'He stamped his feet on the floor and banged his fist on the piano and sang and shouted, all to give us an impression of the rhythms of the music and the colour of the orchestra.'[16]

Georges Barbier's impression of Nijinsky's feminised body as the faun in L'Apres Midi d'un Faune

The ballet was in two scenes and had no specific story, but consisted of a number of primitive rites. Nijinsky had been working on the choreography and the *regisseur* Grigoriev considered, dismissively, that he was as helpless as a child and relied entirely on practical suggestions from Stravinsky and Diaghilev.

The London premiere of *Apres-Midi d'un Faune* took place in February 1913. At the end when the Faun, again danced by Nijinsky, lowers himself on to the scarf, English audiences were as startled as the French. Cyril Beaumont remembered the gasp from the audience at Nijinsky's audacity. Although the ballet was rapturously received, there were also some hisses expressing the outraged feelings of those who thought the Russian ballet was going too far.

However, the hisses came from a minority. There had been radical changes in social behaviour since the death of Queen Victoria over a decade earlier. It would have shocked her to see so many fashionable young women in London currently smoking, drinking, painting their faces and throwing off their corsets. The actor Henry Irving had succeeded in making the stage respectable and the aristocracy now filled the seats, or even went on stage themselves.

Exotic foreign dancers appeared on London's West End stages and equally exotic costume-balls became all the rage, with 'gentlemen with blackened faces, turbans and gold sashes accompanying ladies who were hybrids of Salome, Madam Butterfly and Mary Magdalene.'[17] Along with 'The turkey

Lydia Sokolova, born Hilda Munnings, joined the company in 1913 and became a celebrated member. She is seen here in Chout

trot' and 'the Russian ramp', the Tango was introduced in the spring of 1913 and became an instant trend-setter, inspiring Tango Teas and forcing the makers of the relatively new hobble skirt to slit open these skirts at the front and allow young girls, to the shock of their mothers, to slide around the dance floor showing their stocking-clad legs.

Wealthy young women would tango in exotic dress, in contrast to the economy over costumes practised at the Ballets Russes. One of Serge Grigoriev's responsibilities was to keep a strict eye on the company's wardrobe.

Although he had to decide whether certain costumes had to be repaired or replaced, thrift, with him, was paramount. Once, just before a performance of *L'Apres Midi d'un Faune*, one of its nymphs came to Grigoriev in desperation to ask if she could have a new costume. Her present one, she said, was so ragged that she would soon appear naked. Grigoriev gave a swift glance at the costume and then turning away said 'That will be charming, Madame.'

The 1913 spring season of the Ballets Russes in Paris was launched at the new Theatre des Champs Elysees, with its salmon and gold finish and grey marble and sculpted bas-reliefs. One of the new dancers that year was Lydia Sokolova. Born Hilda Munnings in Essex, England, she was the first English dancer to join Diaghilev's company.

At the start of the season when Diaghilev came to the rehearsals, she was scared stiff by his impressive presence and self-assurance. Everyone stood up, silently, while Diaghilev made a royal progress. The male dancers to whom he spoke would click their heels together and bow. 'He would look for creases in the scenery, make sure the lighting was correct ... carefully shaved and scented, his hair touched up with black dye, except for a white streak left on one side, he looked incredibly distinguished.'[18]

The new season was planned to emphasise Stravinsky's music, Nijinsky's choreography and Fedor Chaliapin as main singer. As the Russian singers could not get to Paris in time for the opening, Diaghilev decided to open with the new ballet *Jeux*, composed by Debussy and choreographed by Nijinsky. It was a sporting, amorous theme and Debussy complained that his score was expected to make a rather improper situation acceptable. He commented that 'in ballet immorality escapes through the dancers' legs and ends in a pirouette.'

Diaghilev took exception to Bakst's design for Nijinsky's costume, which showed him in knee-length, red-bordered shorts, thinking they made Nijinsky look ridiculous. He promptly redesigned these himself, giving Nijinsky long white trousers. To Diaghilev's annoyance the ballet was still unfinished as Nijinsky had been waiting for the arrival of the two ballerinas who would partner him. Diaghilev insisted it be finished immediately and it was somehow scrambled together.

At one point, during rehearsal, Nijinsky flew into one of his unpredictable rages at a remark by Karsavina. He complained furiously to Diaghilev about her but Diaghilev instead of backing Nijinsky, was equally angry with him for his criticism of Karsavina, telling him he was nothing but a guttersnipe compared to her and to apologise to the ballerina immediately.

The story of *Jeux* scarcely existed: it was of two girls playing tennis, joined by a young man, and then all three playing and dancing until a further tennis ball, thrown onto the set, disrupts them. It was a disappointingly tame start to a much-heralded season. Debussy's music was praised by the audience, but there was little sympathy for the dancers' angular movements, which were considered rather ugly in comparison to classical ballet. Far more successful was the first night of *Boris Gudunov* on 22 May, with its spectacular costumes and the brilliant Russian singer Chaliapin.

The Russian composer Sergei Prokofiev, in Paris at the time, considered Chaliapin a musical genius and was delighted that the singer's name was on everyone's lips. He thought that operatic subjects based on the era of Ivan the Terrible realistically portrayed the harsh life of those times. Chaliapin, aged forty, who was from a peasant background, had himself been starved and constantly beaten as a child and had faced destitution. Although actors then were dismissed as of little importance, the stage offered him a certain brotherhood, a possible way out of serfdom. Ultimately, his musical brilliance was recognised.

Although Diaghilev's early cultured years in no way resembled Chaliapin's, the two men shared one significant similarity: they both in adult life made determined efforts to educate themselves further. Through his extensive travel, Diaghilev saw many artistic treasures and met a cultivated circle. He groomed himself into sophisticated elegance and continued all his life to study paintings and music.

Chaliapin, totally lacking in education and culture, learnt table manners from his music tutor, who told him 'if you continue to eat with your knife you will slit your mouth to the ears.'[19]. As he made new and more cultured friends, they introduced him to literature and instructed him how to behave in society. He got them to agree that 'if he did something wrong they would snap shut their cigarette cases. It would be a warning signal that he should stop and think.'[20] There was a constant flurry of snapping, but by the time Chaliapin reached Paris, his manners could not be faulted.

Prokofiev, who greatly admired the new Champs Elysees Theatre where Chaliapin was to appear, was impressed by Parisian chic: 'One is not admitted to the stalls except in full evening dress; during the interval the men wear top hats.'[21]

Paris was buzzing with activity. The year 1913 saw the first volume of Proust's sequence of novels known as *A la Recherché du Temps Perdu*. But it was the premiere of *Le Sacre du Printemps*, subtitled *A Tableau of Pagan Russia*, that set Paris alight. Diaghilev had rehearsed the ballet 200 times. He was very aware that the music might provoke a demonstration and warned

the cast that whatever happened they must continue to the end. But the final dress rehearsal of this two-act ballet, which was attended by writers, painters, actors, musicians and friends, went so well that warnings were forgotten and the riot it provoked was totally unexpected.

The high point of the ballet was the selection of the Chosen Maiden. Once chosen, she would then be offered as a sacrifice to the goddess of spring. As all the maidens dance, one of them falls into a trance and then, in a state of ecstasy, begins to whirl around faster and faster. The rhythm of the music is vital but remorseless and dominating, a maelstrom of ever-increasing sound. The maiden's movements become increasingly frenzied, she spins violently out of control until, exhausted, she falls to the ground, dead. The sacrifice has been made.

The first night audience on 29th May 1913 was alive with excitement: they were at the new Theatre des Champs-Elysees, seeing a ballet choreographed by Nijinsky with music by Stravinsky. The décor and costumes had been designed by the relatively unknown painter Nicholas Roerich. It

Nicholas Roerich's tranquil, idyllic landscape created as the set to Le Sacre du Printemps was a celebration: all the bright stars in the social firmament were there, all expecting to see the Russians performing 'a sort of elegant gymnastics in ballet form, composed largely of graceful poses and timid improvisations. It was an illusion cruelly shattered by the black mass that exploded on the stage.'[22]

Alice B. Toklas, there with Gertrude Stein, was initially intrigued by seeing the French poet, Guillaume Apollinaire, in evening clothes 'industriously kissing various important-looking ladies' hands'. The two women were very amused: 'after the war they all did those things but he was the only one to commence before the war.' Their attention was then drawn to a man in the adjacent box 'flourishing his cane, and finally in a violent altercation with an enthusiast in the box next to him, his cane came down and smashed the opera hat the other had just put on in defiance. It was all incredibly fierce.'[23]

The disruption began almost as soon as the music started. There was jeering, which developed into shouts of protest, followed by equally loud shouts requesting order. The demonstrations and counter-demonstrations soon developed into uproar, drowning the orchestra. Nothing could be heard and, as half the audience were now on their feet, nothing could be seen either. Nijinsky was standing on a chair off-stage screaming to the dancers, ' … sixteen, seventeen, eighteen … ' as this was the method he used to keep the dancers in time with the music.

However the louder he screamed, the louder the uproar became: the dancers could not hear him and indeed the sound of their own heavy clumping steps helped drown his voice. Nijinsky, furious, had to be physically held back from dashing on to the stage. Diaghilev meanwhile had ordered the electricians to turn the lights on and off in an attempt to quell the noise. He shouted to the audience to let the dancers finish the performance, but the furore continued and only towards the end of the ballet did the audience start to calm down.

Coco Chanel recalled the scene with amazement and disbelief. All the upper echelons of society were there, bejewelled and silk-wrapped – but shrieking like banshees. She watched aristocratic ladies in their fashionable turbans turning purple with rage, one of them 'bellowing her lungs out, her tiara all askew.' There was shouting and confusion and the audience at times seemed to take centre stage.

The Comtesse Edmond de Pourtales said she feared the imminence of cataclysm. 'I felt as one does in the first shock of an earthquake, or at the coming of an eclipse, when animals near a farm crowd together, filled with terror.'[24] Regardless of the social standing of those in the audience, there was a general scrimmage, blows were exchanged and women fainted.

Shocked at the almost immediate derisive laughter, Stravinsky left his seat in the stalls and rushed backstage. 'I have never again been that angry. The music was so familiar to me; I loved it, and I could not understand why people who had not yet heard it wanted to protest in advance.'[25]

Stravinsky's revolutionary music of wilful, purposeful dissonance made baffled audiences reassess what they had hitherto regarded as musically enjoyable. Initial reaction spread beyond France: America's *Baltimore Herald* devoted its front page to the following verse:

Who wrote this fiendish Rite of Spring?
What right had he to write the thing
Against our helpless ears to fling
Its crash, crash, cling, clang, bing bang, bing

However, tastes were about to change. Audiences began to realise that music did not have to be romantic and gentle to be artistically acceptable. In Paris, the young Francis Poulenc, hearing the music of *The Rite of Spring* for the first time, was amazed by Stravinsky's strange, dissonant harmonies. The sounds were so new to him that he later asked himself whether, if he had not heard them, he would ever have written any music himself.

There were other enthusiasts. Count Kessler wrote to his friend Hofmannsthal to say, 'What Nijinsky has accomplished here sticks out from the choreography like a Gaugin from a Bouguereau. I have the feeling that we have before us in Nijinsky's choreographic fantasy something as surprisingly new, strong, and revolutionary as Poe for the literary, and Beardsley for the graphic fantasy.'[26]

Nijinsky's sister Bronislava was a strong supporter of her brother's new and controversial choreographic ideas and was acknowledged herself as a leading exponent of neo-classical choreography.

Underlying the mayhem that greeted *The Rite of Spring* was a reactionary protest against Modernism, against what was considered a new wave in the arts. There had been an equal uproar in Berlin the previous year by the audience listening to Schonberg's *Pierrot Lunaire*. It was a rearguard action against an apparent attempt to demolish the old order.

The wish to preserve the status quo was combined with fears that Decadents and Nihilists were behind the new creativity and exuberance that had been bursting through the arts for the last half dozen years.

Yet musicians and artists were not, as was believed, being deliberately destructive but were looking to the past for inspiration. Many of the present ideas were inspired by previous culture. Picasso's magnificent Cubist painting, *Les demoiselles d'Avignon* in 1907, which allegedly inaugurated Modernism, and his paintings of that time, were stimulated by exhibitions in Paris of primitive African masks and prehistoric Iberian sculpture.

Back in 1910, Stravinsky's brilliantly conceived ballet, *The Firebird*, had had the corps de ballet crawling on all fours, portraying Russian folklore monsters, while barefoot dancers imitated Russian folk dancers. *The Rite of Spring* was based on the pagan rites and dances of ancient Russia and Slav folklore was used to rediscover a vigorous, more primitive form of art. These creators were building on the past, not demolishing it.

9

Nijinsky's 'Treachery'

To Diaghilev's delight, the uproar about *The Rite of Spring* generated such wide publicity that it packed the new theatre in the ensuing weeks. Nevertheless, it was with some trepidation that he included this ballet in the company's season that summer in London, a season again sponsored by the Beechams.

Diaghilev went ahead to London while Nijinsky and Nouvel followed, travelling separately from the company. Romola de Pulszky booked herself on the same boat and train as Nijinsky. By standing outside the compartment he shared with Nouvel she occasionally managed to exchange a few words with him. She also went up on the deck of the boat in order to be able to sit near him. His French was still limited, but sign language helped out.

Nijinsky was becoming more aware of her and when he was met off the train by Diaghilev, soigné in a straw hat, he had the temerity to raise his cap to her to say goodbye. Diaghilev looked round at her in surprise – and indeed Romola herself was surprised at Nijinsky's unexpected courage.

The English premiere of *The Rite of Spring* was on the 11th July at the Theatre Royal, Drury Lane. Diaghilev had asked his friend, the music critic Edwin Evans, to appear on stage in front of the audience and explain the music and the aim of the new ballet. Evans did as best as he could, but the audience was so anxious to see this much-heralded production that he was given short shrift.

Anyone who expected the graceful steps of classical ballet and enjoyed dreamlike languors of the preceding ballet, *Les Sylphides,* was horrified at the deliberately angular movements of the dancers and the thudding intensity of the music – which many claimed gave them a headache.

They thought the leg wrappings, scarlet and flaxen smocks and the daubed make-up was an affront to taste. They sat bemused, considering it a scandalous production. Some hissed; others, however, interpreting the intentions of the composer and choreographer, applauded. The audience was almost equally divided. W.A. Propert commented that 'the active hostility of the French was at least more intelligent than the polite indifference of the English audiences.'[1]

Diaghilev was again pleased at the publicity it created. *The Times*, referring to Stravinsky's music, commented that it 'ought to convince Mr Gordon Craig that even if the Russian ballet belongs, as he has lately being telling us it does, to the theatre of yesterday, the music is not always exactly retrospective ...'[2] *The Morning Post* was more hostile: 'These early individuals, clothed in picturesque dresses of many centuries later, indulge in gestures that are supposed to be "of the period". They better suggest a physical culture class ...'[3] The Ballets Russes was again on everyone's lips.

Hilda Munnings, the dancer re-named Sokolova, watching Nijinsky in London, noticed he seemed incapable of mixing with people and only spoke to someone with whom he was dancing, 'and then he would talk softly and shyly, without looking at the person, and move away as quickly as possible.' He had a habit, before starting work, of walking around on the tips of his toes, first moving a few steps to the right and then to the left, 'holding his hands up in a curious characteristic way with the backs touching his cheeks, his head tilted downward.'[4]

At a luncheon party given by Lady Ripon, Lady Ottoline Morrell again met Nijinsky finding him 'a pure artist' and as such quite different from the other smart guests. It was at one of her lunches that Diaghilev allegedly was horrified to hear Nijinsky comparing Ottoline to a giraffe before innocently asking when he could come to lunch again.

Lady Juliet Duff also found herself sitting next to Nijinsky, although her few words of Russian convulsed him with laughter. Like Diaghilev, Nijinsky only knew one or two words of English. One was an attempt at Piccadilly which he called 'Piccadill' and the other was 'Littler' – which was his attempt at saying 'Little Tich' (the comedian Harry Relph).

An extraordinary figure, just four and a half foot high with a head bald as polished ivory and galvanic legs, Little Tich was lionised in Britain and idolised in France. He sang a song saying he was 'highly educated in the feet' and delighted his music hall fans by dancing in long flat wooden shoes

(28 inches long, half his own height) using astounding acrobatic steps and finally raising himself up on the toes of his wooden shoes. If his act was on in London when Nijinsky and Diaghilev were there, the two men delightedly went off to see him, watching spellbound.

Such gentle scenes contrasted with the current clash of English politics, with the furore of the Home Rule Bill for Ireland being rejected and rioting suffragettes trying to blow up the Chancellor of the Exchequer's house.

However, first nights at the ballet still remained a priority for Diaghilev's close society friends. Lady Diana Cooper, for example, was not only a fanatical supporter but thought nothing of donning a costume and joining the Drury Lane chorus. Gertrude Stein also attended frequently and Thomas Beecham remembered her 'always dressed in a thick skirt, white silk shirt and with a little hat perched on top of her huge head ... Ethel Smyth was there too, of course, dressed in a mannish way.'[5] Gertrude Stein would come to London for the Russian season where she was remembered as 'sitting in Buddhistic calm' until she became interested in some topic of conversation 'and then she would talk for hours.'[6]

Behind the scenes at the ballet, life was less fun. Diaghilev was having doubts about Nijinsky's choreography and considered altering the direction in which the company was going. According to Count Harry Kessler, Diaghilev 'had lost his nerve temporarily, in the face of the reaction to *Le Sacre du Printemps* and wondered whether Nijinsky was not alienating his audience. Besides, he was tiring of his protégé.'[7] Nijinsky's sister said Diaghilev told her he was no longer able to endure her brother's unpredictable behaviour and his violent outbursts.

However this did not prevent Diaghilev and Nijinsky going to Baden Baden at the end of the season, where they were joined by Benois. They were enthusiastically planning a ballet set to the music of Bach and hired a pianist to play them Bach selections. Nijinsky and Diaghilev were also talking about visiting Paris and Venice on Nijinsky's return from the South American tour.

The autumn of 1913 saw most of the company, including Nijinsky and the stage manager Serge Grigoriev, set sail for the Argentine, where the company was booked to appear. Diaghilev stayed in Europe, along with a dozen or so dancers who disliked the idea of a long sea voyage and asked to be released from their contracts.

Romola de Pulska, however, applied to go to South America and was so eager to do so she said she would pay her own fare if necessary.

Serge Grigoriev would be managing the company and Diaghilev was represented by Baron Gunzburg. Although Romola was booked into a second-class cabin, she paid to be upgraded to a first class state-room near to Nijinsky.

Romola was 23 and her determined pursuit of Nijinsky was essentially fun for her. She was not in love with him, but she did idolise his dancing. Nijinsky himself had no intention of leaving Diaghilev, or the Ballets Russes which had bought him such fame, but he too felt released at being away from Diaghilev's possessiveness. However, whenever Romola walked past his deckchair he seemed immersed in his book and otherwise spent his time working on the Bach ballet.

Nijinsky remained reserved, but after a couple of weeks the company was surprised to see him once or twice in apparent animated conversation with Romola. What was even more astonishing, according to Romola's account, was that she was then visited by Baron Gunzburg who said that Nijinsky had requested her hand in marriage. She assumed it was a joke, but when she went on deck Nijinsky emerged and said in his rather halting French, 'Mademoiselle, voulez-vous, vous et moi?' and pantomimed, indicating on the fourth finger of the left hand, a ring.' Romola nodded and, waving with both hands, said, 'Oui, oui, oui.'[8]

The Baron gave a dinner on board to celebrate the engagement and Lydia Sokolova later commented 'We all guessed that Romola had prevailed on Gunzburg, who was a friend of hers, to help her organise this affair ... the rest of us thought it was tragic and dreaded Diaghilev's reaction.'[9] There were rumours that Gunzburg wanted Diaghilev's hold over Nijinsky to be weakened or cut, so that he could set up a new ballet enterprise headed by Nijinsky.

Nijinsky married Romola de Pulska in Buenos Aires on 10 September and the whole company went to the wedding breakfast. Sokolova said that 'It was an extremely awkward occasion, for there was not a single person – except possibly Gunzburg, who was either blind or mad – who could honestly congratulate bride or groom ... Nijinsky just smiled and picked his fingers, while Romola looked as pleased with herself as was possible in the circumstances; she must have sensed our disapproval. I think they were both as worried and uncomfortable as we were.'[10]

The couple had dinner in their hotel bedroom 'both,' said his wife, 'so embarrassed that we could not even express ourselves in pantomime.' When Nijinsky finally kissed Romola's hand and left her, she admitted she was so relieved 'I almost cried from thankfulness.'[11]

Nijinsky informed Diaghilev, then in Venice, of his marriage. Misia and Jose-Maria Sert were with Diaghilev when the telegram arrived. He read it and understandably went deathly pale. According to her 'Sobbing shamelessly in Russian despair, he bellowed accusations and recriminations; he cursed Nijinsky's ingratitude, Romola's treachery, and his own stupidity in allowing Nijinsky to travel without him.'[12]

Diaghilev held a council of war with his friends, raging that the marriage must somehow be terminated; but it was too late. Nijinsky had unpardonably yielded to a woman.

Misia and Jose-Maria Sert took Diaghilev to Florence and Naples to divert his mind where 'overcome by sadness and fury, he gave himself to a wild orgy of dissipation. But he was beyond consolation.'[13]

When Diaghilev told Stravinsky in Montreaux, Switzerland, that autumn the whole sorry tale, Stravinsky said that Diaghilev turned 'into a madman who begged me and my wife not to leave him alone'.[14]

Though their marriage may have been conceived in haste, the long-suffering Romola remained with Nijinsky for life

Bronislava Nijinska, who was understandably highly emotional about the whole affair, claimed that Anna Fedorava, a dancer with the company, told her that after receiving the news Diaghilev had avoided people and became reclusive. Seeing him in Montreux when he was sitting alone on the terrace of a hotel overlooking the lake Fedorava noticed he was quite preoccupied, his hands grasping the top of his cane and his chin resting on them. She told Bronislava Nijinska that after he lifted his head she was quite frightened by the way his face was so distorted by grief. He did not answer her, but said nothing.

Diaghilev's old acquaintance Count Kessler observed that 'Diaghilev is mortified in his vanity, in his sentiment, in his pocket, in *everything*.'[15]

Nijinsky had continued to dance with the company, which performed for a month in Buenos Aires before going on to Montvideo and then Rio de Janiero. Ballet as an art was virtually unknown in South America, so the initial reaction was somewhat tepid, but gradually its popularity grew.

One night while the company was in Rio, however, Nijinsky refused to dance in *Le Carnaval*, although he had been billed to appear. For a dancer to miss a performance, without a doctor's certificate, was regarded as a very serious offence. Despite Grigoriev warning Nijinsky that Diaghilev would not forgive his non-appearance, and it could lead to dismissal, Nijinsky still refused to dance. Baron Gunzburg sent a telegraph to Diaghilev to inform him of the incident.

Grigoriev was summoned to meet Diaghilev in St Petersburg immediately the company returned there, which was shortly before Christmas. Diaghilev then showed him a telegram from Nijinsky – who had remained in South America. It asked Diaghilev when rehearsals for the new ballet were to start and requested that during these rehearsals the company took on no other work. Diaghilev, putting his monocle into his eye and biting his tongue which he always did when he was upset, handed Gregoriev the reply he wished him to send. The translation from the original French read:

'In reply to your telegram to Monsieur Diaghilev, I wish to inform you of the following. Monsieur Diaghilev considers that by missing a performance at Rio and refusing to dance in the ballet *Carnaval* you broke your contract. He will not therefore require your further services. Serge Grigoriev, *Regisseur* of the Diaghilev Company.'[16] The man that Diaghilev had once called 'Le dieu de danse', with his miraculous elevation, would dance no longer for the Ballets Russes.

Diaghilev was known for his jealous rage when he thought a lover, or indeed any member of his staff, had betrayed him. Nijinsky was apparently bewildered by his dismissal on the grounds of breaking his contract as he had not had one since 1909. He wrote to Stravinsky to say he was now in Budapest, where he and his wife were visiting her parents, and had just heard he had been dismissed.

'Write to me please, is this true or not?' he asked Stravinsky anxiously. 'I can't believe that Seriozha [Diaghilev] could treat me so basely. Seriozha owes me a lot of money. He has paid me absolutely nothing for two years, neither for my dancing nor for the new productions of *Faune, Jeux* and the *Rite of Spring*. I worked without contract. If it's true that Seriozha doesn't want to work with me any more, I've lost everything.'[17] Diaghilev had, however, always paid the bills for Nijinsky's hotel and his clothes and had also given him enough money to meet his mother's needs.

Nijinsky told Stravinsky that since the split with Diaghilev had been reported in the European press, he had received various proposals including one from a rich German who was offering him a million francs to commission the designs and the music for a rival Ballets Russes. However, Nijinsky said that he would make no decision until he heard the truth from Stravinsky.

Naively he appeared unable to link his marriage to Diaghilev's furious reaction. His wife, more aware, admitted 'Now, for the first time, it dawned on me that perhaps I had made a mistake.'[18]

Nijinsky may have been dismissed from the company, but not from Diaghilev's personal or professional thoughts. The dancer had virtually symbolised Diaghilev's ballet company as premier danseur and then as choreographer.

The problem now facing Diaghilev was finding a replacement. Despite the cavalier way in which he had treated Fokine, he decided to ask him back to act as both dancer and choreographer. Fokine, still bitter about Diaghilev's conduct, at first indignantly refused. It took Diaghilev more than four hours on the telephone to persuade him to return. He was offered the job of taking over from Nijinsky as premier danseur and choreographer. Although Fokine eventually agreed, he insisted that if he did so no ballets that Nijinsky had choreographed were to be performed.

Rejected by Diaghilev, Nijinsky decided to form and tour a company of his own, which would include his sister Bronislava. Although he had complained that Diaghilev had not paid him, he had made a substantial amount of money through private engagements – such as dancing for the Aga Khan – and was thus able to finance this idea. In late February 1914 the Palace Theatre in London delightedly advertised a Nijinsky season. Lady Ottoline Morrell took flowers to the Savoy to welcome Nijinsky and his wife and the season, which was to include a new version of *Les Sylphides*, was soon sold out. All seemed well.

However, problems mounted. Nijinsky felt humiliated at having to dance at a music hall venue, sandwiched between a popular singer and a clown's act. Diaghilev brought a court action against Bronislava Nijinska to prevent her dancing with Nijinsky, claiming she had broken her contract to do so. He lost, but Nijinsky's nerves were wearing thin. He fell out with the management and at one point smashed a table. A bad attack of influenza prevented Nijinsky from dancing and the season came to an abrupt end.

Lady Ripon had no sympathy, angry with Nijinsky for having married a woman she called an 'avaricious, anaemic Hungarian', but Ottoline Morrell was kinder, 'touched by the plight of the little dancer and his pregnant wife. In 1913, everybody had wanted to know him, now nobody did.'[19]

Bronislava Nijinska claimed she saw Diaghilev in the audience when Nijinsky was dancing in *Les Sylphides*. Diaghilev was nonchalantly sprawled in his seat in the stalls, 'his large head leaning to the right, his lower lip protruding with great self-assurance in a sardonic smile. I do not believe he applauded once.'[20]

Mikhail
Larionov
painting
his face in
prepartion
for a Futurist
event in St
Petersburg

Diaghilev and Fokine went off to visit the painter Nataliya Goncharova in Moscow. They intended to ask her to design the new ballet-opera they were planning called *Le Coq d'Or* in which there would be a choir as well as ballet. Diaghilev liked to surround himself with people with creative ideas and Fokine had heard that Goncharova and her life-long partner, the painter Mikhail Larionov, were in the forefront of Russia's avant-garde.

The two artists, both aged 32, belonged to a set of Moscow Futurists 'who painted their faces, organised violent lectures on New Art and that at these lectures pitchers full of water were tossed into the audience.'[21] Fokine was anxious about collaborating with these two young futurists (or hooligans as some dubbed them) but found them quiet and charming.

According to Larionov's biographer Anthony Parton, Larionov had first

met Diaghilev back in the winter of 1902 when Diaghilev was reviewing the Charles Rennie Mackintosh exhibition at the Moscow Society of Architecture for his magazine, *Mir Iskusstva*. Diaghilev invited Larionov to lunch and Larionov commented: 'Our conversation flowed quickly and fascinatingly. Diaghilev broached the topics of most relevance to me: painting, artists, and the theatre.'[22]

Mikhail Larionov's caricature of Diaghilev and his circle about 1920

Diaghilev called for Larionov's assistance in 1906 when mounting an exhibition and their friendship was to last over the years – despite Larionov's notorious temper, which was so violent that he once knocked Diaghilev down.

Larionov, a huge blond man, had met Natalya Goncharova, a descendent of Pushkin's wife, when the two were young students at the Moscow School of Painting, Sculpture and Architecture. Their influence at the time was immense. The two were of particular interest to Diaghilev as they were trying to create a truly Russian style of art, neo-primitivism, to compete with Europe's own avant-garde movement.

It was a momentous meeting for the Russian painters. Goncharova agreed to do the designs for *Le Coq d'Or* and although she did the majority of these, Larionov also contributed. From now on the two concentrated on theatrical design rather than painting. Diaghilev invited them to attend the opening of the *Coq d'Or* in Paris in the May of the following year, 1914, at the Opera House. As the dancer Lydia Lopokova commented, Diaghilev 'had the cunning ... to combine the excellent with the chic, and revolutionary art with the atmosphere of the old regime.'[23]

In the February of 1914, before the opening of the Paris season, the company assembled in Prague where some learnt for the first time that Nijinsky had been dismissed and Fokine re-instated. The company then toured Germany, but without Nijinsky there was a shortage of male dancers. Diaghilev promptly went to Russia – on what turned out to be his last trip there – to engage some more.

With the 1914 Paris season in mind, Diaghilev had previously asked the Russian composer Nikolai Tcherepnin to compose the ballet *La Masque de la Mort Rouge*, based on Edgar Allen Poe's macabre story *The Mask of the Red Death*. He had naturally intended Nijinsky to dance in it, but this was now abandoned.

However, Diaghilev had also commissioned the celebrated Richard Strauss to compose a new ballet, *La Legende de Joseph* and, all going well, conduct it himself. Diaghilev still wanted to go ahead with this, but the role of Joseph, also originally planned for Nijinsky, would have to be recast. Fokine wanted to replace Nijinsky himself, but Diaghilev considered him too old at 34 to do so and gave the part to a new young dancer, Leonide Massine.

Diaghilev had seen Massine when he visited Moscow during the winter of 1913–14 and, full of energy and enthusiasm, had spent his time organising the operas and ballets he intended to stage during the forthcoming Paris and London seasons.

He spotted the eighteen-year-old Leonide Massine carrying a ham on a platter at the Bolshoi Theatre in Moscow. Massine was then 'a boy of compelling presence and beauty' and Diaghilev saw him again a couple of nights later dancing the tarantella in *Swan Lake*. He promptly whisked him off to St Petersburg to audition for Fokine for Strauss's *La Legende de Joseph*. Fokine had doubts but Diaghilev offered Massine the role of Joseph. After the audition, according to Misia Sert, 'Diaghilev took the boy straight to the Hermitage Museum and from there presumably to bed.'[24]

Grigoriev, in the corridor outside Diaghilev's hotel room, noticed 'a young man in a long overcoat, wearing a hat pulled low over his face, which I nevertheless noticed was strikingly handsome.'[25] It was Leonide Massine

Diaghilev first spotted the strikingly handsome Leonide Massine at the Bolshoi Theatre in Moscow and quickly put him under a long-term contract. Massine replaced Nijinsky in Diaghilev's affections and became an outstanding choreographer

and Diaghilev had given him a night to think over joining the Ballets Russes. Massine, after asking friends' advice, returned the next day meaning to refuse the offer, but found himself accepting it. Diaghilev quickly put him under a long-term contract.

Fokine was to oversee Massine's dancing and when Diaghilev asked him how he judged the younger man's progress, Fokine said he was 'a talented young man, but a poor dancer. I'm afraid I shall have to simplify his part.'[26] The film director Michael Powell, a great admirer of Massine in later years, thought him 'intensely musical, a superb mime and a good actor. He could pass from dignity to buffoonery in a flash, one moment a monk, the next a monkey.'[27] In recognising Massine's abilities, Diaghilev showed that as well as being able to discover talent, he could develop, refine and inspire it.

Massine was an eager and receptive pupil and not only fulfilled Diaghilev's emotional needs but over the years became an indispensable interpreter of Diaghilev's ideas. As a lover, he provided balm to Diaghilev by replacing Nijinsky. He was lively and intelligent and a good musician, so could offer Diaghilev a mature companionship. He was also breathtakingly beautiful: slender and dark-eyed.

Massine was impressed by Diaghilev's vast knowledge of art and music. Diaghilev explained that Jose-Maria Sert's décor for *La Legende de Joseph* had been inspired by artists like Titian, Veronese and Tintoretto and told Massine he could learn invaluable lessons in choreography from paintings by such artists.

The two were travelling to Cologne by train at the time for the rehearsals of *La Legende de Joseph* and, noticing Diaghilev's elegant appearance, Massine was surprised to see there were holes in the soles of his shoes. Poverty? Or indifference? Hard to say. Yet when they arrived at Cologne's opulent Domhof Hotel, Diaghilev was totally at home, 'conferring in his suite with artists and musicians, making endless long-distance telephone calls, and enjoying his lobster dinners.'[28]

Larionov and Goncharova arrived in Paris at the end of April 1914 for the new season of the Ballets Russes with delighted anticipation. They were met by Diaghilev and welcomed generally as Diaghilev had heavily publicised the opening of *Le Coq d'Or*. In addition, there was to be an exhibition of their work in June.

They were to supervise rehearsals and once installed at their hotel began completing work on the décor for the *Coq d'Or*. Fokine thought it touching to see how the two of them painted by hand all the stage props. Benois considered Larionov 'a very gifted artist but one in whom a strange sterility is combined with a remarkable eagerness to show himself in the foreground.'[29]

For the two artists, it was a time of intense interest and excitement as they met the core of the Ballets Russes including Stravinsky, Fokine and Karsavina and revived their friendship with Benois and Bakst. They moved in the café society of the time, mixing with Diaghilev's wide circle of dancers, composers designers, artists and writers. The poet Apollinaire became a close friend.

The opening night of *Le Coq d'Or* at the Opera was an outstanding success. The audiences were delighted by Rimsky-Korsakov's music and the neo-primitive scenery and costumes by Goncharova, based on Russian folk art, were vividly eye-catching. Propert recalled rainbow-coloured dancers flanked by purple rows of singers and the 'procession of fabulous creatures that heralded the returning king and queen in their monstrous chariot.'[30]

One of the best dancers in the ballet was the Italian dancer, teacher and choreographer, Enrico Cecchetti, whose occasional bursts of southern temperament only added depth to the parts he played. In *Le Coq d'Or* he was convincingly mysterious as the Astrologer.

On 17th June, at the close of the season, the exhibition by Goncharova and Larionov opened. The whole of the Parisian art world seemed to attend, including Constantine Brancusi, Georges Braque, Pablo Picasso, Andre Derain and Amedeo Modigliani. They all looked intently at the artists' neo-primitive works – which reflected their work for the Ballets Russes.

At the end of June the Archduke Ferdinand and his wife were assassinated at Sarajevo: the events leading to the first world war had begun.

More important to Diaghilev, the following month, was the opening in London of the Grand Season of Russian Opera and Ballet. It was at the Theatre Royal, Drury Lane and lasted nine weeks. Chaliapin sang the chief opera parts outstandingly in *Ivan the Terrible*, *Prince Igor* and *Boris Gudonov*.

It was during a performance of *Boris Gudonov* at Drury Lane in front of the royal family that Diaghilev had a fierce row with the Russian chorus about payment of their salary. When Chaliapin was about to go on, he found there was no chorus on stage. In an angry exchange with them, he struck one member. According to Sir Thomas Beecham, 'Like a pack of wolves the rest of the chorus flung themselves upon him [Chaliapin], brandishing the tall staves they were to use in the next scene.'[31] When Chaliapin left the theatre, he was protected by the police, but in case of emergency he had a loaded revolver in each pocket.

The season had taken a lot of organising. Diaghilev had wanted Stravinsky to compose another ballet, but after his shock at the reception of *The Rite of Spring*, Stravinsky demurred. Instead he composed *The Nightingale*, an opera based on a story by Hans Andersen.

Staged along with Borodin's *Prince Igor* were three ballets, one of which was the premiere of *Daphnis and Chloe* by the French composer, Maurice Ravel. The conductor Eugene Goosens considered that Diaghilev antagonised Ravel by removing the off-stage chorus on the grounds that the singers took up too much room and got in the way of the scene shifters. Diaghilev thought nothing of being so high-handed.

Ravel, who had intended to come to London that June, was so annoyed at the cut version of *Daphnis et Chloe*, which he now considered a haphazard, makeshift production, that he cancelled his visit. However, *Daphnis and Chloe* was very successful, with audiences being particularly impressed by the last scene featuring the Moscow chorus.

The set design for Daphnis and Chloe, *by Maurice Ravel. Diaghilev cut back the production so severely that Ravel refused to attend the ballet*

Another row took place between Diaghilev and Benois over the first performance that season of the opera and ballet *Le Rossignol*. It was a luxurious production with Chinese marches, enormous blue lanterns and fantastic costumes. Benois had objected to certain details when *Le Rossignol* was premiered in Paris and although Diaghilev had promised to correct these, he had not bothered.

Benois shouted at Diaghilev loudly enough for it to be heard in the auditorium, but the quarrel was made up the following day over lunch at the Savoy. Benois remembered that they parted as friends, embracing each other Russian-style. They were not to meet again for nine years.

Diaghilev got in touch with Prokofiev early in 1914, with Prokofiev writing in his diary 'Perhaps he will commission a ballet for his Paris season?! Oho!'[32] His hopes were dashed, but when he went to London during the height of the Ballets Russes season in June that year, when Stravinsky's *The Nightingale* was playing, he did at least meet Diaghilev. Prokofiev was impressed by this 'supremely elegant figure in top hat and tails' who extended a white-gloved hand and said he would be interested in his opinion of *The Nightingale*.

Diaghilev, who 'appeared accompanied by Massine, his latest love,'[33] did indeed want a ballet from Prokofiev. It was to be *Chout*, a modern treatment of a Russian fairy tale. *Chout* was how the French spelt *Shut*, the Russian word for 'The Buffoon'.

The summer season of 1914 at the Drury Lane Theatre had been brilliant. It seemed all London society had attended the various performances and Diaghilev had been a focal point of attention as he moved from box to box, listening to compliments and receiving plaudits. July saw the first night of the much publicised *La Legende de Joseph*, conducted by Strauss himself and with the new young dancer, Massine, in the title role. It was the final first night of the season.

Diaghilev received a congratulatory telegram from Count Kessler, who had written the ballet's scenario with Hugo von Hofmannstal, but Kessler added that he feared the autumn tour planned for Germany might now not take place.

Diaghilev read this with surprise, wondering aloud why Kessler should think the carefully planned tour might be cancelled ('the dear count must be sick'). Meanwhile the impresario was pleased at the success of his company, particularly at the ovation for *Le Coq d'Or*, given the fact that the famed Nijinsky had not been there to attract audiences. The company broke up, expecting to meet again in October in Berlin.

Benois had left for the French countryside in order to collaborate on a ballet with Maurice Ravel. He recalled their lightheartedness, with Ravel boarding a high, large merry-go-round and shouting down remarks when he passed his friend.

Kessler, however, moved in political circles in Berlin and knew that war was imminent. On 1 August 1914, just two weeks after Diaghilev received his telegram, Germany declared war against Russia and then, two days later, against France. On 4th August Great Britain declared war against Germany.

The war stopped the Ballets Russes in its tracks. Diaghilev had achieved an enormous amount. He had revolutionised the old classical Imperial Ballet, replacing the formal ballets always seen at the Maryinsky Theatre by more dramatic, stylish and emotional ballets. Peformances were daring and the images were beautiful to see.

For the next four years, however, as the Ballet Russes struggled to survive and very nearly went under, these images were replaced by those of the wounded, the dying and the dead.

10

America to the Rescue

At the start of 1914, there was little or no awareness of what the year would bring. It was a time of optimism and excitement in the arts: the future beckoned. The cultured Harold Acton, whose interests embraced Europe, modernism and the exotic, believed the Russian ballet was then at its zenith, its influence felt all over Europe. 'The great galas of colour organised by Diaghilev were being imitated even in private entertainments: fancy-dress balls and tableaux vivants became sumptuous and spectacular to a degree unrealised since.'[1]

Although there were rumours of war in the July of 1914, earlier that year the critic Clive Bell thought that not since the French revolution 'have days seemed more full of promise than those spring days of 1914.' And after seeing the Russian ballet Rupert Brooke wrote that 'They, if anything can, redeem our civilisation.'

The shadow of the first world war remained a shadow: no one guessed the end of *la belle époque* was on the horizon and that Diaghilev, the magnet for young musicians, painters and writers of western Europe, was to see so many of them go off to fight.

At the end of the London summer season, Diaghilev went first to Paris where, at Misia Sert's apartment on 28 July, he was listening to a composition by Erik Satie when a friend burst in to say Austria had declared war on Serbia. Misia admitted that her first reaction was one of excitement. It was shared by other Parisians: when on 3 August Germany declared war on France, enthusiastic crowds filled the boulevards.

Diaghilev left Paris and went to Viareggio on the Italian Riviera with Massine, who noticed that 'in this frivolous sun-drenched resort' the carefree crowd in the shops and the beaches seemed quite unaware of the political ferment outside Italy.

Colette, too, in St Malo in the August of 1914, felt that the war was not there, but very far away, on the other side of the world. Yet on one beautiful summer's day, with children in red bathing suits paddling in the sea, 'in the centre of town, the uproar bursts forth all at once: alarm bell, drum, the shouts of the crowd, the crying of children... '[2] The town drummer then read the edict announcing war.

Diaghilev was not predisposed to take the war too seriously, being convinced that Germany would not hold out long. He was forty-two and light-hearted. He and the eighteen-year-old Massine drove in a leisurely fashion through Italy and Diaghilev introduced Massine to the paintings and sculptures that he so loved. They went to see the mosaics in Ravenna and the early Italian paintings in Florence. Diaghilev taught Massine the influence painting could have on choreography. The two went on to Rome where Massine, who had little training in appreciating painting, was strongly affected by the Byzantine art he saw there and was struck by the unbelievably beautiful mosaics.

The war may have seemed far away in Italy but in Paris Misia, like other Parisians, became fearfully aware of its nearness. Cannons could be heard in the Bois de Boulogne and in September the first of several German planes flew over the city, dropping bombs. Frightened and bedraggled Belgian refugees were arriving, restaurants and places of entertainment were closed, and the streets were deserted.

The Russian ballet was due to reassemble in Berlin in the October of 1914 and Diaghilev was slow to realise that this was simply not going to happen: that, for a start, there was now no company. He was preoccupied with finding a ballet-master to replace Fokine. Brilliant in detecting the promise of young people Diaghilev unhesitatingly gave this responsible post to the eighteen-year-old Massine. Although Massine was a dancer, Diaghilev intended to mould him into a choreographer as he had done with Nijinsky.

Both Nijinsky and Massine, and later Serge Lifar, may never have become choreographers without Diaghilev's help. As Lynn Garafola points out: 'His generosity was boundless: he gave them all the accumulated wisdom of his years and all the fruits of his broad experience, in addition to a knowledge of the arts, an appreciation of aesthetics, and an introduction to everyone who was anyone in the circles of High Bohemia.'[3]

Massine became the first in western Europe to try to interpret symphonic music in terms of classical dance. He said of himself, 'I was amazed to see how at the very beginning of my experience as a choreographer I had that desire to get away from the conventional lines and established symmetry of ballet ... it was certainly a very, very vital thing to the future of choreography.'[4]

Meanwhile the casualties of the war in Europe were mounting with appalling speed. The Battle of Mons in August 1914 was followed by the Battle of the Marne in September, which in turn was followed by the first battle of Ypres in October. Misia, in Paris, arranged for delivery vans to be converted into ambulances and, along with Jose-Maria Sert and Jean Cocteau, organised and helped transport the wounded from the front. Trips were made in the dark, on poorly marked roads: orders were that the wounded were to be virtually smuggled into Paris at night so that people would not realise the extent of the casualties.

Financially, the first world war was disastrous for the Ballets Russes: Diaghilev, the dancers, the whole edifice, nearly folded. At its outbreak, Covent Garden Opera House announced it was closing and did not reopen until 1919. The company's forthcoming tour of Germany was cancelled – with casualties in their hundreds of thousands, no one was interested in *pas de deux* and pirouettes and contracts dried up. Diaghilev began to watch expenses and even asked Grigoriev to keep account books – telling him not to show them to anyone. There was very little money to account for. Diaghilev constantly contacted previous patrons in Europe in the hope of raising more. It was a hand to mouth existence.

He was faced with the apparently insurmountable problem of reassembling his company in an uncertain future. His dancers had left for their summer break after the end of the season in London and at the start of war were scattered around different European countries whose frontiers were now closed.

Diaghilev remained sublimely confident he could get his company back together, even though the Fokines were in Paris and Karsavina (forced to travel at one point in a goods truck) in Russia. Serge Grigoriev, too, had left for St Petersburg straight after the end of the London season and two days after he arrived there Russia declared war on Germany. For health reasons he was rejected for military service and spent the rest of 1914 at his Russian home.

Diaghilev's tight circle broke up. Fokine and other senior members of the Ballets Russes returned to Russia and Fokine stayed in St Petersburg throughout the war, acting as ballet master. Stravinsky, who at the time war broke out was returning from a visit to Russia, was caught in Switzerland. The Nijinskys – Vaslav, Romola and their new baby daughter – were about to leave Budapest but found the frontier closed and were arrested and detained as prisoners of war.

Larionov and Goncharova also returned to Moscow immediately Russia declared war as Larionov was called up. He was wounded in October 1914 and sent to hospital.

That month Diaghilev wrote to Stravinsky from his rented villa in Florence to say, 'You awful pig! I wire you that the American contract is signed ... and from you not a word. You force me, an old man, to take up a pen.'[5] Diaghilev was forty-two at the time.

The comment about an American contract is surprising, given that Diaghilev had no company to take there. Despite this fact, he was constantly bullying Stravinsky into finishing *Les Noces* – a ballet based on mid 19th century Russian wedding rites. Diaghilev had been delighted with the music when he first heard it and now asked Stravinsky urgently to come to Florence before he and Massine moved to Rome – ignoring Stravinsky's desperate pleas for money

Grigoriev at his home in the small provincial town of Tiklivin, considered going back to St Petersburg's Maryinsky Theatre. He contacted Diaghilev, who after leaving Rome had gone on to Switzerland to see Stravinsky. He had taken a villa near to him – despite his concern at Stravinsky's daughter having measles.

Grigoriev was acting as Diaghilev's recruitment manager and at the beginning of May 1915 was summoned to meet Diaghilev in Switzerland. It meant having to travel via Finland, Sweden, Norway, England and France, but somehow, staunchly, he managed it.

Larionov and Goncharova were also being besieged by telegrams from Diaghilev asking them too to meet him in Geneva. In the summer of 1915 he blithely sent them an ultimatum, telling them to leave immediately. It succeeded and the couple left Russia for Switzerland. They were never to return to their homeland.

Stravinsky was living at Montreux at the time, working on *Les Noces*. He played the beginnings of it to Diaghilev who burst into tears and said that this cantata would be 'the most beautiful and the most purely Russian creation' of his company. Stravinsky was pleased, though he would have been more pleased if Diaghilev had mentioned payment for it. Diaghilev expected everyone to live on air, working for the good of the company, and dismissed mundane requests for money. He himself must have been getting some money through from Russia: he lived on that and bad debts.

The effects of the war continued to be devastating. The liner the *Lusitania* was sunk and the Allied landings at Gallipoli, in the Dardanelles campaign ended in evacuation. Yet Colette, in Rome in 1915, went to the villa-hospital set aside for wounded Italians, with its palm trees and climbing roses. What was lacking was the wounded soldiers: to keep Rome serene, war casualties so far had been kept away. No wonder visitors like Diaghilev and Massine were able to ignore the war.

That summer Diaghilev's entourage at Lausanne included Stravinsky,

Massine, Grigoriev, Bakst and the dancing *maestro* Enrico Cecchetti who
Goncharova, was giving lessons in dance to Massine. Diaghilev thought highly of the arch-
Larionov, conservative Cecchetti even though Cecchetti disliked the more modern
Stravinsky choreography because the movements it required affected his dancers' limbs.
and Bakst, After Larionov and Goncharova joined the group Diaghilev asked Larionov
Switzerland, to teach Massine the art of choreography. The group became an important
1915 nucleus, with whom Diaghilev discussed future productions – ignoring the
fact that he still lacked a company.

A great friend of Stravinsky joined them at Lausanne: Ernest Ansermet,
the conductor of the Geneva Symphony Orchestra, whom Stravinsky had
met in 1911 when Ansermet was 28. Ansermet reminded Grigoriev of a
Byzantine Christ figure, while Cyril Beaumont described him as having a
Svengali-like air, being 'tall and spare, with a pale face, high brow, luxuriant
tapering beard and magnetic eyes ... He was a dominating, energetic personality.'[6] When younger, Ansermet used to teach and admirably learned how to
conduct during tea-time concerts for English ladies in Montreux.

Diaghilev had managed to sign a contract with Otto Kahn, Chairman of
the Board of Directors of the Metropolitan Opera House in New York for
a Ballets Russes season there. The problem was that the contract specified,

first, that Diaghilev was to accompany his troupe and, secondly, that certain dancers, like Nijinsky and Karsavina, should appear with the company.

Diaghilev asked Grigoriev to persuade Fokine and Karsavina to leave Russia and rejoin the company and then had to use all his influence to extract Nijinsky from his internment. Diaghilev also needed new dancers and while he planned to engage some from Europe, Grigoriev was entrusted with the task of finding Russian ones.

Back in Russia, Grigoriev found that Karsavina was expecting a child and that Fokine would not leave the country in wartime. However, he engaged young dancers from St Petersburg and Moscow who were not away fighting, and took them over to Diaghilev in Switzerland. There was still no sign of Nijinsky's release.

Diaghilev seemed relatively unperturbed about Fokine's absence, as Massine was clearly developing into a good choreographer. Diaghilev also believed, with his usual acumen, that choreography should now take a new direction.

Stravinsky, in Switzerland, met the French musicologist Romain Rolland and told him of his dislike of the showier aspects of the Russian ballet. In his diary, Rolland described Stravinsky as 'small, sickly looking, ugly, yellow faced, thin and tired, with a narrow brow, thin, receding hair, his eyes screwed up behind a pince-nez, a fleshy nose, big lips, a disproportionately long face in relation to his forehead. He is very intelligent and simple in his manners; he speaks easily … and everything he says is personal and thought-out …'[7]

One reason for Diaghilev's continued success was that he worked incredibly hard to retain his position. He was under constant financial pressure to find the money to pay for theatre hire and the salaries of all the members of his company. This meant constantly seeking new patrons, as well as making sure he retained the goodwill of those who had sponsored him in the past and, hopefully, the present. He did not take a salary himself, but he had a number of expenses: staying at good hotels, eating at expensive restaurants, dressing stylishly.

He also was under artistic pressure to find new ideas: a new musical score, a new way of choreographing, new painters to design the décors. He was a shrewd and discerning critic, with an instinctive feel for what was good and what bad. He needed to be aware of up-and-coming young musicians, artists and dancers, so that he could discuss new ideas with them. Much though he enjoyed it, the financial and creative responsibility of running the Ballets Russes was a constant strain.

Although Diaghilev preferred the works of the masters of the Romantic

period, his knowledge of musical compositions, their styles and history, was immense. He could instantly detect the quality of a piece of music and, more important, recognise whether it was suitable for his company.

The composer Nicolas Nabokov was once arguing the merits of what he claimed was a good fugato in the style of the 18th century French overtures. Diaghilev, listening, replied that it may well be a fugato, even a fugue, but it certainly wasn't any good. On another occasion, when listening to a new ballet, he reacted explosively, saying the work was drivel, stupid, dull and slimy. Through his detailed knowledge, he could immediately spot any plagiarism – a crucial attribute as it prevented him from being sued.

Diaghilev in his early maturity, his attention to his personal style was clearly evident

When he was presented with a new work, he would listen respectfully and if it appealed to him would go over it page by page and discuss it point by point, wanting to hear sections played repeatedly. But if he did not like it, 'his face would immediately take on a sour and worn expression; he would look bored and sleepy.'[8] When the composer had finished playing the piece, Diaghilev would thank him with scant courtesy and leave the room. Even if he approved of a score, he delighted in cutting it.

At the end of the year, to test out the ballets chosen for America, Diaghilev held two charity gala performances for the Red Cross, in Geneva (Switzerland was neutral) and then Paris. It seems strange he should consider staging a ballet in Paris during the terrible bloodshed of the war, when the city was barely 100 or so miles from the battlefields. Colette wrote painfully of the wounded in hospital in Paris: 'The man with the shattered jaw and eye says, from time to time, "Oh!" with an accent of dismay and disgust... Is that a death rattle from that other man with the bandaged throat? ...'[9]

One of the company's ballets, *Le Soleil de Nuit*, based on Rimsky-Korsakov's *Snow Maiden*, marked Massine's first – and successful – venture as choreographer. He was helped by Larionov, who suggested he base his choreography on Russian peasant dances. It was also Ansermet's debut as conductor. Stravinsky commented on how gloomy Paris was in those sinister days, but the gala was a triumphant success.

Diaghilev's confidence in Massine grew. He believed, or convinced himself, that he and Fokine had ultimately been moving in different directions and said rather dismissively of Fokine's choreography that it would probably be rediscovered in 50 years' time, 'then it will be thought amusing, and finally be considered classical. But now what's wanted is something quite different: a movement of liberation in choreography; some fresh form of achievement, with new music.'[10]

This 'restructured' Ballets Russes featured Massine as the young choreographer and a new generation of young dancers for whom Diaghilev had spent much of 1915 searching. One of these was Leon Woidzowsky, discovered by Diaghilev in Warsaw, whose great leaps in the air were worthy of Nijinsky.

Diaghilev renewed his own youth (he was 43 in 1915) by surrounding himself with much younger artistes whom he could mould to his design. As Massine took over from Fokine and danced some of Nijinsky's roles, so in turn were Benois and Bakst superseded by Larionov and Goncharova. Such rebirths transcended the loss of fundamental supports like Fokine, Karsavina and Nijinsky.

On 1st January 1916 the company sailed for New York where they were due to perform at the Century Theatre before going on tour. Diaghilev had pressurised Stravinsky to accompany them, so that he could conduct his own work, but he refused. However, Diaghilev was thankful to hear that Nijinsky and his wife had arrived in Vienna from Budapest. It still took hard work to get them extricated from there – both the Pope and King Alfonso of Spain interceded – but Nijinsky was now expected to rejoin the company in New York. In the event, the couple were not released until the spring.

In the absence of Nijinsky, Diaghilev relied heavily on Adolph Bolm, who took over the duties of ballet master, training the dancers, as well as dancing various of Nijinsky's roles.

The voyage to America was rough but although this did not affect Diaghilev too badly, he would not leave his cabin for fear of catching cold. He and his company had not been to New York before and were impressed with the city. It was a time of prosperity there, with orders for war materials pouring in. Musical entertainments like the Ziegfeld Frolics were packed out.

The Ballets Russes opened on 17 January 1916 to an audience flashing with diamonds. An observer saw Diaghilev at a rehearsal walk to centre stage slowly and languidly. Wearing evening dress, 'his famous white quiff peeps out from the side of his sloping top hat. In his hand he carries a walking stick surmounted with a gold knob, in his eye is a monocle... From time to time he draws the attention of a workman, with his stick, to some forgotten trifle which has been left on the stage.'[11] Whenever he knew he was observed, Diaghilev was careful to keep up appearances.

The company's repertoire included *The Firebird*, *The Sleeping Princess* and *Scheherazade*. The America audiences – and more important the critics – for whom the Russian ballet was a new event, were enthusiastic. Massine successfully took over the part that Nijinsky would have danced in *L'Apres Midi d'un Faune*.

The day before the opening night, the *New York Times* enthusiastically welcomed the first appearance of the company, saying advance interest in its appearance exceeded that of all other performances that season. The reason for this was that 'Diaghilev's dancers do not occupy the stage in undisputed sway. The arts of painting and decoration and of music go hand in hand with choreographic art.'

It pointed out that 'highly imaginative colourists' like the famous Leon Bakst, had provided scene settings and costumes to create the atmosphere. Much of the music had been specially commissioned from the 'younger generation of moderns like Igor Stravinsky'. Tomorrow, it said, the audience would have a chance to see the effect of all these elements together.

Diaghilev, the *New York Times* informed its readers, was 'the son of a noble Russian family', who had been honoured with a position at the Imperial Court. It gave a resume of his career to date, emphasising how with Fokine he had changed classical ballet choreography to a 'modern idea of freedom', and recalled that the ballet skirt was seen for the first time at the Bowery Theatre, the centre for fashionable theatre going, a century ago. When the dancers appeared on stage, 'the ladies in boxes arose and left the theatre. The ballet skirt was officially snubbed.'

The four ballets the company was to present on the first night were *The Firebird*, *The Sleeping Princess*, *Soleil de Nuit* and *Scheherazade*. And the paper's expectations were fulfilled. The day after the opening, it enthusiastically reported that every seat had been filled and the Russian dancers' performance was 'the most elaborate ever seen here'. For months, it claimed, American papers and magazines had been printing bright-hued costume-plates, black and white reproductions of artists and reams of material about the ballets until there was nothing left to say. 'What was shown on the stage of the Century Theatre last night constitutes the most elaborate and impressive offering that has yet been made in this country in the name of the ballet as an art form... it made good its title to being an organisation with an impressive individuality ... there is always a sensitive and broadminded artistic intelligence at work.'

The sets were considered arresting, with gorgeous crimson landscapes, and the music was particularly praised, 'presented practically without a blemish.' Stravinsky, said the critic thankfully, was no wild futurist, but a very talented young man with a decided gift for vivid orchestral colouring and great skill in writing descriptive music.

On leaving New York, the company went on a gruelling 16-town tour round America, soon getting exhausted by the constant travelling and the one-night appearances. Returning to New York they opened on 3rd April at the Metropolitan Opera House. Nijinsky arrived a few days later. According to his wife, Diaghilev met them both, gave Romola flowers and kissed the twenty-eight-year-old dancer on both cheeks. Nijinsky placed his daughter in Diaghilev's arms and the two men walked off. Grigoriev's account was quite different: he considered that Diaghilev's attitude was cold and formal.

Certainly relations between the two men remained frosty – not helped by Nijinsky refusing to dance until Diaghilev had paid the money Nijinsky insisted was owed to him. An agreement was made that this would be paid off gradually from receipts.

At the time Nijinsky arrived in New York he told the press he was in excellent condition, having constantly practised on board. One critic, spotting him in the audience before he made his first appearance on stage, described him as a 'dark little man, exquisitely groomed in dead black, with a lustreless top hat.'

Nijinsky did not really empathise with anyone. His lack of communication with the company began to degenerate into a more active hostility. Grigoriev noticed his vagueness and unfriendliness and Sokolova said that he already showed signs of abnormality, never speaking a word to anyone and picking his fingers more than ever. She also noticed that he had grown heavier, possibly because of his lack of practice during the last two years, and that his dancing had deteriorated. However, Massine, watching him dance, was impressed by the effortless control Nijinsky had over his body and considered he had seen a genius.

The *New York Times* gave the first night a rather lukewarm reception, saying that though the theatre was full and the audience receptive, there was no overwhelming enthusiasm.

The dancer Sokolova thought Nijinsky had grown heavier, looked sad, and that his dancing had deteriorated. However, when Nijinsky danced in *Le Spectre de la Rose* in New York for the first time on 12 April, one headline read 'Nijinsky Puts Life into Ballet Russe', considering this was due to his grace and finish and his intelligence as a stage director.

Nevertheless, the critic of the *New York Times* went on to say that though his debut was a success, he was not as sensational as the public expected. One discordant note was his super-refined gestures and posture 'that amounted to effeminacy'. His costume, 'fashioned about the shoulders exactly like a woman's décolleté, with shoulder-and-arm straps, helped to emphasise this'. The way he danced on his toes was also rare in America.

The season in New York lasted until the end of April. Ideally, Diaghilev would then have liked to arrange his usual European tour, but with the war raging he had no option but to book another American tour for the autumn.

He was again faced with the American insistence that Nijinsky be included in the company. Nijinsky then told Diaghilev that he would only agree to this if given complete control of the company. He wanted neither Massine nor Grigoriev and he insisted that Diaghilev himself remain in Europe. There was no option. The company thought it madness but realised how difficult it was for Diaghilev to manage the Ballets Russes financially in wartime and understood that he was forced to agree.

Nijinsky's lack of empathy with those around him was noticed by Charlie Chaplin, who invited him on one occasion to watch the film, *The Cure*, which he was making. Chaplin thought that Nijinsky, with his high cheekbones and sad eyes, looked like a monk in civilian clothing. 'He sat behind the camera, watching me at work on a scene which I thought was funny, but he never smiled. Although the other onlookers laughed, Nijinsky sat looking sadder and sadder.'[12] Nijinsky turned up for two more days, but finally Chaplin did not put a film in the camera, 'knowing Nijinsky's doleful presence would ruin my attempts to be funny.'

Nijinsky then asked Chaplin to come to see him perform at the ballet. Chaplin found his performance hypnotic and god-like, but joining him in his dressing room on another occasion was surprised by his banal questions and his disregard of a waiting audience. 'I witnessed the beginning of a sensitive mind on its way out of a brutal war-torn world into another of its own dreaming.'[13]

The season ended on 29 April, but earlier that month Diaghilev had with relief received an invitation for the company to dance in Madrid. Spain was neutral in the war and he accepted with alacrity.

Once the season was over, Nijinsky remained in New York but Diaghilev and the rest of the company promptly left America for Spain.

Diaghilev confided to Stravinsky the terrible fears he had experienced on board on the return voyage, as the ship was laden with munitions and was forced to veer around to avoid submarines. He showed Stravinsky a picture of himself wearing life-saving apparatus. A further blow for him was that when the company arrived in Cadiz the Spaniards accidentally dropped the magnificent décor by Bakst for the ballet *Thamar* into the sea, sadly never to be seen again.

The company's first performance in the May of 1916 was greeted appreciatively and Diaghilev was congratulated by the Spanish royal family. King Alfonso in particular was an enthusiastic supporter of the ballet. Diaghilev was captivated by Spain, where he stayed during the company's two-month break that summer.

Larionov and Goncharova joined Diaghilev at San Sebastian and Massine was busy choreographing a new Spanish-based

ballet, again assisted by Larionov with costumes designed by Goncharova. Another ballet on which he was working was *Kikimora,* based on the well-known witch of Russian folklore.

On 1st July 1916 the number of British soldiers killed in the Battle of the Somme reached 19,240. The horrors of the first world war, and the carnage taking place, were a surreal background to the activities of the Ballets Russes. The company remained in an involved world of its own.

The second American tour was regarded with apprehension. The company felt Diaghilev's presence essential, both from the artistic and social point of view and had no confidence in Nijinsky who, according to Sokolova, 'We now judged to be not quite right in the head.' Unlike Diaghilev, who kept the company under a tight rein, Nijinsky left it feeling directionless as he failed to turn up for anything unless fetched.

Edward Ziegler, who became assistant manager of the Metropolitan Opera House, wrote the following pointed verse:

O Mr Nijinsky
Where have you binsky?
And if you are here
Why don't you appear
And save the ballet from ruinsky?[14]

Diaghilev himself felt as though he had sent his favourite child off to America to be looked after by someone else – though he had no option, as the company desperately needed any engagement it could get. After their

It is difficult to judge whether or not this life-saving apparatus would have been any help to Diaghilev, in the event of his ship sinking

arrival, telegrams from America arrived for Diaghilev daily, requesting advice for problems. Nothing seemed to go smoothly without Diaghilev in charge.

The saviour was Adolph Bolm. Despite not wishing to participate in this second tour, he had done so simply because Otto Kahn insisted he did. Because of his extreme efforts, and despite the lacklustre Nijinsky, the ballet battled through, the *New York Times* rightly detecting Bolm as being 'the brains' behind it. After a three-week season at the Metropolitan Theatre in New York, the American tour which followed was, according to Sokolova, a failure. Nijinsky on occasion locked himself in his dressing room, or refused to perform an advertised ballet.

Sokolova heavily criticised the 'romantic biography' of Nijinsky by his wife, saying her enthusiastic descriptions of the New York ballet under her husband were, to put it mildly, misleading.

The Washington *Star* of 26 November 1916, commenting on the return visit of the Ballets Russes (which it referred to rather sourly as 'the play-toy of a group of wealthy art connoisseurs') said its latest performances had 'drifted slightly towards the conventionality of the usual touring theatrical attraction.' It went on, with reference to Nijinsky, to attack the 'star system', saying that this, once conspicuously reflected in drama, had now moved to dance: 'the name Nijinsky is made so prominent that it overwhelms attention.'

Although it noted Nijinsky's graceful and proficient coordination, the *Star* pointed out that 'the male dancer is still an exception in American attention, save when he appears as the dancing partner of a feminine star... however graceful his poses and delicate his shadings in pantomime, [the male dancing star] is likely to be regarded more as a curiosity than as the artistic marvel which Nijinsky is conceded to be.'

Sokolova, commenting on the two new ballets which Nijinsky was meant to produce during the season thought that he often seemed unable to function creatively and found it hard to explain what he wanted done. Diaghilev received a stream of letters, informing him what was happening.

During the tour of the country, Nijinsky threatened again not to appear, causing anxiety if not chaos, and the takings dropped. The reputation of the company in America went into such a decline that the tour was cut short by the management.

An unfortunate accident on stage left Bolm with fractured vertebrae. After he recovered he decided to stay in America and form his own group which he called 'Petite Ballet Russe.'

The entire ballet company had not been required for America and Diaghilev, who had decided that the remainder should winter in Rome, had managed to secure an advance from the organisers of the American tour to cover the expense. Without this those still in Europe would have been penniless.

In Rome, the company was growing as more dancers had been taken on by Diaghilev. He had been busy researching music for new ballets and commissioned one by Domenico Scarletti, about whose music he was extremely enthusiastic. It was called *The Good-Humoured Ladies*. Massine and Larionov and Goncharova worked on these new projects, with Diaghilev deeply involved at rehearsals, suggesting, criticising and shaping the new works.

Stravinsky, however, who was irritated at the procrastination over contracts and money, took a sour view of the impresario's activities, writing to Misia Sert to say that it was difficult to come to any understanding with Diaghilev and that in his view Diaghilev 'no longer gets any pleasure from his work. His life is burned out ...'[15]

Harold Acton, in Italy at the time, considered that the *Good-Humoured Ladies* was the most Italian in spirit of all Diaghilev's productions and watching it was like looking at a series of paintings. Diaghilev called on him, along with Bakst, and Acton was highly disappointed in Bakst who, known for his flamboyant and magnificent sets, was far less flamboyant himself, being 'short, neat, affable and business-like with a reddish moustache and pince-nez' and, in Acton's view, lacking personal distinction.[16]

It was a highly creative time. Diaghilev gave a large reception in Rome to launch an Exhibition of Russian Artists, with Larionov and Goncharova contributing to the Cubist and Futurist work on show. Stravinsky conducted excerpts from *Petrushka*. Over the Christmas period of 1916–17, Diaghilev went to Milan in the hope of finding a patron who would sponsor the company and was lucky enough to achieve backing for a season in South America.

Early in 1917 the rest of the company returned from America. There was so little money some had to pool their resources to get to Rome. But the shock that ran through the company was the news of the Russian revolution that took place in St Petersburg in the March of 1917. It was sparked off by a shortage of bread in St Petersburg which had led the desperate population to riot, with the result that some 200 were shot.

Some of the Household Guards mutinied, others joined them: they captured the arsenal and supplied the revolutionaries with ammunition. Troops brought to St Petersburg joined them. On 16 March Czar Nicholas II was forced to abdicate and in the November of that year the Bolsheviks declared themselves the ruling authority under the leadership of Lenin.

The political uncertainty resulted in a stream of émigrés heading for Europe. The Bolsheviks used to gather together at La Coupole in the Boulevard Montparnasse, but the Russian aristocrats, turning up in Paris, couldn't even afford this, being faced with an unexpected lack of funds. 'We were all suddenly poor,' said one. 'You wrote a cheque on the Imperial Bank, but no roubles came.' As a result, 'Grand Dukes worked as headwaiters, czarist Colonels became doormen and a great many became taxi drivers.'[17] Diaghilev also lost the small amount of money he had received in the past from Russia and in addition his current Russian passport was now worthless, as passport-holders were required to be Soviet citizens.

Diaghilev could have qualified to be a Soviet citizen as Lenin was to offer him the post of People's Commissar for Soviet Stage Production. The position had its attractions – he would be the artistic director in Moscow. But his friend Alexandre Benois, one of the custodians of the Hermitage Museum, had already found it impossible to work under the regime and left the country. Diaghilev may have toyed with the idea of the job, but he feared living under the aegis of the 'red Czar' as he could not accept the idea of relinquishing control to anyone. If he formed a company there, he could be prevented from taking it out of the country. The idea was anathema.

Tamara Karsavina lost everything in the revolution and could not get out of Russia for months, but said she did not fare too badly at the hands of the Bolsheviks as she found that though they had contempt for the intelligentsia, they profoundly respected the artist. Unexpectedly she retrieved some of her lost possessions, like chandeliers, in England. She once saw a carpet of hers in a Regent Street store. She went in and asked where they had bought it, saying she could tell them the design in detail. They sold it back to her at the price they had paid for it.

The 1917 revolution was deeply unsettling for Russians, many feeling deprived of their identity. Diaghilev, who had summoned Stravinsky to Rome to conduct *The Firebird* and Rimsky-Korsakov's *Fireworks* (for a gala performance in aid of the Italian Red Cross), considered it inappropriate to play the usual Russian Imperial anthem after the Czar's abdication. There was a hasty substitution of *The Song of the Volga Boatmen*.

Diagheliv, Massine and Stravinsky went down to Naples, where they tracked down early Neapolitan water-colours. Diaghilev found some Neapolitan music in Italian conservatoires and, to Massine's delight, also discovered some old Italian choreography.

The poet Jean Cocteau had had an unenthusiastic response from the public when his first ballet for Diaghilev, *Le Dieu bleu*, had been launched in

Paris in 1912. Since early in 1917, when not helping Misia with her ambulance work in Paris, Cocteau had been working on another idea, which he called *Parade*. This one, he convinced himself, was strikingly original and he approached the composer Eric Satie and persuaded him to write the score.

Eric Satie was original and eccentric. Born of French/Scottish parents, he worked as a café composer before studying music. He produced ballets, lyric dramas and whimsical pieces, loathed Wagner's music and virtually lived in poverty-struck hiding, never asking anyone back to the small room in Paris where he lived. Indeed, if anyone asked him for his address, he replied evasively that he lived in a cupboard. He slept in a hammock, surrounded by a vast collection of old umbrellas, derby hats and new shoes.

Artur Rubinstein the pianist recalled him as being small, 'with little hair left, bearded and with eyeglasses which sat unsafely on his nose. When he spoke he would hold his hand in front of his mouth, apparently to cover some bad teeth.'[18] He rarely brushed his clothes, or even washed them.

However, although there was an all-over greyness to him, especially his high-necked collar, 'when he began to talk it became evident that a most uncommon and entirely modern spirit inhabited the dusty, old-fashioned shell.'[19] Debussy considered him a fine medieval musician, who had just happened to have wandered into this century.

Cocteau was desperately anxious to get the Ballets Russes to stage *Parade* and, as an admirer of the experimental painter, Pablo Picasso, he persuaded him to design the costumes and scenery.

Picasso, who had shocked the French art world with his cubist paintings, had come to Paris from his native country of Spain in 1901. A highly-regarded and at the time traditional painter, he had a small studio in Montmartre and quickly entered the bohemian life of Montmartre and Montparnasse.

Cocteau's theme for a ballet appealed to him. It was based on a show staged outside a vaudeville theatre aimed at luring in passers-by and the performers included a Chinese conjuror and acrobats. It was in effect a series of circus turns treated choreographically.

Picasso had never seen a ballet and, despite Cocteau bombarding him with requests, hesitated about the vast task of designing the stage décor and costumes. However he, like Diaghilev, always had an antenna out for new directions and could see that the ballet could launch an era for avant-garde art. He was a frequent visitor to music halls and circuses, with their flamboyant characters and colour, and the idea of vaudeville characters appealed to him.

However, Picasso was reluctant to leave Paris and Cocteau had trouble in persuading him. As Cocteau remarked sourly about the austere period of Cubism, 'The objects which could stand on a café table and the Spanish guitar were the only pleasures allowed. To paint a stage set, especially for the Ballets Russes (those prim young people had never heard of Stravinsky) was a crime ... The worst of it was that we had to join Sergei Diaghilev in Rome and the Cubist Code forbade all journeys other than the one on the North-South line between the Place des Abbesses and the Boulevard Raspail.'[20]

Picasso's decision to go to Rome was influenced by two close friends, the painter Georges Braque and the poet Apollinaire, both of whom were

away on the war front. After making a model of his stage set, he set off with Cocteau to Rome arriving there in the February of 1917.

There they discussed the ballet with Diaghilev, who had established his wartime headquarters in Rome. He stayed at the Grand Hotel when he wasn't at the flat he had rented for Leonide Massine, who had now been the forty-five-year-old Diaghilev's lover for some three years.

Diaghilev, ever intent on keeping up with contemporary movements in European art, was delighted to have Picasso designing a ballet for the company. The two were both pace-setters, known for initiating new ideas, so Diaghilev was prepared to consider Cocteau's proposal.

Picasso showed his model to Diaghilev and when the two, together with Massine, examined it, Picasso realised the limitations of the standard stage set he had designed. He decided to include two gigantic figures (the 'managers' of the performers), some ten foot high, 'who would lurch around the stage imposing an essentially Cubist conception on his otherwise fairly traditional sets, costumes and curtain.'[21]

Massine was to dance the part of the Conjuror and Picasso's costume design for him lit up the stage as it was in orange, yellow, black and white with asymmetric spirals and curves. The only problem was that although the Cubist-style costumes were dazzling to see, they were also extremely cumbersome for the dancers to wear and made any attempt at graceful movement almost impossible.

Diaghilev, Massine and Picasso in Pompei in 1917. They had taken time off from the razzmatazz of rehearsals in Rome for the ballet Parade *in order to explore the art in other Italian cities*

Picasso enjoyed the frenetic razzmatazz atmosphere of the company. Rehearsals went on around him as he worked in the great hall of the Palazzo Theodori. The drop curtain he designed was vast, some 1,500 square feet. Even though he had a team of Italians to help him, it was surprising it was ever finished.

Cocteau himself resented Diaghilev's admiration and encouragement of both Picasso and Massine, often at the expense of Cocteau's own ideas. Cocteau wrote to a friend to say, 'I could give you a picture of myself spitting in Diaghilev's face in Rome, when he tried to cheat me out of my role as choreographer.'[22]

Diaghilev took Picasso and Massine around Rome to sample everything from paintings by masters like Michelangelo, to the circus – where Diaghilev fell asleep, only waking when an elephant put its feet on his knees. Diaghilev also whisked Picasso and Massine further afield to see the art in Florence and Pompeii and introduced the two men to Roman society.

John Richardson describes how Diaghilev – no doubt in search of a new patron – dragged off Picasso and Massine to dine with the 'excessively rich, prodigiously extravagant, perversely exhibitionistic Marchesa Casati' whose aim was to be 'a living work of art'.

The Marchesa 'dramatised herself by ringing her huge mesmerising eyes with kohl and dilating the pupils with belladonna' and in order to emphasise the Medusa look, she coloured her hair blood orange and arranged it in serpentine coils. Her *coup de foudre* was to take her dog for a walk, startling passers-by by appearing 'naked except for ropes of pearls, a sable wrap, and a mass of make-up.'[23] Occasionally, says Richardson, her pearls were replaced by a necklace of lovebites.

Picasso returned to Paris in the November of 1917. Picasso regretfully had to leave all the work he had done in Barcelona behind, apart from a couple of sketchbooks: 'Officials at the frontier still mistook cubist works for plans of fortifications, and Picasso – the most fearful of men in the face of officialdom – did not want any trouble at the frontier.'[24]

He was pleased to be back at his house in Montrouge, a suburb of Paris, with his dogs, but the war seemed ominously close, with bombings and rationing. Eric Satie, who lived near Picasso, had a narrow escape, writing to a friend to say: 'The shells were terribly close to me. I thought I was done for! People were killed but not me.'[25]

Crucially for Picasso, when he was in Italy he met and fell in love with the auburn-haired and talented Russian ballerina Olga Khoklova, who had the part of an American girl in *Parade*. Picasso was fascinated by her doll-like face

Olga Khoklova, the ballerina whose doll-like face captivated Picasso. Diaghilev warned him that Russian girls expected marriage, not an affair

and figure and her delicacy of movement. He was impressed too by her upper class background: she was the daughter of an officer in the Czar's army. Olga, in turn, was ready to settle down, particularly with a well-known painter, and encouraged Picasso.

Diaghilev watched the growing involvement with amusement, warning Picasso that Russian girls had stricter morals than the lax Parisians. With Russian girls, he said, you have to marry them. Picasso was to find this out.

After the Rome rehearsals, *Parade* was premiered on 18th May 1917 at the Theatre du Chatelet in Paris. Diaghilev was there in his usual top hat and tails along with Misia Sert who wore diamonds. There were so many people that to get into his seat Picasso had to shout his name repeatedly so that guests would give way. The designer Coco Chanel was there, now accepted by the beau monde who had earlier rejected her for being 'in trade.' She and Picasso were to become long-lasting friends.

Picasso, uncaring about such first night splendour, wore a red roll-neck sweater. Apollinaire had written the programme notes and the house was crowded because Diaghilev had handed out a number of tickets to soldiers who had been fighting in the Russian divisions in France. His motive could have been to give them an entertaining night out and, in wartime, to make the ballet seem less elitist. He may also have wanted to ensure the company received some applause, as the ballet was likely to invite noisy criticism – there had already been ructions at the rehearsals when the orchestra refused to play Satie's score, considering it 'circus music'.

Although Satie's overture was applauded, as was Massine's outstanding dancing as the Conjuror, there was a hostile reception to the entrance of Picasso's giant figures. The Cubist figure of an American, combining metallic tubes, skyscrapers and cowboy boots, and a metal-clanking stamping dance, was greeted with angry shouts – even though America had now entered the war.

Cocteau had asked Satie if he could intersperse the sounds of everyday life with the music and Satie 'provided a score for typewriter, ship's siren, the running spiel of a circus barker, and other sound effects, one of which resembled machine-gun fire, to the outrage of the audience.'[26]

Their anger was understandable. The war was raging nearby and the French had just lost 140,000 men in two weeks. A fortnight before the first night of *Parade* the Hindenburg Line was broken at Arras – a town less than 100 miles away from Paris. The year 1917 also saw the battle of Vimy Ridge, the second battle of Verdun and the third battle of Ypres, lasting for three months in appalling water-logged conditions. Mustard gas was used for the first time. Paschendaele Ridge was ultimately taken, with British casualties there reaching a horrific 240,000.

The first night of *Parade* was reminiscent of that of *The Rite of Spring*. There were the beginnings of a riot, with the crowd at the end starting to threaten Picasso, Satie and Cocteau. Fortunately, Apollinaire was there 'bandaged, in uniform, with his Croix de Guerre' and he harangued the audience passionately and 'persuaded them that *Parade* was not the work of Huns.'[27] Cocteau thought that without his presence women armed with hatpins would have gouged out their eyes. Even so, shouts of 'Down with Foreigners' were heard at the end of the performance.

The ballet had its supporters. Proust and his friends, for instance, had been totally entranced by it. However, at the end Satie abused a critic who claimed criminal defamation and took him to court. Satie – and modern art along with him – was sent for trial and he was jailed for a week. Cocteau hit the critic's lawyer and the police moved in.

The critics were unenthusiastic about *Parade* and Diaghilev took it off after two days. Nevertheless, it was a crucially original ballet for the company. Explosive, it changed the perception of ballet and revolutionised its settings. When it was performed again in Paris after the first world war, it was a triumph, hailed as an inspiring innovation.

While in Paris, Stravinsky had introduced Massine to the composer Maurice Ravel, who was then in his thirties. He had already written the score for *Daphnis and Chloe* and Massine found him a witty and erudite conversationalist. The two discussed the possibility of a contemporary ballet based on football, an idea inspired by Robert Delaunay's paintings. Massine was fascinated by the movements of the game, the idea of a football flying around from one group of dancers to another. Although the ballet never came to anything, Diaghilev had the gift of generating in others his own excitement at new ideas.

The company left Paris in the summer of 1917, delighted that their reputation for stimulation, which had suffered because of their long wartime absence, had been resurrected.

11

Nijinsky: the Final Split

After leaving Paris in 1917 the company returned to Spain for a season in Madrid and it was there that Nijinsky joined them.

After having had complete control over the company in America, on his arrival in Spain he expected to find himself indispensable to Diaghilev. He was taken aback to discover that Massine, though in no way able to challenge Nijinsky's incomparable dancing, had by sheer hard work turned himself into an excellent dancer and choreographer.

Diaghilev and Nijinsky had a wary but amicable relationship, despite the New York tensions. They discussed the revolution in Russia as Nijinsky had hopes not only of returning there himself but of persuading Diaghilev to join him. Nijinsky then danced various roles in Madrid and King Alfonso of Spain was so enthusiastic that he turned up not only for the first nights, but also for most of the rehearsals.

However, Nijinsky's wife Romola became convinced that Diaghilev's aim was to separate her from Nijinsky. There was a further problem: Nijinsky had cabled Diaghilev from New York to agree in principle to a tour of South America. He now told Diaghilev he preferred not to leave his baby daughter and needed a rest. He was told in turn that in Spain a cable, such as his regarding South America, was binding in law. Legally, he had to make the trip.

The company at the time was in Barcelona. Happening to walk through the foyer of the Nijinskys' hotel, Diaghilev saw their luggage piled up and was told they planned to leave Barcelona that day. In shock, as Nijinsky was billed to appear in the Ballets Russes that night, Diaghilev consulted the governor of the city, who confirmed that Nijinsky was legally prohibited from leaving the city if he was advertised to appear at the theatre. Police were sent to the hotel to warn Nijinsky that he could not leave. Nijinsky was forced to finish the season but the episode naturally exacerbated tension between the two men.

On 30th June in Barcelona Diaghilev, though unaware of this, was to see Nijinsky dance for the last time.

Grigoriev believed that Diaghilev's publicity for the season, which emphasised the contribution of the whole company, irritated Nijinsky who considered he should have had prime billing. The twenty-nine-year-old Nijinsky, now in a highly nervous and excitable state, prepared to go to South America with the company in the July of 1917.

While the company was away Diaghilev met Stravinsky to ask how the scenario and score of *Les Noces* was progressing. Since 1914, when Stravinsky first proposed the idea, Diaghilev had bombarded him with telegrams to ask how he was getting on. Stravinsky in turn wrote angrily to Benois saying how sick he was of 'this elderly director with his monocle and his Myasin boy' [Nijinsky][1]

His outburst was mainly fuelled by Diaghilev's insatiable hunger for new ideas failing to match his willingness to pay for work in progress. Or even finished work. Money was again discussed between the two men and Stravinsky was left reasonably assured.

The South American tour initially went well – the whole company, including Grigoriev and the conductor Ansermet, bursting merrily into Harold Acton's small room the day they arrived in Montevideo to greet him – even though this brief stop in Uraguay was unplanned. There was a great welcome for the company in Rio de Janeiro as since its first tour the news of its achievements had spread and as there was a serious risk of ships going to South America being torpedoed, visiting companies were scarce.

Grigoriev, however, was having trouble with both Nijinskys. Romola considered any minor accident her husband had was deliberately engineered and at one stage hired a private detective to guard him. Nijinsky's own behaviour was becoming more and more erratic: he would sometimes pace the stage, refusing to dance and although this was furiously denied by his wife, Grigoriev and others thought his mind was clouding and he was showing signs of mental disorder.

While travelling through South America, a spark caught the scenery of some of the ballets and much of it was destroyed. The company finally arrived in Buenos Aires in September 1917, where the Nijinskys celebrated their fourth anniversary.

On the 26th of that month the company ended its tour of South America and Nijinsky – though he did not yet know it – danced for the Ballets Russes for the last time. Once back in Europe, he and his wife and daughter rented a house in St Moritz, where they lived quietly for the rest of the war, although Nijinsky still dreamed of going back to live in Russia.

The company returned to Barcelona in November to be greeted by an anxious Diaghilev who told the assembled artistes that the long-running war was curtailing his chances of making advance engagements. He was optimistic about the future but German troops had broken through the Italian lines, so no bookings could be made in Italy. Neither, with such losses of French soldiers, could they return to Paris. He did, however, have contracts for Spain and Portugal.

Meanwhile he had been working on a revival of *La Boutique Fantasque,* a ballet based on dolls who come to life, which he now put into rehearsal. Despite the incredible difficulties in getting around Europe, he had somehow managed to visit libraries in Paris and Rome to research new music for the ballet. He was excited at discovering some little known compositions by Rossini.

The company was pleased to hear about the bookings in Spain, as the Russians shared with the Spanish a love of spectacle and a delight in bullfights and Spanish dancing. In turn, the Spanish enthusiastically welcomed the company and its performances were invariably sold out.

Eventually, the company moved on to Portugal although its planned opening there was delayed as there was an unexpected uprising. It was promptly suppressed but until order was restored about a week later, all the members of the company were forced to sleep in their clothes under the main staircase of their hotel, using their mattresses as a protective wall against bursting shells from the firing. Diaghilev was annoyed, rather than frightened, saying irritably that it was a waste of good rehearsal time.

The victorious general of the revolution, Sidonio Paes, became the President of Portugal, only to be assassinated a year later. Apart from this uprising, Diaghilev was still digesting news of the October Revolution by the Bolsheviks in Russia, which made him stamp around, furious at all revolutionaries.

Although he was a professed monarchist, Diaghilev was in many ways a revolutionary himself. Despite requests he had never taken his company to dance in Russia during the czarist regime, in case his ideas on all aspects of the ballet, from the music to the choreography, were too advanced for the 'imperialistic' audiences there.

Diaghilev said later of this time that it was very strange 'to have been born and to have lived in a great country, to think that you knew by sight, or at least by name, every prominent leader of opinion, and then to wake up suddenly one day and find your country ruled by men of whose very names, both real and assumed, you and the large majority of your fellow countrymen were totally ignorant.'[2]

The immediate problem for Diaghilev at the beginning of 1918 was the next booking for the company. Because of the uprising the Portuguese had more on their minds than ballet, the season had not gone well and another tour was not welcome. Travelling was highly restricted and the Russians were now dubbed 'revolutionaries' and looked on as undesirable. The contracts for the members of the company allowed one month a year for rehearsals at half pay, so *Daphnis and Chloe* was rehearsed. However, there was little expectation of it being shown. It was, all suspected, merely a way of marking time.

Diaghilev made frequent trips to Spain, trying to negotiate another contract, reappearing in the mid-February of 1918. He needed to reassure his company, but could only tell them that though he had negotiated another contract for Spain, it was not for another two months and he could not pay them in advance.

The company returned to Barcelona in April to find Diaghilev enthusiastically intent on organising a ballet to be called *Le Tricorne* (*The Three-Cornered Hat*), based on authentic Spanish dancing. He was busy commissioning the Spanish composer Manuel de Falla to write the music, Picasso to design the décor and costumes and Spanish dancers to take the main roles.

Picasso, who had travelled to Spain, sat in on the rehearsals, liking to watch the dancers in repose and doing fast thumbnail sketches of them. When he, Massine and Diaghilev met at the Ritz Hotel in Madrid to discuss *Le Tricorne*, Massine was highly impressed by his quick sketches of Karsavina and Massine dancing.

At the time the spy, Mata Hari, was staying in the Madrid Ritz Hotel. Finding Diaghilev a frequent visitor, she asked if she could join his company, saying she deeply admired Stravinsky's music. Diaghilev refused her request, but she still sent him pleading letters. Massine was greatly amused when Diaghilev told him and the two wondered whether she really considered herself a dancer or if the move was part of her scheming.[3]

Meanwhile, everyone's money was dwindling to nothing and there were still no further bookings on the horizon. As there was no actual fighting in England, Diaghilev decided to see if he could go there with a smaller company than usual. He pulled it off, managing not only to make a booking with Oswald Stoll, the manager of the London Coliseum, but also overcoming the refusal of the Premier of France, Georges Clemenceau, to allow the company to travel to England via France.

Permission was finally given after King Alfonso of Spain interceded. Diaghilev never forgot the King's generous sponsorship over the years and always arranged a special gala for him whenever he came to London. Without him, the Ballets Russes would quite possibly not have survived. When Count Harry Kessler was lunching with Misia Sert and Poulenc, Misia told him how Diaghilev and his company had been so desperately poor in Spain they had nearly starved.

In July 1918 Diaghilev and the company were shocked by the assassination of Czar Nicholas II and all his family by the Red Guards. Diaghilev at the time was negotiating the company's departure from Spain and as France had delayed giving Diaghilev a visa for so long, Misia Sert's husband, Jose-Maria Sert, took Diaghilev to the French frontier to smooth the way.

Sert first checked with him that he had nothing compromising on him. Diaghilev denied this but eventually produced a wad of papers which included two letters from Mata Hari. As the French had just arrested her for espionage, the two men only just had time to destroy them before reaching the frontier.[4]

Massine's version of events differed. He claimed that he and Diaghilev were travelling together and when they reached the French border two sinister Spaniards demanded their credentials and asked Diaghilev a stream of questions as to his association with Mata Hari: had she been a member of the company? Had she written any letters to him? Massine remembered thankfully that the letters were still in Madrid and Diaghilev was allowed through.

On 12 July 1918 Picasso married Olga Khoklova in Paris with Max Jacob and Apollinaire as his witnesses. Misia Sert was present and Jean Cocteau was one of those who, in accordance with the rites of the Russian Orthodox Church, helped hold the gold crowns over the couple's heads.

The honeymoon was spent in Biarritz, now becoming a fashionable resort. This, along with the couple then moving to a more elegant area of Paris, was a sign that Picasso's previous unconventional lifestyle, when he shunned the monied and propertied classes, was coming to an end. His new wife expected a higher standard of living.

The wife of the painter Andre Derain wrote dismissively of her: 'The first time I saw her I took her for a chambermaid; she was a plain little woman with freckles all over her face'. The reaction to her from Picasso's old friends might have been irritation at the change in Picasso, who was now dressing 'like a well-to-do businessman, in a well-cut suit with a bow-tie, white pocket handkerchief and gold watch chain, giving smart lunches and dinners ...'.[5]

The Ballets Russes arrived in England in the August of 1918, which allowed them a month to prepare for their opening on 5 September. Diaghilev was busy, not only in preparing for the current productions, but also for future ones. A large amount of scenery for the ballet *Contes Russes*, for example, had been accidentally burnt in a train while the company was in South America and before the ballet could be re-staged, the scene painter had to recreate these.

Ethel Sands, the painter, was very conscious of the food shortages in London in 1918 and dreaded having to satisfy the 'determined greed' of Diaghilev. However, 'his repeated visits vouchsafed that she and her cook succeeded in the task.'[6] Diaghilev may have tired of the only other offer of food, which was having tea at Garland's Hotel in Suffolk Street with Lady Ottoline in her plush old-world sitting room where ballerinas ate 'strawberry or raspberry jam in silver spoons, dipped previously, after the Russian mode, in tea without milk.'[7]

It was not only food that Diaghilev required on first coming to London, it was an entire new set of clothes. His lounge suit and Homburg hat were bedraggled and he quickly bought an impressive new outfit: bowler, overcoat and suit with dove-gray spats, along with a smart walking stick. How fortunate that Stoll had paid an advance. Beaumont said that when the company first saw Diaghilev's transformation, they 'crowded round him with expressions of admiration, fingering his clothes and praising the quality of the materials.'[8] It made Diaghilev smile.

The Ballets Russes opened on 5 September 1918 at the Coliseum and the event was the expected glittering affair. The company performed *The Good-Humoured Ladies*, with music arranged by Vincente Tommasini and simple settings by Bakst. Massine and Lydia Lopokova danced the main parts – Lopokova having returned to the company in 1916 after working in America for five years. It was an anxious evening for Diaghilev as both dancers were unknown to London audiences and he also did not know if Massine's new choreography would be well received.

He had no need to fear as it was the start of a triumphant season for the Ballets Russes. Lopokova was a major success. Lady Ottoline Morrell remembered meeting her when she came to her house at Garsington with Diaghilev: 'She is a most charming and perfect little woman,' she wrote on 14 October, 'full of spirit and affection and intellect and enthusiasm – so different from the English sticks who keep and guard themselves so well – I love her.'[9]

The charming and talented Lydia Lopokova would later marry the celebrated economist John Maynard Keynes

The novelist Osbert Sitwell, a devoted adherent of the Russian Ballet, also praised her grace, pathos and comic genius, and liked her inquisitive, bird-like face which seemed to him to be the personification of gaiety and spontaneity. He considered that the productions that year 'manifested a new accent, a new emphasis, more modern and with a Spanish tang.'

Osbert, Sacheverell and Edith Sitwell were symbols of ultra-modernism, the arbiters of fashion in music, art and interior decoration. Sacheverell, writer and art critic, used to recall the music of certain ballets when in the trenches to keep himself sane and on hearing the Ballets Russes was returning to London that autumn believed that it augured peace. And indeed the Armistice was signed on 11 November 1918.

That day, by chance, Osbert Sitwell had asked a group of friends to his house in Swan Walk, Chelsea, including Diaghilev and Massine. Hearing the uproar in the street, they went to investigate and then joined the crowds where revellers were climbing lamp-posts and riding – or dancing – on the roofs of taxis. Sitwell watched Diaghilev, big, burly and bear-like in his fur coat, gazing with melancholy exhaustion at the crowds, without revealing what he was thinking. Sitwell found his solemn pathos quickly banished by the intense energy of his eyes and his very charming smile.

Massine, meanwhile, was intently and professionally watching the steps and gestures of the dancing couples. He always had work in mind and had created the choreography for *The Three-Cornered Hat* by watching Andalusian festival dancers.

Sitwell and his circle then went to the art collector Monty Shearman's flat in the Adelphi, where there was a pre-arranged party. Osbert Sitwell noticed the rooms were thick with paintings by Matisse and the Paris school, along with some by the Bloomsbury Group and Mark Gertler, the in-vogue painter, whose still-lives were of 'apples and pears of an incomparable rosy rotundity falling sideways off cardboard cloths'.[10]

Gertler himself was there, along with the elite of the intellectual and artistic world. They included Lytton Strachey, Clive Bell, Roger Fry, Lady Ottoline Morrell, Dora Carrington, Nina Hamnett, Maynard Keynes, Duncan Grant, Sacheverell Sitwell, Diaghilev, Leonide Massine and the ballerina Lydia Lopokova – later to marry Maynard Keynes. D.H. Lawrence and his wife joined them, as did Augustus John in uniform and surrounded by a bevy of land-girls in leggings and breeches.

It was a bacchanalian scene of rejoicing. Everyone but Diaghilev danced – Dora Carrington non-stop for three hours, mostly with David Garnett whose novel *Lady into Fox* was to win prestigious prizes. Osbert Sitwell saw the tall, flagging figure of Lytton Strachey 'with his rather narrow, angular beard, long, inquisitive nose, and air of someone pleasantly awakening from a trance, jigging about with an amiable debility.'[11] He reminded Sitwell of a benevolent but rather irritable pelican.

The Bloomsbury Group were bandying phrases like '*ex*-quisitely civilised' and 'How *simply too* extraordinary.' Civilised living, it appeared, was back. Osbert Sitwell commented that 'to everyone here, as to those outside, the evening brought unbelievable solace ... No one, I am sure, was more happy than myself at the end of so long, so horrible, and so more than usually famous a war.'[12]

The writer Vera Brittain found solace harder to find. As she walked down Whitehall that night, she felt only cold dismay. 'Already this was a different world from the one that I had known during four life-long years, a world in which people would be light-hearted and forgetful, in which themselves and their careers and their amusements would blot out political ideals and great national issues.'[13]

Elsewhere, the dancing went on. Sacheverell Sitwell, who had met and become very friendly with Diaghilev after the impresario arrived in London, had joined the Shearman party late, having been preoccupied with military manoeuvres at Aldershot. His constant disappearances down there puzzled Diaghilev who asked Sacheverell one night 'Who is this Aldershot? Is she your mistress?'

Sacheverell Sitwell had a strong admiration for Diaghilev's poise and presence. He saw the impeccable and impassive impresario, with his massive head, at the Shearman party, watching the dancers. His expression was distant, his face pale, fleshy and sensuous. The description recalls the sensuality of Oscar Wilde, an early believer like Diaghilev of art for art's sake.

Like Wilde, Diaghilev's homosexuality was part of his creativity. Cyril Connolly considered Diaghilev one of the great homosexual trailblazers in the arts, together with figures like Proust and Cocteau, who in the early 20th century avenged himself on the bourgeoisie for 'killing' Oscar Wilde.

To Sitwell, Diaghilev represented an exciting future as the most important and influential figure in the early post-war years.

12

Picking up the Pieces

Diaghilev had a horror of anniversaries, of the realisation of time going by. He therefore refused to mark the fact that a week after the Armistice the company celebrated its thousandth performance.

Despite that achievement, after the war the Ballets Russes was struggling to survive. Following the initial euphoria, audiences dropped off and theatres were often only half full. Diaghilev sent constant, desperate pleas to possible patrons for financial help to keep the company going.

Europe was no place for cultural enjoyment, for ballet premieres. Before the war, its power and prestige in culture, arts, economics and science had been dominant. After the war, its political, military and economic power had virtually vanished: much of the continent was a desolate area of starvation, anarchy and revolution.

What else could be expected? Ten million men had been killed in the last four years: the effect on bereaved families, on jobs, on the economy, was shocking and Europe was still in a desperate state. Leonard Woolf considered the war had destroyed the bases of European civilisation. 'In 1914 in the background of one's life and one's mind there were light and hope; by 1918 one had ... admitted into the privacy of one's mind or soul an iron fatalistic acquiescence in insecurity and barbarism.'[1]

There was a certain hectic enjoyment in London, an escapist reaction, as people danced frantically and nightly in the Grafton Galleries, ignoring the pictures on the walls of Canadian soldiers' wartime agony. Alfred Noyes' chilling verse summed it up: 'The cymbals crash/and the dancers walk/with long silk stockings/and arms of chalk/butterfly skirts/and white breasts bare/ and shades of dead men/watching 'em there.'[2]

The peace of Versailles was unwillingly signed by Germany in the June of 1919. A further string of peace treaties signed between the successful allies and the defeated states dramatically altered the boundaries of the new Europe. There was also widespread threat to civil order, with uprisings in Russia (1918–20), Hungary (1919) and Germany (1918–23), where both the extreme right and left threatened the new democratic government. Hyper-inflation began to run riot in Germany and certain central European countries. Mussolini's fascist government seized control of Italy in 1922, when the country was in political turmoil.

When travelling in Italy the previous year, Vera Brittain did not take the growing rumours of *fascismo* very seriously. She thought Rome colourful and very different from the 'tense, austere capital of 1917,' but when she went to Amiens, to the cathedral with its boarded-up windows smashed by German shells, she felt as if she had strayed into a tragic legend. Everything had deliberately been left as it was after the 1918 offensive: the sight of the battlefields, the shell-racked roads, the roofless houses and skeleton trees was a sad, depressing experience.

Against this background came the scourge of the Spanish flu. It began in March 1918 and lasted till June 1920, spread as far as the Arctic and soon became the worst epidemic since the Black Death of the 14th century.

Those who died from Spanish flu numbered far more than the military casualties of the Great War, with estimates varying from 20 to 30 million deaths. It was initially thought to be cholera, or dengue, or typhoid. Rumours grew, panic took over: it was said to be a re-visitation of the twelve plagues of Egypt and there was fearful remembrance of prophesied pestilence and sorrows.

Because of the anti-German feeling still sweeping Europe, it was also widely held that the disease had been criminally started in German laboratories. Other theories linked it to war-time European trenches and to a coastal village in Africa. A fast killer, it took less than six months to spread round the world. First noticed in the army camps in Kansas in the March of 1918, it was quickly carried by soldiers to Europe, India, China and Africa.

As the virus caused an over-reaction of the immune system, healthy young people were more likely to die of it than the old and frail with their weaker immune systems.

The symptoms were typically those of influenza: sore throat, high temperature, headache, aching limbs. There was also haemorrhaging and patients could turn a strange violet colour. Death might follow within a couple of days.

Two of those struck down by the flu in the October of 1918 were Ansermet and Stravinsky. According to Stravinsky's biographer, Stephen Walsh, the Stravinsky household in Switzerland got off lightly, but Stravinsky's eldest son recalled 'everyone had to take to their beds, and I can still see Father buried under piles of blankets, his teeth chattering, a big beret pulled down over his eyes and in a very bad temper while my mother staggered round in her dressing-gown handing out medicines, infusions and linctuses to the whole family.'[2] Stravinsky still had a violent fever after eight days.

Countries anxious not to frighten the public with the number of deaths asked newspapers to conceal these. However, there was no such censorship in Spain and when the papers there revealed the news of millions of deaths, other countries promptly and unfairly dubbed the epidemic 'Spanish Flu.'

The disease was highly contagious with infection spread through coughing. Various measures were taken: public meeting places like schools, universities, cinemas and theatres were closed; drinking fountains and telephones were sterilised; street car passengers in parts of America were only allowed on if wearing masks. Mediterranean countries disinfected everything in sight from public baths to pubs; swept streets, cleared rubbish and protected food from flies and dust as these were thought to spread the lethal germs.

When no medically accepted cure was found, people tried out their own remedies: eating garlic, smoking, drinking alcohol.

One of those who died of Spanish flu, two days before the Armistice, was Guillaume Apollinaire, the French poet who spurned traditional verse and whose work had nuances of the Cubist school in painting. Picasso drew a self-portrait of himself on hearing the news, looking mournful. The flu was no respecter of persons: amongst others who died were the Austrian painter Egon Schiele, and his pregnant wife; the German political economist, Max Weber; Freud's daughter, Sophie; and the Bolshevik party leader, Yakov Sverdlov.

At the same time, families in Europe were also having to come to terms with their war-time bereavements: war memorials in the French countryside, unlike the engraved pillars in England, portrayed grieving mothers. Families also had to cope with wounded soldiers and those who were shell-shocked.

The shell-shocked were subject to screaming fits, chattering teeth, panic attacks and constant shaking. Some had complete mental breakdowns. As shell-shock was barely understood, those affected had usually been classified as malingerers and sent back to the front line, where some committed suicide.

Two who received treatment at Craiglockhart War Hospital, where the respected wartime psychiatrist W.H. Rivers worked, were the poets Siegfried Sassoon and Wilfred Owen. Treatment after the war was still primitive and families of shell-shocked soldiers were left to cope on their own.

Slowly the mood in Paris and London changed. Post-war depression gradually lifted: everyone wanted to start afresh. There was a feeling of optimism, of barriers falling.

In post-war London in the summer of 1919 Osbert and Sacheverell Sitwell were busy organising an exhibition of Modern French Art. It was to include paintings by Andre Derain, Henri Matisse, Pablo Picasso, Amedeo Modigliani, Maurice Utrillo, Fernand Leger and Raoul Dufy, along with sculpture by Ossip Zadkine. The venue was the Mansard Gallery in Heal's store, London, but the paintings only arrived shortly before the opening and the two men had to help unpack them as there were too few gallery staff to do so quickly enough.

The work of such artists had naturally not been seen throughout the war and friends of the Sitwells like Roger Fry, author of *Vision and Design*, dropped by with delight to watch the unpacking. At one point a currant was found in a painting by Derain, stuck in between the glass and the painting. Roger Fry looked at it and said, 'Better leave it alone. He probably placed it there intentionally. It makes rather a swagger contour.'[4]

On hand to help was the Parisian-Polish dealer Zborowski, described by Osbert Sitwell as having 'flat, Slavonic features, brown almond-shaped eyes, and a beard which might have been shaped out of beaver's fur.'[5] At the end of the war the Royal Academicians were the dominant group in paintings, but tastes were changing. Victorian paintings, once fetching thousands of pounds, fell dramatically in price while those by artists like Jean Jacques Rousseau, Paul Cezanne, Vincent Van Gogh and Eduourd Manet rose.

The critics were impressed with the exhibition, but the public filled newspapers with their moral complaints. One called the exhibition 'a glorying in prostitution.'

The Salon des Independants in Paris held an exhibition in 1919 of pre-war Cubists. However Picasso refused to show and in denouncing Cubism broke off his friendship with Braque and Derain. Picasso claimed he had seen his friends off to war, but had never found them again.

Clive Bell believed that society, preoccupied just the year before with military and political intrigues, was now focusing its interest on the arts. The Ballets Russes remained high on the artistic list. A critic in 1919 commented

Coco Chanel, a dear friend and generous patron of Diaghilev, was a fashion leader whose designs were used by the Ballets Russes

that the appeal of the Russian ballet, which had regained its pre-war popularity, rested on a solid foundation: 'the beauty of its *ideal* is undimmed. It is always offering something new and strange. It is never content to rest solely on its past laurels. Moreover, its variety is truly remarkable.'[6]

Paris after the war was a different city from the one in which Diaghilev first launched the *Ballets Russes*. Post-war nerves were apparent in the almost frenzied behaviour of café society.

The dress designer Coco Chanel was revolutionising fashion with her new design, the 'sheath' dress – promptly noted by artists creating costumes and décor for the latest productions for the Ballets Russes. Alice B. Toklas pointed out the relationship between fashion and economics: she considered the sheath was no creation, just 'a revival of the Middle Ages when the poor wore them.'

She and Gertrude Stein had returned to Paris in the summer of 1919, to find that 'friends were gone, an era had passed. Matisse had moved south; Picasso ... was playing the successful, suave husband; Apollinaire was dead.'[7]

Jean Cocteau at the time had fallen out with Diaghilev after Diaghilev cut some of Cocteau's sound effects in *Parade*. Cocteau's mother wrote to a friend to say that though the Russians were there, her son seldom went to the ballet as, after Diaghilev's intervention in *Parade*, he now detested him. Instead, Cocteau was writing weekly articles for the paper *Paris-Midi*. He lightheartedly described the parade of the Allied Armies down the Champs-Elysees on Bastille Day, 14 July 1919: 'Here is General Pershing, rigid on his pink horse. His troops halt, mark time, and are off again, like chorus girls. The Marines, entwined in their silver horns, play the latest fox-trot.'[8]

His articles focused on the current artistic scene in Paris. He moved from Futurism to Cubism, from jazz to Charlie Chaplin and one of his interests was the six young composers, known as 'Le Six', many of whom set Cocteau's poems to music. Cocteau collaborated with one of them, Darius Milhaud, on a show called *Le Boeuf sur le Toit*, a farce set in America during prohibition. He would normally have gone to Diaghilev to stage this, had the two not fallen out.

While the peace conference continued in Paris that year, current political events surrounding Britain were less peaceful. The IRA was founded in Ireland; feeling against Britain in Afghanistan developed into war; and in Amritsar, the sacred city of the Sikhs, Indian nationalists were massacred by troops under British control. There were shipbuilding strikes in Belfast and on the Clyde and a railway strike in England.

However, as Britain had been victorious in the war despite the cost in lives, there was a bullish, underlying spirit of optimism. When the Ballets Russes was booked to tour Germany a whole six years later, they found the country changed and shabby, with the Germans no longer friendly to foreigners.

Yet in London, just months after the end of the war, Diaghilev and his company were lightheartedly welcomed as a star attraction.

13

The Lord of the Dance Brought Down

Nijinsky and his wife and daughter were still living in St Moritz at Christmas 1918, just after the war ended. They entered into the spirit of the occasion, decorating the Christmas tree themselves and taking presents to the village children. A horrified maid rushed in the next morning to tell Romola the tree had collapsed, which she warned was a prophecy of bad luck.

Nijinsky's state of mind now worsened. His brother had developed schizophrenia when just a child. Nijinsky may have escaped the same early fate by being under the protective, cosseting care of Diaghilev, who made the daily decisions for him and shielded him from problems.

His behaviour became so irrational it seriously worried his wife and she wrote about it in detail in her book about her husband.[1] Twice he took her and his small daughter on a sleigh journey: on the first occasion he proceeded to drive at other sleighs and nearly crash; on the second he drove so fast both his wife and daughter were thrown from the sleigh. On a third occasion he pushed the two of them down the stairs – before reverting to his usual gentle, affectionate nature.

The servants complained to his wife that Nijinsky was behaving strangely: his voice was hoarse, his eyes hazy. He announced he was giving up dancing in order to farm in Russia and one of the servants told Romola that he was walking around the village wearing a large golden cross over his necktie, stopping everyone to ask if they had been to mass and sending them off to church.

Romola, now seriously concerned, took him to see a psychiatrist in

Romola Nijinsky in St Moritz. She took her husband, Vaslav, back to their home there after his diagnosis as schizophrenic

Zurich, a Professor Bleuler. The couple had waited till the war was over to have another child and she told her husband that their visit was merely to check whether a second child would be mentally and physically sound. Professor Bleuler, who had invented the word schizophrenia in 1911, saw Nijinsky and then, after smilingly shaking his hand in dismissal, told Romola privately that she needed to take her child away and get a divorce as Nijinsky was incurably insane. She was almost too shocked to take this in. It was March 1919 and Nijinsky was 31 years old.

Diaghilev was in London when he was told of Nijinsky's diagnosis. He had long thought Nijinsky's mental health suspect and told Massine with sadness that he was only surprised that the illness had worsened relatively suddenly.[2]

Romola refused to give up hope about her husband. But her parents, now with her, tried to persuade her to divorce Nijinsky and when she refused they briefly got her out of the hotel while they called in the police ambulance. The fire brigade turned up to prevent Nijinsky from jumping out of the window and he was taken away to a state asylum.

The effect was immense: it resulted in his first catatonic attack and brought on the acute development of his illness. His wife quickly arranged for him to leave the state asylum and he spent the next six months at the Sanatorium Bellevue Kreuzlingen. Specialists from America and Europe were called in, all agreeing that the diagnosis was schizophrenia.

The time Nijinsky spent at the Kreuzlingen sanatorium, despite hopes, did not lead to any improvement in his mental state. Indeed, he grew worse, becoming violent, having hallucinations and refusing his food. Romola tried taking him home in case his own surroundings helped him but his condition did not improve.

Coincidentally, in London at the time Nijinsky was declared insane in 1919 was the young and brilliant Flamenco dancer Felix Fernandez Garcia, who had been discovered by Diaghilev and Massine taking part in a Spanish dance exhibition in Seville. Diaghilev wanted a Spanish lead dancer in the ballet *Le Tricorne* and brought him over to London.

To everyone's shock, he was suddenly arrested. He had been found dancing in front of the altar of St Martin's in the Fields in London, having smashed some of its windows. It was a sad parallel with Nijinsky and, like him, the Spanish dancer was declared incurably insane.

Romola took Nijinsky back to their house in St Moritz and over the next seven years tried to give him some sense of freedom there and, later, in Vienna and Paris.

It was the start of years of consultation, but none of the doctors could help. In Switzerland the couple saw Dr Jung and then moved to live in Vienna where Professor Freud's psycho-analysis could not cure schizophrenia. No one could offer any hope. Even a desperate trip to Lourdes was unsuccessful.

Once when Romola briefly left Austria on a trip, her parents were quick to have Nijinsky committed to a state asylum outside Budapest where he was treated badly. Fortunately for Nijinsky, Romola on return was quick to have him released and take him back to their home in Austria.

She faced a difficult and uncertain future, particularly as on 14 June 1920 in Vienna she gave birth to their second child, another daughter. Nevertheless,

In an
unsuccessful
attempt to
help Nijinsky,
Diaghilev
took him to a
performance of
Petrushka *in*
Paris in 1928.
Left to right:
Kremnev,
Benois,
Grigoriev,
Karsavina,
Diaghilev,
Nijinsky and
Lifar

she resolved that if at all possible she would look after her husband herself and try to prevent him from being taken to an asylum.

That same year, 1920, Diaghilev revived Stravinsky's ballet, *Le Sacre du Printemps*, as the original sets and costumes had survived the war. Nijinsky's original choreography had been lost so it was re-choreographed by Massine. Grigoriev thought the new version lacked pathos. Sadly, Nijinsky was now a figure of pathos himself. When the following year his sister escaped the revolution in Russia to come to Europe, he did not appear to recognise her.

Two years later, in 1923, Romola rented a flat in Paris near the Eiffel Tower and tried taking her husband to various outings: the theatre, the ballet and Cossack dancers. He did show certain signs of interest, but they did not last and he returned to his silent state. He stayed in the flat, with Romola's sister looking after him if she was away. Nijinsky's own sister, Bronislava, also had a nearby flat.

Diaghilev went to see Nijinsky in Paris. It was the first time the two had met since they had fallen out in Barcelona over Nijinsky's refusal to dance six years before. He asked Nijinsky if he would dance again for the Russian ballet and said he needed him. Nijinsky allegedly replied, 'I cannot because I am mad.'[3]

Years later Diaghilev made one more attempt to try to encourage Nijinsky out of his schizophrenic state. It was when the Ballets Russes returned to L'Opera in Paris in December 1928. One of the last performances they staged was a revival of *Petrushka*, the role Nijinsky had once danced so brilliantly. Karsavina had made her debut with Nijinsky in this ballet and she now repeated her performance.

Diaghilev had the idea that if Nijinsky saw her again in *Petrushka* it was just possible the memory would jolt him out of his present inert state. He therefore arranged for him to be present for one performance. But first he and Lifar went to visit Nijinsky in the apartment in Paris where he lived. Lifar noted the hospital atmosphere, the silence and the attendants dressed in white. Nijinsky himself lay half-clothed on a low divan.

Count Harry Kessler, at the ballet that night, was asked by Diaghilev to help him take Nijinsky down three flights of stairs. Kessler sadly saw that Nijinsky 'who formerly seemed able to leap over roof-tops, now feels his way, uncertainly, anxiously, from step to step. I held him fast, pressed his thin fingers ... the look he gave me from his great eyes was mindless but infinitely touching, like that of a sick animal.'[4]

Karsavina, standing next to Nijinsky for a photograph at the end of the performance, said that he looked into her face, 'but on meeting my eyes he again turned his head like a child that wants to hide tears.' Diaghilev told her later that Nijinsky had asked who Lifar was when he came on stage. When told it was the principal dancer, he asked, after a pause, 'Can he jump?'[5] Nijinsky watched the ballet intensely and had not wanted to leave the theatre. When he did so, Diaghilev kissed him on the brow.

Kessler joined a group which included Diaghilev, Karsavina, Misia Sert and Gordon Craig for a meal at the Restaurant de la Paix, but remained shocked by Nijinsky's plight.

'Let him dream his dreams,' said the specialists. Nijinsky lived on in his dream world until he died in April 1950.

14

The Vogue for Vogue

The composer and conductor Constant Lambert was to say, cuttingly, that before the war Diaghilev had created a vogue for Russian ballet but that after the war he had simply created a vogue for vogue.

Taper, biographer of Georgi Balanchine, the Russian-born American choreographer, agreed. He argued that, post-war, the Ballets Russes reflected 'a restless search for novelty, for modernism at any cost' and that the artists around Diaghilev 'deliberately cultivated the banal and the trivial for shock effect.' In this way, he thought, they represented the spirit of the post-war age, 'anti-heroic and contemptuous of bourgeois morality ... the era of *So What?*'[1]

Diaghilev was regarded as *le dernier cri*, the king of all that was most progressive in theatrical art, the leader of the great 20th century trailblazers. He achieved his position by his sensitivity to changing fashion. He was always aware of its direction, but this time the path ahead of him was unclear. After the war years, he had little energy for intellectual experiments. Indeed, Harold Acton saw him at the theatre and commented, 'Somewhere at the back, a bear wrapped in Russian gloom, Diaghilev sat biting his nails, remote and lonely among his satellites.'[2] He commissioned the music for a new ballet, *La Valse,* from the composer Maurice Ravel, of whom he was a great admirer. He liked the result but felt it lacked scenic action. The two men fell out and the friendship was not resumed.

Diaghilev now rose from the ashes and began producing artistic and ingenious work. Two years after the war his company had virtually regained the position it had held in 1914. He may have lacked a little of his early passionate creativity, but individual ballets were still outstanding.

Although the company was having a successful season at the Coliseum, Stoll unexpectedly terminated its contract in the March of 1919. Fortunately for a startled Diaghilev, a revue failed at another of Stoll's theatres, the Alhambra, and the company was able to transfer there.

The company received a tremendous reception when it moved to the Alhambra. Shortly after opening there was further jubiliation from the audience as one of London's favourite ballerinas, Tamara Karsavina, had managed to get out of Russia and now rejoined the ballet in London. The first time she again danced with the company, Diaghilev presented her with a wreath bearing the inscription 'In celebration of the day on which you returned to your Father's embrace.'

John Gielgud nostalgically recalled how he would play truant from Westminster School and climb to the top of the gallery in his top hat and jampot collar to watch the Russian ballets – on one occasion going twice in one day. He loved it all: Stravinsky's music, Massine's choreography, Bakst's exotic sets and was particularly entranced by the passionate dancing of the ballerina Liubov Tchernicheva – Grigoriev's wife – in her role as the Swan Princess. At the Alhambra, 'standing in the promenade beside my father, and walking about with him in the intervals among the cigar smoke and clinking glasses all around me, I felt I had really grown up at last.'[3]

Stoll wanted some new ballets added to the repertoire and Diaghilev decided to put on *Parade*, which had not yet been seen in London along with *La Boutique Fantasque* (The Fantastic Shop), and *Le Tricorne* (*The Three Cornered Hat*), which featured Flamenco dancing.

Diaghilev had long admired the imaginative décor of French painters. He had originally asked Bakst to design the décor for *La Boutique Fantasque*, but felt the results lacked charm and gaiety. Hearing Andre Derain was interested in stage design he sent Massine to see him in Paris.

Derain was instantly fascinated by the idea of *La Boutique Fantasque*, waving his large hands around excitedly and showing Massine the marionette theatre he had built in his flat with all the little puppets he had bought at a country fair.

When Derain arrived in London in 1919 with his designs, Grigoriev thought them unrealistic but Diaghilev was highly enthusiastic, pleased with their aesthetic appeal. Derain was intensely interested in the play of light on solid structures and had created 'an enchanting, totally unrealistic shop, with large arched windows opening on to a fantastic view – a harbour with exotic plants and an old-fashioned paddle steamer with white wheels.'[4] It was witty and charming and it cleverly gave the impression of a toyshop seen through a child's eyes. Derain painted the drop-curtain himself with brightly coloured *trompe d'oeil* chairs and tables.

Bakst was offended at being ruthlessly dropped, but Massine told Diaghilev that 'the artistic perfection of his productions was the most important thing in his life and he would allow nothing, not even a long-standing friendship, to stand in the way of it.'[5] He reminded Diaghilev that he had told him that in the theatre, there were no such things as friends.

W.A. Propert considered Derain's designs the work of a man 'who had come fresh to his work unspoilt by any acquaintance with stage conventions.'[6] Its immense feeling of air and space and delightfully painted fruits and flowers made it the most painter-like décor ever seen in the Ballets Russes.

Diaghilev kept a careful eye on Derain's ideas, inspecting through his eyeglass such decorations as a long pole with a bunch of dolls tied to one end, and gravely examining the sketches for costume and curtains Derain brought to him for approval.

Derain was a charming, good-humoured man. He looked more like a farmer than a painter, being large and tall with fair hair and weather-beaten complexion. He rarely went to any social occasions, disapproving of these as he took his work as a painter too seriously to leave it for mere jollification.

The English art and literary critic Clive Bell knew him well and considered he 'was a man of natural authority, which he exerted without a glimmer of self-consciousness. He spoke slowly, as became his bulk, and with distinctive humour; though a habit of talking with a pipe in his mouth sometimes muffled his voice and distressed his friends.'[7]

When Derain was working on *La Boutique Fantasque* he lived in a modest lodging in Regent's Square in London. Unlike Picasso, elegant in his smoking jacket, Derain remained wedded to his blue serge suit. Clive Bell recalled the first night of *La Boutique Fantasque* when the theatre was packed with white-tie'd, tail-coated enthusiasts. Derain, forced by Diaghilev and Massine to take a bow on stage, still wore his blue serge suit.

Picasso's scenic colours for *Le Tricorne*, premiered in July that year, were pale blues and pinks and whites and greys which Diaghilev liked though, always interested in detail, he asked Picasso to paint a vine growing up the side of a house. There was an argument over whether Massine was to wear the traditional Spanish tight trousers or, as Picasso wanted, knee breeches. A compromise was reached whereby he wore tight trousers for the first half of the ballet then changed to knee breeches for the second.

Osbert Sitwell, who went to the first nights of *La Boutique Fantasque* and *Le Tricorne*, never forgot his excitement at the sight of such modern works of scenic art. He thought Andre Derain's drop-scene for *La Boutique Fantasque* and Picasso's for *Le Tricorne* the most inspired and original creations for over a century. He believed both ballets highlighted the satire, panache and comic audacity of such outstanding dancers as Leonid Massine and Lopokova. The way the two danced the can-can in *La Boutique Fantasque* invariably brought the house to its feet.

Lopokova had a wonderful *elevation* and a certain eccentricity in her dancing and was a great favourite. All the more extraordinary, therefore, when she suddenly disappeared in July, leaving her husband and the company to run off with a Russian officer. Diaghilev, in Paris, was astounced by the news and a replacement was hurriedly found. She returned equally unexpectedly two years later, welcomed by Diaghilev and even more vociferously by English audiences.

Osbert and Sacheverell Sitwell met Picasso when he came to London in the summer of 1919 to oversee his work. They had gone along to his studio in Leicester Square where his brightly coloured drop curtain took up the whole of the floor, and found him and his scene painter casually sitting on it eating their lunch. The curtain design showed a bullring with a dead bull being dragged away, watched by Spanish women wearing mantillas and men in cloaks.

Sacheverell Sitwell was especially taken with the costumes, his favourite being the glittering red and gold Torero-Harlequin, with his cocked hat. Neither settings nor costumes were quite ready on the first night, so Picasso stood by in the wings, dubbing paint on the dancers before they went on stage.

The ballet was hailed as a great success and Picasso, staying at the Savoy Hotel with his wife Olga, was showered with invitations by London's social elite, including the Bloomsbury Group. With enormous vitality he accepted them all.

Not everyone shared Osbert Sitwell's liking for modern works. Charles Ricketts, the painter and stage designer, protested at Robert Delaunay's set for *Cleopatra*: 'The hideous setting was by the post-Impressionist round the corner, pink and purple columns, a pea-green Hathor cow, and yellow pyramids with a green shadow with a red spot.' He was more approving of Massine, whom he considered danced well, even if stark naked except for rather nice bathing-drawers.[8]

Stravinsky was still working on his ballet, *Les Noces*, planned for the

Diaghilev,
Grigoriev and
Picasso in 1919
at the studio
in Covent
Garden, where
Picasso's drop
curtain for Le
Tricorne *was*
being made

Matisse and
Massine
alongside the
Nightingale
(danced by
Karsavina) at
a rehearsal in
Paris in 1920 of
Le Chant du
Rossignol

next Paris season. That year, 1919, he had been conducting a bad-tempered correspondence with Diaghilev over the money for this. Both men were financially pressed and Diaghilev wrote to Ansermet, who had been acting as go-between, to say that before the war 'I could lose 120,000 francs a season in London. I knew I would always find resources in Russia. Some merchant would be ennobled, and I would get the consideration, out of which I could create art. Now there are no Excellencies or Grand Dukes left; a year ago I had debts of a million; London has saved me, but I'm not rich ...'⁹

Massine, with whom Diaghilev appeared as infatuated as he had previously been with Nijinsky, accompanied Diaghilev to the social occasions he attended. Diaghilev found the Bloomsbury Group rather too heavily intellectual for his taste, but still turned up at Lady Ottoline's 17th century mansion, Garsington, in the hope of meeting a possible patron. Lady Ottoline found that she was expected to provide both gourmet food and well-connected guests. Once, finding a lack of celebrities, he was placated by being introduced to a 'princess' – in reality Dorothy Brett, the sister-in-law of 'The White Rajah of Sarawak'.

On one occasion Diaghilev and Massine accompanied Lady Ottoline and Aldous Huxley to Hampton Court. Diaghilev 'whose energy made him rather an exhausting companion, divided his enthusiasm between the pictures and his lunch, for which he showed an appetite which left Ottoline

and Aldous gazing in astonishment.' Massine was neither interested in paintings nor lunch, but Lady Ottoline wrote in her diary that if he could only be siphoned away from Diaghilev 'he might be quite young and gay. He is terribly overworked, poor boy.'[10]

The season at the Alhambra ended in the autumn of 1919 and the company moved to the Princes Theatre, opening there on 29 September. The only new ballet shown was *Parade*, the ballet Picasso had designed during the war and which had originally been premiered in Spain. Whenever *Parade* was staged, reactions varied widely. One critic reviewing it at the Princes Theatre said: 'This is craziness with a touch of genius. The Russians have descended to the "stunt" ballet. It is queer satirical foolery without beauty, charm or grace.'[11]

It amused the public but was not a favourite. Despite postwar hardships the ballet was still expected to be a source of gaiety. The King of Spain came over and his favourite ballets, like *Scheherazade*, were staged for him and there were visits from King George V and the Shah of Persia.

Aware how long the Ballets Russes had spent in London and anxious not to overstay his welcome, Diaghilev negotiated a new season in Paris at L'Opera, where the company opened on Christmas Eve. Unfortunately as the new year of 1920 dawned, the orchestra at L'Opera went on strike for three weeks.

Diaghilev was currently spending much of his time planning new work for the company, aware it was in need of a renaissance. He asked Stravinsky to remodel the music of his opera *Le Rossignol* for a new ballet, *Le Chant du Rossignol*. The two men had not worked together for some six years but this reignited their friendship. The ballet, with its exquisite white and turquoise décor by Henri Matisse, premiered some months later in April 1920 and was a huge success.

Diaghilev had an evening out with Stravinky and two friends of Diaghilev's, Vera Sudeykina and her husband Sergey, who had fled from the civil war in Russia. Stravinsky was moody that evening and Diaghilev asked Vera to be nice to him. The end result was that Stravinsky fell madly in love with Vera and the affair continued for two decades. Her husband was furiously jealous, warning Stravinsky he could not be responsible for his actions.

Diaghilev was more concerned that Stravinsky work on another score, the story of *Pulcinella* based on the popular and ancient Italian comedy, *commedia dell'arte*, developed during the 16th to 18th centuries. Performances usually involved amorous intrigues and were known for their stock characters like Pulcinello, Harlequin and Colombine.

Massine was commissioned as choreographer. He was now at the height

of his powers and after the Paris season ended and the company went to Italy and then Monte Carlo, the forty-eight-year-old Diaghilev bestowed on him the prestigious title of *Maitre de Ballet*.

Picasso agreed to do the décor for *Pulcinella*, but quixotically updated his designs to the 19th century: side-whiskers replaced the traditional black masks. Diaghilev objected to this and became so angry that he allegedly 'flung the drawings down, stamped on them and left the room, slamming the door behind him.'[12] Diaghilev was stubborn, Picasso full of Spanish pride and the quarrel continued. It was only patched up by Diaghilev's close friend Misia Sert.

W.A. Propert thought the ballet fell awkwardly between ancient and modern, citing Picasso's distorted houses in the background and the way Stravinsky had knocked Pergolesi's original music 'out of shape'. But *Pulcinella*, which opened on 15 May 1920, was a critical success. The Ballets Russes was yet again the talking point of Paris.

Diaghilev, however, was only too conscious of his use of Spanish painters

Picasso did the décor for Pulcinella *but Diaghilev dismissed his designs for the costumes which led to an immediate quarrel*

and Italian composers, saying to Grigoriev rather despairingly, 'How can we find young Russian musicians and painters abroad? Oh, how I long to be back in Russia: to breathe in its air and gain new energy from its soil. But shall I ever be able to? I wonder.'[13]

The company's ninth season in Paris began in May 1920: despite the recent war memories, spring was not spring in Paris without an elegant audience attending the Ballets Russes, with its fusion of music, dance and décor.

The company then left Paris for a short season at Covent Garden in London. The ballerina Lydia Sokolova, caught up in an adulterous affair with male dancer Leon Woizikovsky, recalled Diaghilev's kindness at its sudden break-up. Calling her to the Savoy, he asked her to explain her apparent collapse – she had been overdosing on laudanum – and then said to her: 'I want you to think of me as a father, and remember I will come to you at any time of day or night if you should need me.'[14]

Despite the avuncular approach, when Sokolova later hit her lover on stage – though after the curtain had descended – as despite the break-up he had stroked her, Diaghilev promptly fined her £5 'For Assault.' It was the largest fine ever paid by a member of his company.

When at the end of the season, the company took its summer break, Diaghilev went off to his beloved Venice. He was again in financial straits. One reason for this was that Massine was currently rehearsing a new and costly production of *The Rite of Spring*, with different choreography from the original by Nijinsky. Diaghilev wanted the production for the next season in Paris but there was not enough money to re-stage it and pay for the large orchestra it required.

Fortunately for Diaghilev, his guardian angel was as usual hovering overhead. The impresario was lunching with the Duchess Maria Pavlovna, a patron of his from his old days with the Imperial Theatres, when Misia Sert and her friend Coco Chanel joined them. Later, back in his Paris hotel, still without funds, Diaghilev was told a woman wished to see him. It turned out to be Chanel who gave him a cheque that would cover all the ballet's expenses, on condition he told no one. She helped him further by having the costumes for the production made in her own famous fashion establishment.

Jean Cocteau gave his opinion of Chanel with her 'tantrums, her spitefulness, her fabulous jewels, her creations, her caprices, her extravagances, the lovable things about her like her humour and generosity, composing a unique character, winning, attractive, hateful, excessive ...'[15] In a word, human.

Cocteau's show, *Le Boeuf sur Le Toit,* first staged in Paris was successful enough to be retitled *The Nothing-Doing Bar* and staged at London's

Coliseum theatre in the July of 1920. Cocteau found London a tranquil city: Diaghilev found the whole country too tranquil. Because the war had left Europe impoverished, the company's usual mid-European tour that autumn had been cancelled. Instead Diaghilev dubiously followed the suggestion of an employee and arranged for the company to tour the English provinces.

This, as he feared, turned out disastrously: the provinces proved uninterested in ballet. To make matters worse the agent in Birmingham went off with the company's takings.

The company left England with relief.

15

Exit Leonide Massine

The company returned to Paris but Sokolova, who had been chosen to perform the dance of the doomed maiden in *The Rite of Spring*, stayed in London with Massine for a week's hard rehearsal. Only one other dancer was with them, an English girl called Vera Clarke, whose surname was changed to Savina, after a famous Russian tragedienne. She was known for her delicate hand and arm movements, a quality of lightness and a graceful long jump.

What happened next was totally unexpected. Massine, dedicated it was thought to a life with Diaghilev, fell in love with Savina. Massine was highly attractive to women, according to Sokolova, and many of the dancers were a little in love with him. With Diaghilev ever watchful, that was highly dangerous. Sokolova well remembered one time in America when a dancer flirted obviously with Massine. Diaghilev immediately sent an abrupt message to the company that anyone who disturbed Massine in his work would be expelled immediately.

Mid December saw the Paris opening of Massine's *Le Sacre du Printemps*. In Grigoriev's view, Massine's version concentrated too much on the rhythm and lacked the pathos that Nijinsky had created. Sokolova was so exhausted at the end of her dance that she collapsed as the curtain came down.

Diaghilev then restaged *Parade* in Paris, restoring some

sound effects, and a gleeful Cocteau wrote that Diaghilev was now as sweet as sugar.

W.A. Propert in summing up the following year, 1921, for the Ballets Russes said that it had to be considered as one of the most memorable in the company's history. Diaghilev started off at the height of his powers, 'full of energy and ambition and royally extravagant,' but by the end, claimed Propert, he was 'disappointed, broken in health and spirit, and almost penniless.'[1]

The company went off to Rome where they opened on New Year's Day. The city housed a large number of aristocrats from Russia, who had sought refuge there from the revolution and tried to recreate their old life by meeting together at a Russian library.

Savina and Massine went on several local trips together: Sokolova did not think they realised that Diaghilev was having them followed by two private detectives. However, once Diaghilev suspected Massine of infidelity, he had one of his temper tantrums. When this happened, he would 'attack the furniture with his stick, tear the telephone out of the wall and smash it.'[3]

Diaghilev told Savina that if she agreed to renounce Massine he would make her his prima ballerina. This would have been a great honour but Savina, feeling too pressurised, declined to sign such a contract and Diaghilev ruthlessly removed her from her main roles and demoted her to the corps de ballet. Massine, too, about to take the part of Petrushka, was deprived of the role.

Worse was to come as Diaghilev, calling for Grigoriev in a great state of agitation and walking up and down the room with flushed face, told him to terminate Massine's services. He angrily asserted that he had done everything for Massine, had indeed *made* him, this dancer and choreographer who had merely 'a good-looking face and poor legs!'

Massine and Savina had little option but to leave the company, managing to get a three-month contract to go to South America with the well-known Walter Mocchi Opera Company. On their return the two married. Diaghilev felt totally betrayed. The dancer Lydia Sokolova, staying in a room above Diaghilev's, overheard him on a lower terrace telling Misia Sert of 'his hopelessness, aimlessness and sense of loss.'[3] The Russian composer Nicolas Nabokov thought that after Diaghilev's lovers deserted him, 'then suddenly his love turned to a sense of frustration, not hatred, but a strange feeling of being deprived of the object or subject you love ...'[4]

The dancer Frederick Ashton believed Massine only became Diaghilev's lover to further his career. He said that he asked one of Massine's mistresses what Massine had thought about going to bed with Diaghilev. She replied, 'Oh it was rather like going to bed with a nice fat old lady.'[5]

Massine had joined those in Diaghilev's entourage who had left over the years in order to establish their personal and professional independence. It was not an easy decision as such defectors knew how much they owed to Diaghilev, who had invariably shaped their careers and talents. In return Diaghilev had regarded them as his exclusive property, expecting unending loyalty and service. If they failed to provide this, Diaghilev was unforgiving.

Grigoriev regretted Massine's departure as he considered that though he had built on Fokine's work, introducing even more complicated movements, he could have risen to even greater heights.

Emotional problems apart, Diaghilev now had the professional difficulty of replacing Massine as choreographer. Despite Grigoriev's doubts, he chose a young man in the company called Taddeus Slavinsky, who was good looking with a slim figure, though bad teeth. The dancers considered him unreliable and boastful.

Diaghilev knew Slavinsky lacked knowledge of choreography, but argued that Massine at the start of his career with the Ballets Russes had been equally untutored. Diaghilev asked the painter Larionov to oversee this young, untutored choreographer. The first choreographic task he gave Slavinsky was to work on Prokofiev's ballet, *Chout*, for which Larionov was the designer.

Diaghilev was preoccupied with the company's opening night in Madrid. He had recovered his equilibrium and was again in energetic spirits. With him came Stravinsky and Walter Nouvel, his old Russian friend of many years' standing. Nouvel was to become the administrator of the company – to Grigoriev's relief as he was seriously overworked.

There was another newcomer, a seventeen-year-old poet called Boris Kochno. Kochno had fled from war-ravished Russia to Paris the previous year. He told his childhood friend, the painter and costume designer Vera Sudeykina who knew Diaghilev, and was known for her long affair with Stravinsky, that he was looking for a higher attachment and his one ambition was to meet Diaghilev. 'I saw him once in the foyer in the Theatre des Champs Elysees and almost fainted. Such an appearance!'[6]

He finally had the chance to knock on Diaghilev's door and the impresario opened it, monocle in place and swathed in a dressing gown. Diaghilev asked Kochno a raft of questions about Russia and, as always when deep in thought, stood chewing his tongue. Diaghilev was missing Massine and a sexual involvement seemed likely but after a few weeks Kochno told Sudeykina, 'Verushka, I can't stand it, but I don't want to go away entirely.' She suggested he become Diaghilev's secretary.[7]

It was an inspired move. They may not have been lovers, but Kochno, intelligent, well-born and artistic, gained Diaghilev's total trust, was established as a librettist and became a member of the inner circle, proving indispensable. The two men were mentally attuned, worked in tandem throughout Diaghilev's life and Kochno was with him when he died. Although he received no salary, his meals, lodgings and clothes were paid for.

John Drummond in his interviews with various members of Diaghilev's circle had reservations about Kochno, considering there was something 'in those untrusting eyes that held me back, even when he was sober.'[8]

Kochno accompanied Diaghilev and Stravinsky on a visit to Seville in 1921 to look for a team of Spanish dancers, musicians and singers whose music could

Boris Kochno, who took much of the burden of work as an assistant to Diaghilev. He was with Diaghilev at his death

be rearranged by Stravinsky in a setting by Picasso. They succeeded in this and also met the theatrical producer C.B. Cochran.

Diaghilev was quick to persuade him to book the company for his Princes Theatre in London. Cochran remembered being wooed at the daily lunch parties held at the Venta Antequera, Diaghilev's favourite restaurant, where they would start with a bottle of Manzanilla and then choose from 50 different kinds of hors d'oeuvres.

Cochran was amused by Diaghilev's negotiations with the classic male dancer, Ramirez, about payment should he come to London to dance. Asking Ramirez what salary he would expect, Ramirez with a noble gesture said he would leave it to Diaghilev. On suggesting a sum, Ramirez bowed and said it was munificent. However the following day he told Diaghilev that he had heard how expensive London was and he would need twice the amount. Diaghilev, anxious to engage him, agreed to a supplementary sum. Then Ramirez spoke eloquently about how lonely he would be in London and would like a friend to accompany him – for the same amount of money that Ramirez himself would be getting. The friend, he said, wasn't a dancer, but he was an excellent horseman. At that point Diaghilev sensibly retired from the fray.[9]

The company briefly visited Monte Carlo, where they met the entertainers

the Dolly Sisters. Larionov was there working on the scenario, décor and choreography for the vivacious ballet, *Chout*. This and the Spanish *Cuadro Flamenco* were the only new works planned for the forthcoming Paris season opening in May 1921. But Diaghilev was disappointed with the early results of the choreography for *Chout* and decided that in future he would need a more innovative choreographer.

Picasso's Spanish costumes for *Cuadro Flamenco* and his delightful décor were immensely popular. His design showed the inside of a small Spanish theatre with painted, smiling spectators in boxes either side. He used some of the designs originally planned for *Pulcinella* and fortunately did not charge Diaghilev for these – as the company was yet again in the middle of a severe financial crisis.

Diaghilev was forced to launch the 1921 Paris spring season at the undistinguished theatre, Gaite Lyrique, having insufficient money for the L'Opera or the Theatre des Champs Elysees. Local people turned up to laugh or jeer at the top-hatted audience who arrived each night. However, the season went well, even if *Chout* made comparatively little impression.

When the season ended, Larionov went straight to London to the newly rebuilt Princes Theatre to supervise the opening of *Chout* on 8 June. It scandalised audiences: *The Observer* dismissed it as 'the worst of bores' and that the new art form the ballet represented 'has not yet learned to walk. It can scream very piercingly whilst waiting for its bottle.' *Vogue* called it 'a nightmare of impudent, bad-boy perversity for which the perpetrators deserved rather to be spanked and put to bed than criticised.'[10]. Diaghilev wrote to *The Times* defending it, but it was quietly dropped from the repertory for some time.

The Princes Theatre was uncomfortably small, but the Spanish dancers were once more enthusiastically received. Massine's version of *The Rite of Spring*, although more calmly greeted than at its first showing, still did not ignite the audience. Diaghilev simply couldn't understand why Stravinsky's music was so unappreciated. He was also annoyed that quite a number of his dancers had defected to Massine, who was setting off to America with his own company.

The first Russian exhibition of Arts and Crafts took place in June 1921 at the Whitechapel Gallery. On show were some 450 works by over 70 Russian artists currently working in London and Paris. Larionov and Goncharova alone showed over 80 paintings and theatre designs. The opening night was crowded with artists and writers and Larionov met Wyndham Lewis who promptly invited him and all the Russian dancers to a cabaret.

It was an enormously hot summer in London: the city was full and there was a constant round of lunches, teas, receptions and country-house weekends. That year the Ballets Russes invaded the Bloomsbury Group's ivory tower when the economist Maynard Keynes married the Russian ballerina, Lydia Lopokova.

Bronislava Nijinska, who had left the company at the same time as her brother Nijinsky, fled from Soviet Russia that year. She had a gruelling journey with her elderly mother and two small children but rejoined the Ballets Russes in 1921 to assist with the choreography. She was a memorable sight in her dark practice clothes, pale face and straw-coloured hair, gesticulating dramatically with her white arms.

At the time the popular musical *Chu Chin Chow* had been running in London for three years, a length of time which amazed Diaghilev as his own company put on short, different ballets each night. He decided to try for a long-running West End hit and revived Tchaikovsky's 30 year old five-act ballet, *The Sleeping Princess*, which would last a whole evening and could be run daily.

It was a lavish and complicated work: Diaghilev imported three Russian ballerinas to share the classical role of Aurora; asked Stravinsky to re-orchestrate the score; and, crucially, persuaded Bakst – still smarting at Derain's appointment as designer for *La Boutique Fantasque* – to design six scenes of imperial splendour and 300 costumes. Noting the phenomenal success of the young conductor Eugene Goossens, Diaghilev asked him to conduct it.

Sir Oswald Stoll had guaranteed £10,000 for the production but inevitably Diaghilev seriously overspent and had to ask Stoll for another £5,000, and then another. Stoll was angry but had to pay out the money or the production could not be staged and he would have lost his entire investment.

The ballet opened on 2 November at Stoll's Alhambra Theatre. Sacheverell Sitwell thought it the most exciting first night he had ever seen in his life, considering the music was an enchantment from the start. It was the last great production by Bakst, whom he intensely admired. Bakst had again fallen out with Diaghilev shortly before the first night and as a gesture of defiance stayed sitting in the stagebox wearing a tweed suit rather than his evening wear.

The actor John Gielgud was entranced by Bakst's décor and the brilliant cast, but recalled, 'The magic wood refused to grow ... while ominous creakings and crackings almost drowned the orchestra. Pieces of wood emerged from the trap only to break off or keel over ... while in the final scene one of the dancers fell on her back during a *pas de deux*.'[11]

In addition, when the Prince stepped into a frail barque to be carried to the mysterious abode of the Sleeping Princess, the machinery failed. There were long delays in moving the vast sets which irritated both audience and critics.

Another difficulty was that London audiences were not used to sitting through a full-length ballet, preferring the usual triple bills. Receipts dropped and though Diaghilev had hoped for a six-month run so that a proportion of the weekly receipts could be used to repay the capital sum Stoll had advanced, the season ended in under two months.

As the dancer Ninette de Valois pointed out, 'England did not have the great ballet public of today and classical ballet of such dimensions was unknown.' However, she regarded its failure as being less important than the interest it rekindled in traditional classical ballet.[12]

The season ended in financial chaos and for once Diaghilev failed to raise the money to cover the shortfall. He even had to sell, not pawn as usual, his treasured black pearl stud, a gift from Lady Ripon. The creditors promptly seized the sets and costumes which were stored under the Coliseum stage.

Diaghilev's plan to open with this ballet in Paris the following spring was therefore ruined – along with many of the sequestered sets and costumes, which perished after a later music hall act at the Coliseum installed a leaky swimming pool on the stage above them. The whole episode, including (in Diaghilev's eyes) the organised hostility of the London critics, greatly depressed him and he left, penniless, for Paris.

There were rumours that the company was closing and in fear of this, four of the main dancers, including Lopokova and Sokolova, defected to Massine's company. This blow could well have broken Diaghilev's spirit, but he had an extraordinary ability to dig his way out of any pit into which he had fallen and he now started to work on new presentations.

He remembered hearing some music by Stravinsky while in the house of Princesse Edmond de Polignac, one of his old friends and patrons. She had commissioned the music herself but gave him permission to use it and he called it *Le Renard*. He then 'borrowed' some dances from *The Sleeping Princess* and with the use of a previous décor from the ballet *Le Pavillon d'Armide*, called the 'new' ballet *Le Mariage d'Aurore*.

The company, or what was left of it, struggled to get to Paris. Diaghilev bore grudges indefinitely, so when Massine unexpectedly offered to return, bringing his own company with him, Diaghilev took malicious pleasure in refusing.

Coco Chanel, commenting on this time, was struck by Diaghilev abandoning his normal use of Russian artists and becoming an ardent propagandist for foreign artists. She did not realise the difficulty Diaghilev was having in raising Russian artists.

The Princesse de Polignac was an early and much valued sponsor of the Ballets Russes

Mikhail Larionov's set design for Le Renard

The season of the Ballets Russes at L'Opera in Paris began on 18 May 1922 with *Le Renard*, which was based on Russian folk stories of Reynard the Fox. It was described as 'Ballet Burlesque avec Chant', but it was really a 16 minute mini opera. which was sung by four singers (banished to the orchestra pit), and performed by four dancers who corresponded to the voices. The animal masks were designed by Larionov and the choreography was by Bronislava Nijinska, who based it on the circus acrobatics she had seen in childhood. She also danced the leading role.

Reactions to it varied: some liked it, others thought the music too harsh, the scenery too childish, or the dancing rather grotesque. It was rarely re-staged.

The season at L'Opera proved a success, but although Diaghilev wanted to extend it, this could not be arranged and he reluctantly agreed to transfer the company to the lesser-known Mogador Theatre. His doubts were justified as the audiences were far more sparse than at L'Opera.

Despite their overall success in Paris, the sword still dangled over the company. It could not return to London at the end of the season because of the money still owed to Stoll and it was proving difficult to get autumn and winter bookings in other countries. The war may have been over, but it had been followed by further insurrection.

That summer saw bitter fighting in Dublin between the Irish and the British; and in October Mussolini organised his Fascist March on Rome. Germany's finance minister, Walter Rathenau, a homosexual Jew, was murdered that year. The Kaiser had linked the first world war to a conspiracy of 'international Jewry' going back to the homosexual trials known as the 'Eulenberg affair' in 1907. The propaganda of the rising Nazi party exploited these events, being virulently anti-homosexual.

The company did a frenzied rush round European towns, a day here, a week there, but everyone's spirits were low and the future once more seemed bleak. Salaries were in arrears and even Diaghilev could hardly afford to eat. Members of the company had also cut down their meals to virtually nothing and some began to split from the company and look elsewhere for work.

A short season in Monte Carlo was booked for the spring of 1923, when yet another disaster hit the company. The scenery of the ballets had been sent from Paris to Nice where the freight charges had to be paid. As the company was in such low financial waters, there was a delay and the trucks were shunted into an open siding. Inevitably, there was a violent thunderstorm and when the bill was ultimately paid and the trucks were opened, the décor for one of the scenes was completely ruined and others badly damaged.

With problems like this, along with key dancers like Karsavina, Lopokova and Massine having left the company, and Bakst being ill, Diaghilev seemed to lose heart, wondering if ballet had anything further to offer.

However, he then managed to pull a substantial rabbit out of the hat. The Prince of Monaco had recently died and his successor, Louis II, had a daughter who was married to the Prince de Polignac who, in turn, was a nephew of Diaghilev's close friend, Princesse Edmond de Polignac. The young couple were cultivated, interested in the arts, and the Princesse agreed to help persuade them to let Diaghilev establish a permanent six-month winter base for his company in Monte Carlo.

It was the much-needed lifeline. When the long-term contract was signed the company suddenly experienced a blessed and most unusual feeling of permanence. After a roller-coaster ride, the last half-dozen years of the Ballets Russes were positively calm.

16

Paris in the Twenties

The *New Yorker* Paris correspondent called Paris in the 1920s 'the capital of hedonism'. It was the time of bobbed hair, short skirts, and the overthrow of morality. There was truth in the lighthearted refrain, 'Ashes to ashes, dust to dust/if the cocktail don't get you, then the cocaine must.' Shimmy-dressed women frequented bars and salons, took lovers – often other women – and avoided marriage.

Young people gaily danced *le fox* (the foxtrot), the one-step, the mambo and the Charleston at the *bals musettes* in the Luxembourg district, or visited the small, licentious *boites* on the Boulevard Montparnasse, while the champagne set thronged the new *clubs de nuit* opening in the Champs Elysees.

In June 1920 Stravinsky and his family, who had spent the war in Switzerland, left what Diaghilev scathingly called 'his alpine colleagues' and came to France. James Joyce and Ezra Pound also came to Paris that summer, heralding a new literary era.

Sylvia Beach, the proprietor of the bookshop Shakespeare & Company, recalled first meeting Pound. He looked, in his velvet jacket, uncombed hair and pointed beard, like an English aesthete. 'I found the acknowledged leader of the modern movement not bumptious,' she said.[1] The work Pound did for the small magazines, which sponsored new literary movements and characterised Paris and London in the twenties, was of immense help to aspiring writers.

Pound became the centre of literary activity along with Sylvia Beach, who was the major source of distribution of small magazines. The thin, stooping James Joyce, who moved into an apartment above Sylvia Beach's bookshop, relied heavily on her. He had no money and complained to Pound that he had to wear his son's boots which were two sizes too large.

In 1922 James Joyce's novel, *Ulysses* was published. Ernest Hemingway and his wife of four months, Hadley, had recently arrived in Paris and discovered Sylvia Beach's bookshop. Hemingway took an instant liking to Beach and helped her collect subscriptions for *Ulysses* in advance of publication. It provoked violent reactions, but Hemingway had unqualified praise for it.

Montparnasse had now replaced Montmartre – whose rents had risen sharply – as the bohemian outpost. The married Picasso was now a relatively rare sight in café society. He had exchanged his old stained corduroys for a dinner jacket – although under the dinner jacket he invariably wore a bullfighter's cummerbund – and with his wife Olga dressed by the designer Coco Chanel, he saw more of the current fashionable world than his old painter friends.

Two of the most famous faces in Paris in the Twenties, Sylvia Beach and James Joyce, stand in the doorway of her bookshop Shakespeare & Company

The couple had now moved into an apartment in rue La Boetie, the new street of modern art. It was a far cry from his old studio in the dilapidated building in Montmartre, which Max Jacob had christened *Bateau Lavoir* because it looked like one of the old laundry boats lining the Seine. Picasso's tea would freeze in the teapot overnight, to be reheated for breakfast the next day.

On 22 May 1922, a celebrated dinner party was given at the Hotel Majestic by the wealthy English couple, Violet and Sydney Schiff for five guests of honour: Diaghilev, Joyce, Proust, Picasso and Stravinsky. There were 40 guests in all and the intention was to celebrate the premiere of Stravinsky's ballet, *Le Renard*.

It was a strange evening. At the top table, Diaghilev looked his usual immaculate self, Proust wore a fur coat and Joyce did not possess a dinner jacket. The conversation was jagged. Proust politely asked Stravinsky if he liked Beethoven and Stravinsky told him abruptly that he hated him.

There are different versions of the conversation between Proust and Joyce. One had Proust ask Joyce if he liked truffles and on Joyce saying he did, Proust said how strange it was that two of the current greatest literary figures on first meeting should discuss whether they liked truffles.

Another version had Joyce and Proust discussing illness. Just as Diaghilev feared speaking to Benois when Benois' children had fever, so Joyce when he heard the concierge's grand-daughter had measles and whooping cough, insisted that his mail be soaked in disinfectant for two hours before opening it.

According to Ronald Hayman, Proust's biographer, Joyce complained at the dinner of 'headaches every day. My eyes are terrible.' Proust answered, 'My poor stomach. What am I going to do? It's killing me. In fact, I must leave at once.' 'I'm in the same situation,' Joyce replied, 'if I can find someone to take me by the arm. Goodbye.' 'Charme,' said Proust. 'Oh, my stomach.'[2] However, according to Schiff the supper-party was matchless, 'precisely because Diaghilev stage-managed the proceedings as if he was directing one of his own ballets.'[3] Proust died that November.

Picasso, one of the five chief guests, was there with his wife Olga, although she was not at the top table. Since the birth of their son Paolo in 1921 the marriage had gone rapidly down hill. Olga had put on weight and become more discontented with her life. Picasso, irritated by her insistence he conform to bourgeois conventions, reacted 'by hanging a sign on his studio door announcing, *Je ne suis pas un gentleman*'.[4]

To be in Paris then was a delight. The *Times* correspondent wrote, in the May of 1922, that 'The café terraces are crowded, the fountains of La Place de la Concorde are spurting their columns of scintillating water exuberantly into the air, and the taxi-men have become more than usually reckless and even more profane to one another when they just miss a collision by inches.'[5]

However, there was still nostalgia for the pre-war days. 'Exit the Fiacre' headed an article by the *Observer's* Paris correspondent that Spring, bewailing the disappearance of the horse-cabs with their red-waistcoated drivers in favour of the new six-wheeled motor buses roaring down the grand boulevards. The small Paris cabs 'built for a race of pygmies' came under criticism, as did the Metro where passengers were 'bundled like cabbages in a crate.'

There was further gloom in the following months at museums and galleries charging one franc entrance fee; the disappearance of musicians in restaurants due to a high entertainment tax; the cinema being threatened, like the tango, with perishing; and the rising divorce figures (84 divorces a day in the last six months of 1921). More cheerfully, bachelors looking for a wife were advised to wear a green ribbon and there was a one-day anti-income tax strike.

However, the Ballets Russes was hardly affected by these happenings. After a successful season in Paris in May and June, they had little booked and zig-zagged around Europe from Marseille to Geneva, from Ostend to San Sebastian.

Diaghilev remained in Paris, where the *Salon d'Automne* that year, 1922, said one newspaper correspondent, showed a marked decline in asserting the 'ism'. The Cubists were less Cubist, the Impressionists less Impressionistic. 'What', he ended airily, 'was either of them but a protest?'

The following year was memorable among the socialites in Paris for a huge dusk-till-dawn party on board a leased barge in the Seine. It was thrown by the wealthy American couple, Gerald and Sara Murphy, for the opening at last of Stravinsky's ballet *Les Noces* on 13th June 1923. The Murphys' families had made their money in high-class trade in America and the couple, reacting against this, decided to relocate and replant themselves in Paris.

The two were central figures in Paris's artistic scene. He was good-looking, she was beautiful, they both loved American folksongs and jazz and on seeing Picasso's work for the first time became passionate about such painting and arranged to study stage design with the Russian artist Natalia Goncharova.

Goncharova was the first woman set designer for the Ballets Russes and, impressed by their work, she recommended them to Diaghilev. He promptly asked them to repair backcloths. 'The Murphys had to spread the canvas curtains and muslin flats on the floor and work with soft brushes at the end of broom handles, then climb thirty-foot-high ladders to judge the effect.'[6] The result was then checked by artists like Picasso and Derain. The Murphys loved it and often went to performances of the ballet. They were the only Americans in Paris at that time who were closely involved with the Ballets Russes.

At the now legendary party they gave to celebrate *Les Noces,* some 40 artists, writers and painters were invited. Guests included Diaghilev and Chanel, Picasso and Jean Cocteau. Cocteau was chary about boarding for fear of seasickness, which started as soon as he saw the barge rocked by passing river traffic. Nevertheless he had dressed himself in full captain's uniform for the occasion and spent his time wandering around the rooms with a lantern in hand, announcing mournfully, 'We're sinking'.

Even Stravinsky threw off his serious side and astounded watchers by making a running leap through a vast laurel wreath, imitating a balletic rite of spring. Meanwhile Picasso amused himself by making sculptures from the children's miniature toys decorating the dinner tables.

Zelda and Scott Fitzgerald returned to Paris from America in the May of 1924. Zelda Fitzgerald had recently told a friend she 'simply must have some Chablis and curry and fraises de bois with peaches in champagne for dessert. Also I want to feel a sense of intrigue which is only in Paris.'[7] Fitzgerald hoped that Paris would help alleviate the tensions in their marriage. Equally important, no American writer was accepted as successful without the Parisian stamp of approval.

The over-riding advantage, however, which drew them and a host of other Americans to Paris was the cheapness with which Americans could live in Paris: the currency exchange was greatly in their favour and a meal with wine cost about three francs – some 16 cents. Diaghilev, ever short of funds, also appreciated the city's relative cheapness: at least he could rely on Americans and wealthy socialites to wine and dine him.

The Fitzgeralds' life in Paris before had been mainly parties and café-life. Both were shocked by the way Montparnasse had lost its old bohemian character under the influx of Americans in Paris. When they had first come to Paris in 1921 there had been 6,000 Americans living there; now, in 1924, there were more than 30,000. 'With each new shipment of Americans spewed up by the boom, the quality fell off ...' wrote Fitzgerald.[8]

The two sought out Gerald and Sara Murphy and that summer went off to Antibes on the Riviera and hired a villa near the Murphys. It was a carefree time. At beach parties, instead of sunbathing guests would don colourful, strange costumes.

It was the Murphys who made the beaches along the Riviera fashionable, a fashion reflected in the Ballet Russes' *Le Train Bleu*, the ballet premiered that year and featuring the in-crowd of the Riviera.

Fitzgerald, busy writing *The Great Gatsby*, left his wife strictly alone: she became bored and started an affair with a French naval pilot. It had a lasting effect on her marriage.

Through the Murphys, Zelda Fitzgerald met the top dancers and choreographers from the Ballets Russes. She had long dreamt of becoming a dancer, a second Pavlova, and Picasso's wife, the former ballet dancer Olga Khoklova, suggested she study Russian classical ballet under Madame Lubov Egorova – director of the ballet school for Diaghilev's Ballets Russes. Fitzgerald laughed at his wife's efforts but was relieved to find something innocuous to occupy her time, even though he begrudged paying the expensive fees.

At the end of December 1924, Bakst died. His work lived on as his extraordinary sumptuous and inventive designs for the Ballets Russes had had such an impact, evident in the internal décor of houses and the clothes people wore.

Scott Fitzgerald called 1925 'the summer of a thousand parties and no work.' In Paris, where he and his wife were then living, the sensation was Josephine Baker, the beautiful black dancer who was performing in *Le Revue Negre* naked from the waist up, but sporting a tutu of bananas.

Lynn Garafola makes the point that in his ballets Diaghilev did not care to undress women, apart from the odd flash of skin from under a tutu: 'At a time when short skirts routinely displayed the leg and tight-fitting bathing suits showed off the torso, when Paris chorus girls and specialty dancers performed their acts in G-strings, Diaghilev's women, for the most part, were as sexy as matrons.'[9]

Diaghilev intensely disliked jazz and its growing influence but Vernon Duke, the Broadway musical composer, claimed that he saw Diaghilev at *Le Revue Negre*, disguised in dark glasses. The 20 year old Duke was introduced to the 53 year old Diaghilev by Misia Sert. Diaghilev promptly told him that he didn't like men aged over 25. 'They lose their adolescent charm and sleep with any woman who gives them the nod. Oh, so you can still blush?'[10]

Everyone – even if not Diaghilev – was singing and dancing to the new American jazz music (though Stravinsky had composed his own *Ragtime* back in 1917). Jazz could be heard from *La Coupole* in Montparnasse, where the dance floor was in the basement, to the Cafes *Flores* and *Deux Magots* in Saint Germain.

Black nightspots were crowded. One of the most well-known was Bricktop's in the rue Pigalle near Montmartre – opened by Ada Smith du Conge, a black woman with dyed orange hair, promptly nicknamed Bricktop. Although protective of her clients, she failed to stop Zelda Fitzgerald giving away her pearl necklace to the black woman with whom she was dancing – a necklace costing $1,700 given to her by her husband with the money he received for a book advance. Fortunately, it was returned the next morning.

Montparnasse artists were now getting involved in film-making. The French painter Fernand Leger had been working on a 15-minute experimental art-film which was a blend of sound and image. It included fragmented images of the face of Kiki (an artists' model and singer) 'spliced together with such diverse images as a mechanical marionette of Charlie Chaplin, pulsating mechanic discs, household appliances, wine bottles, geometric shapes, words, and single letters.'[11]

The Ballets Russes was not filmed as Diaghilev thought motion pictures were merely a cheap form of entertainment and was adamantly against them: 'I have refused because I believe the reality of the ballets to be superior to their reproduction,' he said.[12] The only ballet he thought could be success-fully filmed (though it was not) was *The Sleeping Princess* as he believed it 'the greatest masterpiece of a period which came to an end with the passing of the old regime in Russia'.[13]

It was in November 1925 that the first Surrealist exhibition opened in Paris at the Galerie Pierre. Works shown included those by Paul Klee, Chirico, Max Ernst, Joan Miro. Picasso was regarded as their prophet and some of his paintings were borrowed for the exhibition.

The puritanical Surrealists disliked fashionable society, even extending this to the 'decadent' ballet. When Diaghilev asked Max Ernst and Miro to design the décor and scenery for *Romeo and Juliet*, a number of surrealists protested.

Picasso directed his own irritation towards Matisse, as he had discovered Matisse was doing the curtain sets and costumes for Stravinsky's *Chant du Rossignol*. 'Matisse!' he said. 'What is a Matisse? A balcony with a big red flowerpot falling all over it.'[14]

Picasso's last costume and scenery design for a ballet (a charity performance in 1924 for the war wounded and Russian refugees) showed a more flowing line. The composer in this case was Erik Satie, who died that same year.

Satie was the father figure of the group of musicians known as Le Six: Georges Auric, Francis Poulenc, Germaine Tailleferre, Arthur Honegger, Darius Milhaud and Louis Durey. Satie composed a number of ballets for Diaghilev and was known as a woman-hater. However, he frequently went to the bookshop run by the French writer and publisher, Adrienne Monnier, where he was part of a close group of composers which included Aaron Copland. Adrienne Monnier had a long relationship with Sylvia Beach, the publisher-owner of the bookshop, Shakespeare & Company.

The author of *Sylvia Beach and the Lost Generation* points out how many independent and talented women there were then living in Paris – women involved in journalism or art or publishing. Three of them were Janet Flanner, the *New Yorker* Paris correspondent, Solita Solano (actress, drama critic and short story writer) and Djuna Barnes, author of *A Book*.

More and more writers were flooding into Paris like e.e. cummings and Ford Madox Ford. Ford edited the *transatlantic review* and such literary magazines were a boon to writers, who came to Paris looking for publication.

The poet Hart Crane – who once, fighting drunk in a café, knocked out four waiters and a policeman – told a friend that Paris was a test for an American. He meant that *working* in Paris was a test. The cafes and the bars of Montparnasse and Montmartre seduced many away from their work – including artists and composers for the Ballets Russes.

Who, after all, could resist the distractions and temptations of Paris in the 1920s?

17

Enter Serge Lifar

To open the Monte Carlo season in April 1923, Diaghilev decided to repeat *Le Mariage d'Aurore*. He needed a number of dancers and gave his unwilling permission for Grigoriev to go to London to recruit some, like Sokolova, whom Massine had poached, and who were now out of work. Their defection still rankled with Diaghilev.

Monaco's Princess unexpectedly attended the rehearsals of the ballet and her obvious interest ensured its success. Diaghilev was already planning the spring season in Paris and decided to have just one new ballet, Stravinsky's *Les Noces*. Bronislava Nijinska was the choreographer and the décor was by Larionov and Goncharova. The backcloths they designed showed the interior of a Russian peasant cottage.

The atmosphere behind the scenes was unhappy: the dancers found Stravinsky's music difficult, tempers were fuelled by a rise in the cost of living, and finally there was a demand for a salary rise under threat of resignations. Diaghilev promptly called the company together and told them that they demanded the impossible:

'I take good care of you, you know that, and I do the utmost I can. I know your wages are not sufficient, and should like to be able to increase them, because I value your work; but there are limits that can't be overstepped, if one wishes to preserve our great common cause, which you should love and cherish as much as I do. Calm yourselves, ladies and gentlemen ...'[1] However, he added that if anyone felt they must leave, so be it. As ever, Diaghilev's persuasian worked and rehearsals promptly recommenced.

Les Noces was first performed at the house of Diaghilev's patron, the musician and painter Princesse Edmond de Polignac. It formally opened on 13 June 1923 at the Theatre de la Gaite-Lyrique in Paris and was highly successful, although the dancers were still uneasy with Stravinsky's music. Diaghilev was so pleased with Nijinska's choreography that she was in future known as 'La Nijinska'.

Serge Lifar was to succeed Massine as Diaghilev's lover and protégé

Diaghilev was equally delighted when his company was asked to give a performance at Versailles in front of a distinguished audience which included the French President Poincare, all the Cabinet and most of the Diplomatic Corps.

One of the young dancers in the corps de ballet of *Les Noces* was Serge

Lifar. He had come over from Russia after Nijinska, at Diaghilev's request, had telegraphed the Kiev Opera, where she had taught, to ask for their five best pupils to join the Ballets Russes. The eighteen-year-old Lifar was one of these students – a highly-strung, attractive young dancer, who was ambitious and desperate to succeed in ballet.

He recalled his first meeting, early in 1923, with Diaghilev who wore his usual fur coat and a soft hat and swung a cane. Lifar described his face as fleshy, with his brown eyes giving him a look of a St Bernard dog. Diaghilev asked Lifar about Russia and sat motionless while listening.

Lifar was delighted to have the chance of dancing with the Ballets Russes, even if some of the customs – like the young male dancers in the corps de ballet being expected to run errands for the leading dancers – originated from the days of serfdom. The rehearsals for *Les Noces* were supervised by Stravinsky, and Lifar recalled him gradually livening up, taking off his jacket, sitting at the piano and singing in a rather cracked voice. Diaghilev occasionally appeared at these rehearsals which made everyone nervous, as he was quite likely to order the same step to be repeated some 20 times.

The room Lifar lived in was too small for practising so he would work outside on the pavement, peered at by the girls behind the shutters in the overlooking brothels who would shout out encouragement.

Leaving the heat of Paris in the August of 1923, the company thankfully returned to cooler Switzerland and Belgium, where they revived various ballets. One was *Scheherazade* and Lifar, who played the part of the dying slave, on one occasion did an over-the-top roll down the steps. Diaghilev told him, 'What you've just done, young man, is entirely unartistic, very immature, very callow. I'm sorry you used your talents to wreck the ensemble instead of supporting it by exercising rigorous self-discipline.'[2]

Diaghilev always laid particular significance on the action of the whole ensemble, believing artistes with secondary roles must play their part to perfection, but remain in the background and not draw attention away from those with leading roles.

Cyril Beaumont, on meeting Lifar, said, 'There was something very charming about his infectious high spirits, his evident delight in being alive, his almost boyish eagerness to earn the affection of the public.'

Describing him, Beaumont said, lyrically: 'His dark eyes, thick lips, and golden-brown skin gave him an exotic, almost oriental appearance.'[3] In his view, Lifar's head and torso, with its broad shoulders, rippling muscles and and narrow hips, reminded him of both a faun of classical mythology and a fabled centaur. Carried away, he compared his lithe, sinuous movements to those of a wild animal. Cyril Connolly, however, commenting on Lifar called him "vain, pompous, humourless, spoilt, and exhibitionistic".[4]

John Drummond, author of *Speaking of Diaghilev*, who met Lifar, was of much the same mind, admitting he was a beautiful young man but not, in his opinion, a great dancer. 'He was a sort of monster sacre with a patchy record at the Opera and a dubious role during the Occupation ... there was something so vain, so mindlessly self-vaunting about him ... he was a silly person.'[5]

The fifty-one-year-old Diaghilev, however, admired Lifar's hard work and ambition, and was smitten. He enhanced his 'beauty' by paying for him to get his teeth and nose straightened. Lifar could attract both sexes and was later to marry and have children. He said of himself, 'I have always been a poor lover, like one who is a stranger to the sensual pleasures of the couch.'[6]

Banned from London because the company was still in debt to the Stoll Theatre, Diaghilev concentrated instead on the next season at Monte Carlo. He decided to revive a number of old ballets but also commissioned two young French composers, Francis Poulenc and Georges Auric from the group known as Le Six, to write two new ones – Poulenc's was called *Les Biches* and Auric's *Les Facheux*, after a comedy by Moliere.

Poulenc was delighted with the commission, and wrote in later years, 'My collaboration with the Ballets Russes was an unhoped-for bit of luck, a great happiness, the warmest of the memories of my youth ... Dear Diaghilev, irreplaceable Diaghilev, you were the wonderment of my twenties, not only because you gave me your confidence and your esteem, but because I owe you my most violent aesthetic shocks.'[7]. Poulenc, according to Count Harry Kessler, was a 'big, broad-shouldered farmer's son, rather taciturn and difficult of approach, but likeable.'[8]

Critics and ballet-lovers all came to Monte Carlo to see the new mixed ballet and opera season. Diaghilev, whose aim was to make the city an advanced art centre, decided on a mixture of old and new ballets and operas. Nijinska had been working on Poulenc's *Les Biches* since September, to Poulenc's pleasure. He had written to Diaghilev that month to say, 'What joy that you like the whole of *Les Biches!* Now send me *La Colombe* [The Dove] quickly so that I can get shot of this bird.'[9]

Despite his apparent excitement, Poulenc wrote more anxiously to the French composer, Charles Koechlin to say, 'A most perilous piece of work has come my way – commissioned by Diaghilev. I have had to do the recitation, often too long and eight in number, for a comic opera by Gounod, *La Colombe*, which will be performed this winter in Monte Carlo.'[10]

As a result of all this commissioning, at the end of 1923 Diaghilev was working with uncontained energy, overseeing no fewer than seven ballet productions which were all at different stages. New names alongside the composers Auric and Poulenc included the Spanish painter Juan Gris who was designing three productions and the French artist Marie Laurencin who was responsible for the white and blue décor for Poulenc's *Les Biches*.

This latter ballet was an example of the 'new modernism' inaugurated by Nijinska. Frederick Ashton who saw it later in London found it a revelation. 'I thought it was the most wonderful thing I'd ever seen. The chic, the elegance, the complete evocation of what life was like at that time was staggering to me. And then later when I saw *Les Noces* I realised what a great choreographic genius Nijinska was.'[11]

In London Ashton was at the centre of society. It was Olivia Wyndham, the virtual creator of the 'Bright Young Things' of the 1920s, who introduced Ashton to the group which Cecil Beaton christened 'the illuminati'. Diaghilev asked Ashton to audition for the Ballets Russes and Ashton recalled that he 'felt so inadequate that I couldn't do it. I remember walking round and round the Lyceum Theatre and I couldn't go in because I was in a most terrible state.'[12]

Ashton was under the tutelage of Marie Rambert and Diaghilev visited her studio to see the dancer Diana Gould perform. Ashton remembered him entering the studio, dressed in black and looking imposing and aristocratic. Ashton was also asked to dance, but Diaghilev dismissed him to Rambert as 'plain'. He asked Ashton his plans and was told that Nijinska had accepted him as a dancer in a troupe she was assembling. Diaghilev merely smiled sardonically and said 'Hmm.'

Diaghilev opened his winter season in Monte Carlo in November 1923, but it was not until January 1924 that he launched his seven new productions, starting with the French opera *La Colombe* on New Year's Day.

It was a busy and productive time, enjoyed by everyone. Poulenc and Auric were often to be seen with the rest of the company at the night club *Boeuf sur le Toit* in Montparnasse which opened that month and was the celebrated new meeting place of the mainstays of literary and bohemian life.

Diaghilev was particular about where his artists were seen. 'They were never really off duty,' said one commentator, 'and their private lives were very much his concern' (aesthetically rather than morally). Diaghilev called his artists 'his jewels' and considered them spoilt if not seen in their proper setting.[13]

The last new production of the season, on 19 January 1924, was Auric's ballet, *Les Facheux*. Its décor was by the painter Georges Braque, and although he often worked in browns and blacks, this particular décor was in more spring-like yellows and greens. Braque found working for Diaghilev had its disadvantages, however. As his biographer points out, 'in the Ballets Russes artistic differences were resolved by Diaghilev, in favour of Diaghilev.'[14]

Braque also fell out with the cast. While working on the décor and curtain for *Les Facheux*, he wanted a dancer to act as a naked nymph, dancing a prologue before his verdant curtain. When no dancer would accept the role, he merely painted one onto the curtain.

During rehearsals in Monte Carlo, Braque felt awkward in bowler hat and bow-tie strolling round the casino's exotic gardens with Diaghilev and Kochno. When showing Diaghilev his sketches for a new production of *Les Sylphides*, he asked particularly that they were not made into sets until the entire décor was finished. Diaghilev took no notice and went ahead. Braque promptly asked the police to seize the sets. Diaghilev told him that not only was he difficult to deal with, but that he had no business sense. Braque admitted, sadly, that this was true and did no further designs for 20 years.

Les Facheux caused a great deal of trouble as Diaghilev, who came to watch rehearsals, frequently disagreed with what he saw and had angry arguments with Nijinska, which went on interminably until the rehearsals had to be cancelled.

Sokolova, who had taken a wealthy French woman on as a pupil, complained to her one day of a bad headache. The woman gave her a powder to take and Sokolova, in rehearsal, suddenly felt exhilarated and threw herself into the part. Diaghilev, watching her, called her over to ask why she was so excited. 'Who gave it to you?' he asked. Only then did Sokolova realise the powder was cocaine. She stopped teaching the French woman at once.[15]

Along with the new productions was a revival of *Daphnis and Chloe*. In this a new dancer took the part of Daphnis, with Sokolova as Chloe. The graceful and good-looking new dancer's name was Patrick Healey-Kay, who had first danced under the name Patrikeeff. Trained at Astafieva's Russian School, Astafieva had convinced Diaghilev that Patrikeeff was exceptionally talented. He was promptly taken on by Diaghilev as a potential soloist without having to work his way up from the corps de ballet. His name was changed again, to Anton Dolin.

His dancing was not thought that good at the start, but he improved immensely during the first two months he was with the company. Pleased with his progress, Diaghilev decided to allow him to dance Daphnis and he did so most successfully.

The two men – Diaghilev was 52 and Dolin was 20 – briefly became lovers. Commenting on their sexual relationship In later years, Dolin told John Drummond that Diaghilev's sexual demands 'were straightforward, rather adolescent, and did not involve any form of penetrative intercourse.'[16]

Dolin was a cheerful athletic figure, constantly turning cartwheels in the wings. He amused Jean Cocteau who suggested to Diaghilev that he write a scenario around Dolin's acrobatic antics. It would be called *Le Train Bleu*, the name of the Paris-Riviera express which wafted wealthy travellers down to the Mediterranean, and celebrated the sports they played on the beaches on arrival, like tennis, golf and swimming. Dolin's acrobatics on the beach, Cocteau planned, would then impress a group of bathing beauties of both sexes.

Diaghilev liked the idea, seeing it as a 'choreographed operetta'. Dolin was cast as the Don Juan on the beach, perfect for the part 'with his dead centre part, black hair glued to his scalp, velvet eyes, and acrobat's jersey.'[17]

It was the first ballet to celebrate the cult of the body beautiful, a cult mainly due to the American couple Sara and Gerald Murphy bringing the French Riviera into fashion in the early 1920s. Until then visitors had avoided the heat of the Cote d'Azur in the summer months and hotels closed down.

The Murphys managed to get one hotel there to remain open and the guests who came down included Picasso and his wife Olga, who then bought a villa down there. Others followed suit, the Hemingways making a special visit down there to tell the Murphys that their marriage had come to an end. Antibes, thanks to the Murphys, had changed from a quiet village into a highly fashionable resort. *Le Train Bleu* portrayed the flirtations of the smart set on an equally smart beach on the Riviera.

Lynn Garafola makes the point that whereas before the first world war Diaghilev 'had feminised the male body' he now concentrated on 'making the female body masculine.' For example, the previous year in his revival of *L'Apres-Midi d'un Faune* he had cast Nijinska – with strapped-down breasts and a body stocking – in the role made famous by her brother.

Whatever the directional change, however, Garafola considers that 'by almost any yardstick, women in the Ballets Russes counted for less than men.' In the twenties, she points out, women were dominating other forms of concert dance which underlines 'the anti-female bias implicit in Diaghilev's homosexual radicalism.' From 1923, when Anton Dolin joined the company, through to the years of Serge Lifar, Diaghilev's heroes 'wore their sexual plumage like peacocks' and 'the body was not only bared but its erogenous zones were explicitly sexualised.'[18]

Le Train Bleu is a good example of the way in which Diaghilev thought and worked; of the reactions of those working for him; and the invariable arguments and backbiting behind the scenes.

Diaghilev constantly took risks. In this instance, he wanted the music to imitate that of the ebullient street musicians, to invoke what Cocteau called the 'powerful charm of the pavement'.

Diaghilev with Darius Milhaud who composed the music for Le Train Bleu, *premiered in 1924*

With this in mind it is typical of him that he at once commissioned the unlikely composer Darius Milhaud to write the score – unlikely because Milhaud was known for his cantatas from biblical themes. Milhaud himself said 'In those days the fashion was for a hedonistic and charming kind of music far removed from what I was composing ... which didn't at all suit Diaghilev's taste, as I knew ... it was a gamble and I took it.'[19]

Diaghilev then asked Nijinska to do the choreography, which was also a gamble as the Riviera scenes, with their pleasure-loving, over-indulged, sybaritic occupants were far removed from her experience. Cocteau wanted Nijinska to draw her inspiration from the personalities and events of the worldly milieu of the day – 'a milieu that Nijinska, who led a quiet, secluded life, didn't know and, furthermore, detested.'[20]

Her attitudes were very different from those of Cocteau and the two constantly clashed. Although Diaghilev acted as mediator between them – Nijinska did not speak French – his secretary Boris Kochno found the atmosphere at rehearsals highly charged. There was a constant struggle for power, with Cocteau publically insisting the choreography must be altered and initiating ideas which Nijinska absolutely refused to carry out.

Diaghilev had commissioned the French sculptor Henri Laurens, a friend of Braque and Modigliani, to create the decor, despite the fact that Laurens had no experience in designing a stage set. He produced a décor of angular constructions of cliffs, parasols and bathing tents – a décor which Grigoriev privately thought the worst in all the company's productions. Chanel was asked to design the costumes, which paralleled the bathing dresses worn by the Riviera set: pullovers in a loose-fitting jersey and, below them, trunks reaching down to mid-thigh.

The backstage difficulties continued as the production started to run late. Picasso had agreed to do a series of sketches to illustrate the programme but when asked for them claimed they were lost. Diaghilev also wanted his painting 'The Giants' of two women running in white tunics with torn shoulder drapes to be reproduced for the drop curtain, but Picasso had no interest in this. Diaghilev got a craftsman to do the reproduction, startling Picasso with its success.

The dress rehearsal – held at the Theatre des Champs Elysees only a few hours before the first performance was scheduled – was a disaster. The different views of Cocteau and Nijinska had caused confusion among the dancers and Chanel's costumes were not designed for dancing. Depending on the movement, they sometimes appeared too long, sometimes too short. Diaghilev was watching the dress rehearsal and though he was used to rescuing Titanic-like disasters, quietly asked what other ballet could be substituted for *Le Train Bleu*.

No one left the theatre. Somehow, as ever, the ballet was pulled around. The costumes were altered, the programmes with Picasso's cover and studies of dancers were finally ready. *Le Train Bleu* opened on time, on 20 June 1924. The programme note to this one-act *operette dansee* read, 'You must now accept this poetry of the streets ... Don't be afraid of banality, give all your attention to the birth of this music, the music of tomorrow ...'

The audience, with its usual mixture of artists and aristocrats, wildly applauded Dolin's extraordinary acrobatic leaps (his knees and feet often bled as a result of these) and the press next day were full of praise.

Chanel had invented a new pearl made of china and coated with wax, which Sokolova wore on stage. Later, at a party given to celebrate the ballet,

Chanel wore ropes and ropes of these pearls over a skin-tight, champagne-coloured lace gown with a fish-train and her back bare to below the waist. The fashion for sportswear spread as a result of the ballet. The Ballets Russes was again the talk of the town.

The choreographer Frederick Ashton was exhilarated by the ballet, considering it a thrilling expression of the new age. He had gone to the ballet 'expecting to see someone wearing a dress with a long blue train' but instead had 'encountered 1920s flappers, athletes, tarts and gigolos disporting themselves on a Riviera beach.'[21]

Benois, however, was critical of Diaghilev's current ideas, commenting sourly on some of his plans. He disliked the 'new spirit' of the current work and the inner emptiness of some of Diaghilev's advisers like Jean Cocteau who, said Benois,

Diaghilev backstage with Jean Cocteau, who wrote the scenario for Le Train Bleu

up till 1914 had been considered 'as a sort of enfant terrible.' He also had little time for Boris Kochno, Diaghilev's secretary and frequent source of inspiration, though there could have been more than a hint of jealousy here.

Benois also considered ballets like *Le Train Bleu* to be 'ultra-modern and ultra-snobbish' and senselessly ugly. Grigoriev too had his doubts about this ballet, considering its décor poor and its score insufficiently frivolous for the subject.

Diaghilev was pleased with Dolin's dancing but Sokolova and her husband noticed that the fifty-two-year-old Diaghilev was now no longer exclusively interested in Dolin. He had been seen walking on the boulevard with the new young dancer, Serge Lifar.

Looking at Diaghilev at the time, 'flanked by his youthful companion' and with his 'fur-lined coat with its handsome beaver collar making his big, tall body and his tremendous head look even more majestic, more lordly,' one friend recalled 'his tired, haughty look, his dark eyes and the even darker bags under them.' He noticed the 'sallow, wasted colour of his heavy-set but well-kept face with the neatly trimmed moustache, the protruding lower jaw, and the upturned upper lip, revealing, when he smiled, a row of dubiously new teeth.' His voice, too, was particularly noticeable, with its 'high-pitched, nasal and capricious tone.'[22]

Diaghilev also had a habit of dropping unaccented syllables of long Russian words as if he had swallowed them up. There was invariably an aura of violets around him as he used to chew violet-scented bon-bons.

The hothouse intrigues at the Ballets Russes were always near to the surface. The dancer Serge Lifar claims in his memoirs that Diaghilev assured him that he wished to make him his leading dancer, but that this had to be kept secret. The nineteen-year-old Lifar doubted this claim by Diaghilev and in the June of 1924, while they were having tea, told him that he intended to leave the Ballets Russes and enter a monastery.

According to Lifar's highly-coloured account, Diaghilev 'let his head slump down on the table and he broke into tears ... Why bury yourself alive? Why say goodbye to life, to your abilities?' Scarlet-faced, Diaghilev then grabbed the table and threw it over, causing a terrible crash of broken crockery.

He paid no attention to the people around them, but furiously shouted at Lifar, 'What have you got the nerve to tell me? I get you out of Russia, I teach you how to dance, and now that I am counting on you, you come and calmly tell me that you are going away... You are nineteen years of age, you are just beginning to live. I have told you that you have it in you to become *premier danseur*, but you are mightily mistaken if you think you are already one ... I don't like ungrateful people ... you can go to hell!'[23]

As the Russian singer Chaliapin pointed out, 'The Russian temperament does not appear to know half measures. It is by disposition inclined to extremes of mood and sensitivity. Such is our strange Russian nature that its good and its bad sides know no moderation.'[24]

Diaghilev did indeed have various sides to him: he could be aloof, cold and heartless, gazing with apparent indifference through his monocle; or he could be kind and thoughtful. He could also become incandescent with rage, his Russian temperament coming dramatically to the fore.

Once, discovering how upset Sokolova's husband was when his gold confirmation cross, given to him by his mother, broke and slipped through the stage floorboard, Diaghilev bought him a new beautifully crafted gold cross. It was gestures like this that won him the loyalty and affection of his dancers.

He was equally easily roused to jealousy, frequently behaving in a tyrannical, monopolising way over his current favourites. Lifar claimed that Diaghilev was possessive 'about my childhood's dreams, girl dancers, my partners, people I met casually.' A claimed example was that while rehearsing with a *danseuse* of the company, Diaghilev told Grigoriev, 'Throw that girl out of the troupe, she's making eyes at Lifar.'[25]

Lifar also said that Diaghilev told him that he was the only person who kept him attached to the Ballet. Without Lifar he would – or so Lifar asserted – have disbanded the troupe. Telling Lifar he wanted him to be another Nijinsky, Lifar agreed to stay: if he had ever planned to go.

That July Diaghilev sent Lifar to the famous dancing master, Cecchetti, in Turin, who had taught both Pavlova and Nijinsky, although this irritated Nijinska whose opinion of Lifar was not particularly high. Lifar was also being groomed by Diaghilev: the older man outfitted him, including a straw hat – invariably worn by Diaghilev's lovers. When he wore it the whole company laughed at him ('Look, here comes our own little Maurice Chevalier').

Diaghilev gave him books and, with Mussolini's help, obtained a visa for him. Diaghilev had become friendly with Mussolini after the Italian leader, in his journalist days, had written approvingly of Diaghilev.

Diaghilev and Lifar met again briefly in Milan, where they went to churches and galleries, saw Leonardo da Vinci's *Last Supper* and visited La Scala. Lifar recalled that Diaghilev was wearing his summer outfit, which was narrow white trousers with white shoes and a straw hat that, in the heat, he would lift to sponge his forehead.

He wore a camellia in the buttonhole of his black jacket and his eyeglass dangled against his waistcoat. 'His shirt-collar was stiffly starched (never even in the hottest weather would he consent to wear a soft collar). He leaned on his walking-stick and constantly moved his head about as though he was trying to escape from the collar.'[26]

During the summer of 1924 Diaghilev started to educate Lifar artistically, telling him he would like to take him to Florence where Massine's 'artistic activity' had begun. He sent him pamphlets with reproductions of paintings by famous artists, telling him to look at these carefully to see the differences between the painters. Sacheverell Sitwell recalled being in Florence when Diaghilev praised Lifar for reading *Baedeker* but Sitwell found, inspecting it, that Lifar had slipped photographs of himself between the pages.[27]

In Venice Diaghilev delighted in showing Lifar the treasures of his 'native city'. He was thoroughly at home there, knowing everyone and liking to sit at the cafes in the Piazza San Marco. The two men then went to Padua, both deeply attracted by its Giotto frescoes. It was the city of St Anthony and Diaghilev always had a trinket of the saint in his waistcoat pocket to protect him against pestinential illness.

Because Diaghilev was so passionate about art, architecture and music himself he loved to pass on his knowledge. He would take his protégés and

Serge Lifar with Enrico Cecchetti in Venice. Cecchetti was the pre-eminent professor of ballet

friends to museums and art galleries around Europe so that they could both share his enthusiasm and get ideas.

At the end of the 1924 summer season in Paris, the company toured Germany. It was here that Bronislava Nijinska married. There was little chance of visiting England because of the stand-off with Sir Oswald Stoll about the company's sequestered property, but while in Germany a breakthrough occurred.

Diaghilev had asked his London agent to re-approach Sir Oswald about the sequestration and he now said that if the Ballets Russes agreed to perform for 24 weeks over two seasons at the Coliseum, starting in November, he would release the property. Diaghilev hesitated at first, reluctant to commit the company for such a long season at a rather unsatisfactory theatre. However, he realised that if he did not agree the company would never appear again in London.

The Ballets Russes therefore returned to London that winter, after a gap of three years. Ballet-lovers were delighted. The season opened on 22 November and the ballet premiered that evening was *Le Train Bleu*. It proved highly popular, even more so than in Paris. Because the stage floor was made of teak, stagehands set up a springboard from which Anton Dolin could leap on stage and these soaring leaps of his drew ecstatic applause.

Sokolova remembered New Year's Eve, 1924, when the company was allowed to go to a party. There was usually strict discipline over social events. Diaghilev accepted or rejected party invitations on behalf of the whole company and then decided who would attend.

Diaghilev had taken on an Irish girl called Edris Stannus (her stage name was to be Ninette de Valois) the previous year and during the Coliseum season he employed a number of dancers from both Britain and Russia. They included Vera Savina, a former member of the company and Massine's first wife; and a thin young English girl of 14 years, called Alice Marks, whose name was changed to Alicia Markova. Markova was to work under the tuition of ballet mistress Liubov Tchernicheva, Grigoriev's wife, who according to Diaghilev made Markova 'take wing and fly.'

At the end of the London season, Nijinska decided to leave, furious at discovering Diaghilev had been secretly grooming Serge Lifar, once her own pupil, to act as choreographer. Diaghilev, always looking for new directions, was willing to discard the old in his constant search for the young and the new. 'No one is indispensable,' he said.

Looking back on 1924, Grigoriev thought the company's season in Paris had provoked growing criticism of Diaghilev for abandoning the classic tradition, eliminating plots, making ballets mere suites of dances, pursuing the immediately fashionable and making the element of surprise all-important. Diaghilev dismissed such criticism, continuing with total confidence to look for new forms of expression.

18

New Passions for Old

Diaghilev's inner certainties prevented criticism from wounding him too badly. This was just as well: the year 1925 had its downs as well as ups.

Eugene Goossens, who was having a highly successful career in America, recalled joining the company for its two week season in Barcelona in May that year 'and processing down the Calle de los Ramblas with Diaghilev and his inseparable companions Boris Kochno, his secretary-librettist, and Serge Lifar, his favourite young dancer. They would dine at the Master's favourite restaurant and then watch the best flamenco dancing in Spain at Villa Rosa.'[1]

Lifar was very young, very inexperienced. A more experienced dancer from Russia in whom Diaghilev was currently interested was Georges Balanchivadze, or Balanchine as he became known.

Balanchine had been at the Maryinsky Theatre in St Petersburg where his dancing was acclaimed, particularly his hoop dance as the Jester in the ballet *The Nutcracker.* The ballerina Danilova said he could twist and whirl around the stage like a firecracker. When the company started its season in Monte Carlo early in 1925, Diaghilev was in difficulties without Nijinska as choreographer. He considered Dolin, but decided his temperament was too British, and thought Lifar as yet too inexperienced.

He decided to ask the twenty-one-year-old George Balanchine, who had already composed some dances, to act as a replacement and choreograph some of the dances for the operas the company was staging. Diaghilev may have missed Nijinska but he was intent on having a choreographer who

George Balanchine became a brilliant choreographer with the company. Photographed by Boris Kochno in Venice in 1926

would try out new developments. Balanchine justified Diaghilev's faith in him by showing a real talent for composition.

The season was going well until the dancers, conscious of the rise in the cost of living, asked for more money. Diaghilev said he would do what he could, but the dancers said that without a definite guarantee, they would not dance that night.

An angry Diaghilev went to see them and that night's performance finally took place some half hour after planned. He dismissed two lead dancers and the rest were only paid more when Diaghilev could afford it.

Picasso and his family joined the company there, at Diaghilev's request, but Picasso turned down Diaghilev's blandishments to get him to collaborate on another ballet, as he found it took too much of his time.

The company had a tight schedule that year, leaving for Barcelona after

Monte Carlo and then on to a summer season at the Coliseum in London, broken for a week by a short appearance in Paris.

Dolin left the Ballets Russes after the company's last performance in Paris. He did so quietly, no tears, no remonstrations. His going was a decided loss to the Ballets Russes. Grigoriev asked Diaghilev why Dolin was leaving, but he just shrugged.

Diaghilev had no hesitation in ruthlessly brushing away previously cherished collaborators if they no longer fitted into his pattern. His sacerdotal flame was devotion to art.

The fifty-three-year-old impresario's interest at the time was turning towards Serge Lifar. The Paris papers referred to the next season as 'Lifar's season' and Diaghilev inscribed Lifar's programme with the words, 'For the first among the youngest, to the youngest among the first.'

Diaghilev, who regarded Paris as his second home, suddenly turned against the city and its inhabitants. To Griegoriev's surprise, 'He was continually cursing the Paris public; and there was even a moment when, by way of punishment, he threatened not to indulge them with our presence at all!'[2] He finally 'allowed' them to have a season, but only long enough to remind 'those rotten Parisians' that the Ballets Russes still existed. He refused to explain his attitude, but a year or so later suddenly took against Monte Carlo in exactly the same way.

Life during the London seasons was cheerful enough. Massine recalled dining with the artist Sir William Nicholson, particularly known for the striking posters he and his brother-in-law James Pryde produced under the name of the Beggarstaff Brothers. Nicholson had hung a large collection of hats in his dining room and Massine recalled that between courses guests were trying on Roman helmets, bishops' mitres and jockey caps.

During the London season that summer, there was a new system of giving single ballets each day and allowing people to buy cheap 'roving tickets' allowing them to stand and watch. Lady Ottoline Morrell had one such ticket but noticed an empty seat and promptly sat in it. Equally promptly ejected, she later told Diaghilev this. He said magisterially to an attendant 'This lady may sit down whenever she pleases.' That summer George Gershwin approached Diaghilev about his *Rhapsody in Blue* music, wanting him to stage a ballet using this. Lifar did so, under the title *Sunlight*, but not until 1945.

This was just one of the innumerable requests Diaghilev received. Many were from the public, anxious to work for his company. 'I am strong and of refined appearance, strictly sober, single, and of superior education' said one letter. 'I am prepared to work in any capacity' said another, asking for a generous and helpful hand 'to my urgent need of work.'[3]

In 1925 a pioneering picture of Anna Pavlova dancing in *The Fairy Doll* at Covent Garden appeared in *The Times*. It was the first successful attempt, using special fast plates, to photograph a stage performance with available light rather than flashlight. The photographer was Ulric Van den Bogaerde, the father of the actor Dirk Bogarde.

The company went to Berlin in the December of 1925 for a month and Lifar bought Diaghilev a small Christmas tree. Diaghilev, touched, told him that he had not seen one since childhood. 'He talked about his parents, of his childhood spent at Perm, of his years at high school. He could not think of Russia without shedding tears.'[4]

More important, however, was that the Kunst Theatre where the company was dancing remained only a quarter full. As their programme had been almost entirely by French musicians and painters, the problem could have been Germany's continued hostility to France.

Diaghilev lost a great deal of money over this production and as he was already in financial difficulties through settling the debt with Sir Oswald Stoll, this latest blow rendered him virtually penniless. He became deeply depressed, considering it unlikely he could fund any new ballets for the Monte Carlo season in 1926 as he could hardly afford even to get his company there.

He decided that one way to raise money was to sell the drop curtain designed by Picasso for *The Three Cornered Hat* along with the figure-paintings the artist also did on the décor for the ballet *Cuadro Flamenco*. Diaghilev would also have sold the drop curtain Picasso designed for the ballet *Parade*, but he was forced to give up that idea because no one wanted to buy such a vast curtain. Grigoriev was sad to have to part with Picasso's work but Diaghilev was willing to sacrifice sentiment for practicality. However his depression continued at Monte Carlo, exacerbated by his suffering from boils.

Although Diaghilev constantly over-spent on his ballet productions, he was incredibly careful over his own bills. He would spend a considerable time monitoring the meters of cab drivers and would carefully check restaurant bills in case he had been overcharged by a fraction.

In 1926 Diaghilev commissioned Constant Lambert to write the score for a new ballet, *Romeo et Juliette*. Lambert, later the lover of the ballerina Margot Fonteyn, was the first Englishman to compose a ballet for Diaghilev and he came over to Monte Carlo for the rehearsals. However, a row soon took place, with Lambert defying Diaghilev in order to support the choreographer, Nijinska. Lambert dared to threaten Diaghilev that if he didn't get his way, he would leave and take his score with him.

The next day Lambert was astonished to see his score being taken from the music library to the rehearsal rooms under heavy guard by two casino gendarmes, both dressed in picturesque musical-comedy uniforms. The autocratic Diaghilev was not used to threats, or to independence, and regarded Lambert with suspicion, wondering if he could be a revolutionary. He would have been amazed if he'd known that Lambert thought the whole affair too funny to pursue.

What did upset Lambert, however, was that Diaghilev refused his plea that the painter Christopher Wood be entrusted with the settings and costumes. The ballet was called 'a rehearsal, without scenery' and the drop curtain and 'scenic adjuncts' were carried out by the painters Max Ernst and Joan Miro.

A tall, large man, the English press magnate Lord Rothermere, came with Diaghilev to one of the company's rehearsals in Monte Carlo. He was interested in the ballet and was known to be exceedingly wealthy. His spectacular villa on Cap Martin, La Dragonniere, which overlooked Monte Carlo, stood in two acres of orange groves. Visiting ballerinas were handed gigantic silk-wrapped boxes of chocolates.

A ballerina Rothermere admired at the time was Lydia Sokolova. She had praised the tulips in the gardens of the villa and Lord Rothermere promptly sent armfuls of them daily to her flat.

Diaghilev, planning a season in London and wanting to book the expensive Her Majesty's Theatre, was hoping that Rothermere would finance this. He approached him on this matter but nothing concrete was arranged. Diaghilev asked Sokolova to speak to Rothermere on his behalf at a dinner party he was throwing for Rothermere at the Carlton Hotel in Monte Carlo.

Sokolova disliked this responsibllity 'as I was not by nature a gold-digger and had no experience of extracting large sums of money from rich men'. However, she claimed Diaghilev said to her 'You must realise that on your ability to get this support depends the whole future of the Russian ballet.'

Sokolova said that at a certain stage at dinner Diaghilev whispered to her that she must now go and dance with Rothermere. Nervous, she finally raised the subject. Rothermere did not make it easy for her but said 'All right, I will do what you ask. But I want you to make it clear to Diaghilev that I am doing this for you personally.'[5]

Although Rothermere backed Diaghilev financially a number of times,

Diaghilev was always careful, even if near bankruptcy, not to relinquish control over casting roles or artistic policies.

However, Rothermere could not be relied on always to dance to Diaghilev's tune. A request to him in the March of 1926 regarding publicity elicited an immediate stinging reply from his agent, informing Diaghilev that Lord Rothermere did not concern himself with details of the newspapers and was quite indifferent as to arrangements for Diaghilev's publicity.

There was one dancer to whom Rothermere became seriously attached. She was a ballerina who had joined the Ballets Russes the preceding year, the slim 'piquante and promising' Alice Nikitina. The journalists on the paper Rothermere owned, the *Daily Mail*, promptly joked that he was suffering from 'Nikitina poisoning'. However, Nikitina genuinely returned Rothermere's affection and, according to Beaumont, 'the affair, which lasted almost until Rothermere's death, was far from carnal.'[6]

Romeo et Juliette was premiered on 4 May 1926 in Monte Carlo. From there the company went directly to Paris, where they opened at the Sarah Bernhardt Theatre with several short ballets including *Romeo et Juliette*. This had curtains and scenic adjuncts designed by Max Ernst and Joan Miro and the police warned that there was going to be a protest by the Surrealists against Ernst and Miro ('traitors brought up by the bourgeois') for collaborating with the capitalist Diaghilev. The protesters aimed to manhandle all three of them.

It was to be another theatrical *scandale,* so beloved by the French. Diaghilev gave instructions that the curtain was to be lowered and the houselights put on if there were signs of trouble. After the interval, when the drop curtain of *Romeo et Juliette* came into view, there were shouts and hisses of protest. Fanatics in the gallery flung down a mass of surrealist tracts, which covered the seats below. The curtain was lowered and the gendarmes charged down the centre aisle into the rear of the boxes and dragged out the protestors.

As usual, the publicity ensured full houses. However, although the critics praised the dancers they were less kind about the other two ballets that season, *La Pastorale* with music by Georges Auric and *Jack-in-the-Box,* composed by Eric Satie. The music was judged too difficult for dancers and Diaghilev was accused of caring too little about the tastes of the day and too much about trying to be ahead of the times.

The next stop was London. It was in the May of that year that bitterness erupted in England when landowners with coal mines on their property attempted to cut miners' wages. A General Strike was called and workers at the *Daily Mail* and *The Times* refused to print editorials which condemned

*Lifar and
Nikitina in
Romeo and
Juliet, 1926.
The Surrealists
staged first
night protests
aimed at
the ballet's
designers Max
Ernst and
Joan Miro for
collaborating
with capitalists*

the miners and called for volunteers to man buses and other vehicles. With no pay for the strikers, the strike collapsed after ten days.

Diaghilev had no worries that month as at last the Ballets Russes no longer had to to perform at the Coliseum. The debt to Stoll was finally discharged. Instead from mid June the company, backed by Lord Rothermere, was booked at Her Majesty's Theatre. The season there, conducted by Goossens, was judged by audiences as one of the best ever. *Romeo et Juliette* was welcomed, as the much-loved Tamara Karsavina played Juliet. W.A. Propert said that when the season finished at the end of July, 'the prestige of the ballet stood higher than it had at any time since 1914.'[7]

Surprisingly, the press was more hostile, regarding Diaghilev like a mountebank trying to make the public accept inferior work on the strength of his past reputation. *Romeo et Juliette* was criticised on the grounds that Shakespeare had been burlesqued and that the young composer Constant Lambert 'had betrayed his country and written in the detestable French manner.'[8] A particularly sharp attack was made on the first appearance in London of the ballet, *Les Noces*, composed by Stravinsky.

The novelist H.G. Wells promptly went to its defence, writing in *The Times* that he was 'very much astonished' at its reception by the critics ('guardians of culture' he called them), and by their sneers at 'the elite'. He attacked the 'undercurrent of artistic politics in the business' and said 'I do not know of any other ballet so interesting, so amusing, so fresh or nearly so exciting as *Les Noces*... so I protest against this conspiracy of wilful stupidity that may succeed in driving it out of the programme.'[9] Despite the critics, the season was a financial success and Diaghilev could repay Rothermere, who agreed to subsidise the next season.

It was in 1926 that Diaghilev, for the first time since the revolution, was in contact with Soviet Russia. He had heard about a new form of theatre there. It was based on the theory of 'theatrical constructivism' and Diaghilev, always interested in new forms, found it could be applied to a ballet. He conferred with Prokofiev, asking him to write an appropriate score, and Massine was appointed as choreographer. The ballet, to be called *Le Pas d'Acier*, would be staged the following year.

During the last few weeks of the season, Diaghilev concentrated on producing a ballet on an English theme – in recognition of the generous support the country had invariably given him. Knowing little English music, and with no clear idea of what subject to choose, he asked Sacheverell Sitwell for help.

Sitwell, enthusiastically full of ideas, suggested Elizabethan music, but Diaghilev wanted something more up-to-date. Although he listened to the work of modern composers like William Walton, he remained uncertain. Asked about settings and costumes, he said he wanted to commission a modern painter. Sitwell suggested an English one, to which Diaghilev replied 'Are there any English painters?' Sitwell took him to see paintings by William Roberts, Edward Wadsworth and Wyndham Lewis, but Diaghilev remained unmoved.

However, what did excite him was Sitwell's suggestion of a ballet based on the early 19th century pantomimes. Sitwell took him to Benjamin Pollock's Toy Museum and Diaghilev was delighted by its quaint appearance and its model theatres set amid gaily-coloured scenes and characters. He bought prints there which resembled the Russian popular prints of the Czar Nicholas period. Sitwell agreed to write the scenario and Lord Berners was to provide the music.

Diaghilev became more and more fascinated with the project, at one point going with Sitwell to May's, the famous costumiers in London's Garrick Street, where he discovered two early 19th century foil stone tunics made of hundreds of small squares of glass backed with coloured foil and sewn on to a foundation garment. It was attractive enough to look at, but the ballerina Sokolova who had to wear it was decidedly less happy at having to dance under its weight and warmth.

After the London season, the company went off to Ostend to perform while Diaghilev went to Florence. Sitwell joined him with his script of the ballet-pantomime-harlequinade, in 12 tableaux, to be called *The Triumph of Neptune*. Grigoriev was relieved to find Diaghilev so involved as he had become anxiously aware that his interest in the ballet was beginning to be replaced by his passion for collecting rare books, phonographs and models of decors.

It was in 1926 while in Venice that the young Cecil Beaton spotted Diaghilev. 'Oh! God, there he was ... a marvellous fat pale man, such a funny face and so smartly dressed, and with him was Lifar, so young and smartly dressed too – both in superb white flannel trousers and blue double-breasted coats with tuber- roses in their buttonholes. Diaghilev was as quiet and meek as a lamb – he was rather nice – so furry. I can't think what animal it is he reminds me of – perhaps a mole – perhaps a very nice monkey. He is like a baby – very fat and dignified.'[10]

Beaton was desperately anxious to show Diaghilev his photos and designs. Diaghilev examined his portfolio, looking at every one, but said nothing until Beaton asked his advice on some of them. He found that Diaghilev knew at once where each design went wrong. Sometimes he said 'nice', sometimes 'original'. He asked Beaton if he also took photographs and looking at them said, 'Yes, I like this. It is very curious.' However, after shaking hands Diaghilev walked away and Beaton was in despair. Events proved him right, he would not encounter Diaghilev again.

In November the company returned to London, opening at the Lyceum Theatre. Diaghilev was none too happy about this, considering the Lyceum merely a down-market home for melodrama. He privately thought that only the Covent Garden Opera House was good enough for his company. However London audiences, aware of the expensive seats and uncertain visibility at the Opera House, were quite happy with the cheaper Lyceum.

The season opened with a number of revivals, including *The Firebird*, not staged in London since 1921, with an eye-catching new décor by Natalia Goncharova. Balanchine looked less like a Russian enchanter than an African witch-doctor, with his face made up to look like a ceremonial mask and gloves with long gleaming metal nails. Goncharova's partner, Larionov, came to London to supervise the ballet's production, staying at the Savoy for ten days at Diaghilev's expense.

The Triumph of Neptune was indeed a triumph. Sacheverell Sitwell noted in his diary, 'Mimes of 70 years ago & the curtain & scenery copied exactly from the little toy theatres of that date. The tremendous audience screamed with laughter.'[11] Diaghilev himself was particularly taken with the tableau, 'The Frozen Forest' in which the ballerinas appeared to be flying, raised up on wires, true to the Victorian period.

The year 1927 marked Diaghilev's 20th season in Paris. His friends wanted to commemorate this, but they knew they had to confer secretly as Diaghilev would immediately object if he knew their plans. They finally chose a new work by Stravinsky, to be given in concert form, called *Oedipus Rex*.

The plan was for the main characters to look like statues, standing immobile on a raised stage, masked and wearing sheaths. These 'lonely, petrified and helpless victims of Fate' would chant their tragic tale, helped by a chorus, an interpreter and an orchestra. Impressive this may have been, but perhaps inappropriate for a happy celebration.

Diaghilev, who always found out everything that was going on, objected – not to the opera, but to the occasion. He said that he wasn't dead, 'so why must you read the funeral service over me?'

Going to one of the company's rehearsals he implored them to drop the idea, saying: 'I am afraid I abhor jubilees in general and my own in particular. A jubilee is the beginning of an end: something that rounds off a career. But I am not ready to give up ... I wish to continue working ... I wish to remain always young.'[12]

Right now he was full of vitality and energy and although he was against a specific celebration, he did want the next season in Paris to be a memorable anniversary. He was faced with his usual problems, however, like being unable to pay his hotel bill, which he neatly avoided by changing hotels.

While the ballet toured Italy before returning to Monte Carlo, Diaghilev went to Paris to work on various new projects. He was not interested in *Oedipus Rex* as a personal tribute, but he welcomed the first work that Stravinsky had done for the company for four years. Diaghilev was also overseeing *Le Pas d'Acier* the new 'constructivist' ballet by Prokofiev, along with

Serge Prokofiev composed the music for Le Pas d'Acier *(1927). A 'Soviet' ballet about which it is said 'You either shut your ears and waited as patiently as might be for the end of it, or you sat spellbound'*

a one-act ballet *La Chatte,* based on one of Aesop's fables, by the young, modern French composer Henri Sauguet, and another new ballet by Erik Satie.

This was an enormous amount of work, but Diaghilev thrived on it: such productions were his passion, his *raison d'etre* and he had endless reserves of energy.

The Russian ballet *Le Pas d'Acier* had two scenes of contemporary Soviet Union life, showing the peasants in the fields and workmen in factories. Working on the ballet made Diaghilev homesick and he had long discussions about his homeland with Prokofiev, with whom he was very friendly, whenever the composer visited Europe. At one point Diaghilev even approached the authorities in the Soviet Union about returning. Although the signs were favourable, Diaghilev again feared that once there he might be prevented from returning to Europe.

Le Pas d'Acier was shown in Paris in May, 1927. Diaghilev was slightly nervous of an outcry against this 'Bolshevik' ballet from the Russian émigrés in Paris, but all remained quiet – or, rather, the audience remained quiet. W.A. Propert in discussing Prokofiev's forceful music for it, said 'You either shut your ears and waited as patiently as might be for the end of it, or you sat spellbound, unable to think or to protest, stunned by the mere accumulation of heavy sound and only released when the last crash of the tremendous climax had died away.'[13] The crashing was echoed by the sound of young workers swinging their hammers and wheels, levers and pistons all in clanging motion.

The new Stravinsky work, *Oedipus Rex*, drew a full and enthusiastic first house, but despite costumes by Picasso and a sung text by Jean Cocteau translated into Latin, it raised little excitement from the audience.

Thanks to Lord Rothermere's continued funding, the company returned to London that summer for a season at The Princes Theatre. However the theatre had a small and shallow stage, a limitation worsened by a staff member thinking it helpful to rub it with salad oil. It was polished until it looked like glass and Grigoriev was forced to fling handfuls of sand from the fire buckets onto the stage every time the dancers went on, to stop them from falling.

Diaghilev also received a warning letter from the managers, Walter and Frederick Melville, to say that he had 'failed to make the scenery non-flammable' resulting in a 'very unpleasant strong letter from the Lord Chamberlain.' He was told to rectify this immediately or the theatre could be closed.

That season, while the stage was being set for *La Chatte*, Diaghilev came on stage leaning heavily on a walking stick. Beaumont noticed that 'he had developed a curious habit of moving his jaws with a circular motion as though he was chewing something.'[14] However Diaghilev's eyes were as sharp as ever and he was irritated at the state of the stage cloth which he insisted was swept and cleaned.

La Chatte became a great favourite, with Nikitina dancing the title role ('the most adorable cat who ever danced in a talc petticoat') and a bouncing clockwork mouse which occasionally went on strike and refused to move. Lifar played the youth carried off lifeless at the end, Hamlet-style, on his friends' shoulders to the majestic music of Henri Sauguet.

The criticis were asking why more new music was not being presented. Janet Flanner, the Paris correspondent for the *New Yorker* magazine, claimed it was because they were so badly paid. 'For his charming ballet of *La Chatte*, Sauguet, it is said, received 5,000 francs from Diaghilev ... doubtless as much as the master can afford ... about 75 francs was paid when it was danced in England, where there is no copyright protection for French musicians ... In this day of rich patrons, composers are still supposd to starve.'[15]

At the end of the 1927 season, Diaghilev went off to his beloved Venice but then returned to Monte Carlo to sign a contract for the company's winter sojourn there. He was in an anxious state, as negotiations over the contract had been prolonged and he was worried it might not be signed. He had also cut his finger badly, which was failing to heal.

He was enthused, however, by having visited Stravinsky and heard the score for a new ballet, which had delighted him. He and Kochno, Derain, Balanchine and various dancers frequently had a sumptuous two-hour noisy and cheerful lunch at Girdino's, a small restaurant high up on a hill above Monte Carlo.

On the Lido,
Venice: Max
Reinhardt,
Morris Gest,
Diaghilev and
Otto Kahn

Once the Monte Carlo contract was signed, Diaghilev went back to Venice. For the rest of the year the company toured Europe, with tiny Alicia Markova at last graduating to the title role in *La Chatte*. Lifar was particularly pleased about this as she was so easy to lift in any *pas de deux*. Two gala performances at L'Opera at the end of December in Paris brought a successful end to the year.

At the start of 1928, Grigoriev found Diaghilev 'gloomy and taciturn, and only livened up into his accustomed good humour when tackled on the subject of books.'[16] He told Grigoriev that they were his original love, before he became interested in the theatre, and now he wanted to return to them.

Diaghilev's old student friend, the artist Alexandre Benois, also noticed that Diaghilev was switching his focus from the ballet to collecting rare books. Diaghilev never had any money and it's hard to see how he could afford these unless he was using amounts allotted for the ballet season. Lifar considered this was endangering the future of the ballet.

Diaghilev had long encouraged Boris Kochno to buy early Russian literature and entire editions of Russian classics, which Kochno stored in trunks. Originally Diaghilev just planned to build a private collection of rare books and musical manuscripts.

Profoundly homesick for Russian culture, he became increasingly involved in the search and bought ever more books and spent much of his time cataloguing these. When he went to Poland that year with Kochno, as well as engaging dancers he spent his time in bookshops. He considered setting up a vast Russian library in Europe.

As a result, the Diaghilev-Kochno Russian collection grew so fast that Diaghilev had to hire an apartment in Paris to house it. It could have formed the basis of a Diaghilev Museum, but Diaghilev loathed the idea of his pince-nez and old bedroom slippers being preserved in aspic.

The collection also included a mountain of letters, hotel bills and other ephemera. Diaghilev was especially interested in old letters and one reason he wanted to put on a charity gala in Monte Carlo that year, despite the company being exceptionally busy, was that the organiser was Countess Torby, wife of the Grand Duke Michael and a descendant of Pushkin, who had promised to leave him a letter from Pushkin in her will. As it happened, the Countess died the following year and Diaghilev not only got the letter but persuaded the Grand Duke to sell him a further ten.

Despite his friends speculating on his changing interests, Diaghilev continued to work on new ideas for ballets.

19

The Shadow of Diabetes

One new project interesting Diaghilev early in 1928 was the first commissioned work by a relation of his, the composer Nicolas Nabokov. It was called *Ode* and was based on an 18th century ode by the Russian poet Lomonosov in which a statue of Nature comes to life and shows a young student some of the wonders of nature. The student wants to take part in the beauties he is shown and the statue, frightened, returns to its petrified state. Lifar was to dance the part of the student.

Diaghilev was also busy on a new ballet by Stravinsky about Apollo so he left *Ode* in the hands of Boris Kochno, with whom he had a close friendship. He had already started to call Kochno his successor.

Kochno, however, found *Ode* difficult to manage and irritated Diaghilev by repeatedly turning to him for advice. When Nabokov came to Monte Carlo in April 1928 during the rehearsals he found Diaghilev in one of his most critical moods. The impresario announced that he disliked *Ode*, flew into a tantrum and unfairly attacked Nabokov for indolence. Rehearsals continued, Massine being the choreographer, but when Diaghilev went to see how it was progressing, he announced that it was 'utter rubbish.' The chances of it ever appearing on stage seemed remote.

One reason for Diaghilev's outburst could have been his shock at finding out that Lord Rothermere, who had funded the last two seasons of the ballet in London, had suddenly withdrawn his patronage for that year's season, even though this was already half planned.

Lady Juliet Duff helped out Diaghilev by setting up a committee of patrons who each paid a few hundred pounds and finally enough backers were found for the season to take place. However, it was an unnerving time for Diaghilev. He took some of his anger out on Rothermere's favourite ballerina, Nikitina, 'and addressed her rudely making cutting remarks to her in front of the whole company.'[1]

Throughout rehearsals, right up to a few days before *Ode* was due to be premiered in Paris in June, Diaghilev showed no interest at all. He then telephoned Nabokov and shouted, 'Get up right away and come to the theatre. This mess can't go on any longer. I have ordered a full stage rehearsal at ten, a full orchestra rehearsal at two, a full chorus rehearsal at five, and all evening we will rehearse the lights.'[2]

Nabokov, despite Diaghilev's initial offhand reception of his ballet, remained full of admiration for his ability. Those who believed that Diaghilev's interest in ballet was waning were given proof of his enormous reserves of energy and interest. In this case, with casual sang froid, he took over the whole direction of *Ode*, making all the decisions and taking total responsibility.

His energy seemed limitless. 'He ran to the prefect of police to have him over-rule the fire department's decision forbidding the use of neon lights on stage ... He supervised the dyeing, cutting and sewing of costumes. He was present at every orchestra and choral rehearsal and made the conductor, Desormiere, the soloists, the chorus, repeat sections of the music over and over again until they blended well with the choreographic movements and the light-play of Tchelitchev's scenery.'[3]

He also bullied the recalcitrant stagehands into working harder, physically helped with painting props and scenery and spent two entire nights directing the lighting rehearsals. All this was at the expense of his temper. He shouted at Tchelitchev when the lighting went wrong, at Nabokov if he played the piano unevenly and at Lifar when his steps faltered.

Naturally enough, this frenetic activity exhausted Diaghilev. He finally left the theatre only a couple of hours before the ballet was premiered at Paris's Sarah Bernhardt Theatre on 6 June 1928 looking 'worn, grey and sallow as he crossed the stage, his face covered with a two-day growth of beard.' Fifteen minutes before curtain-up he returned, 'in full evening dress, be-monocled, his famous rose pearl shining on a snow-white shirt ... calm, confident and resplendent.'[4]

Despite Diaghilev's frenzied work, *Ode* was a failure. Lifar did his best, but his part gave him little chance to display his dancing and the ballet failed to ignite the audience. To Grigoriev's surprise, Diaghilev seemed curiously indifferent to this disappointing result. It was the last time that Massine acted as choreographer.

Another new ballet, composed by Stravinsky, had its premiere a week later: *Apollon Musagete*. In it, Apollo is born, reveals his creative powers, teaches three Muses their arts and ascends with them to Parnassus. The ballet owed much of its success to Balanchine's choreography. Diaghilev told Andre Derain that what Balanchine was doing was magnificent, that it was pure classicism, 'such as we have not seen since Petipa's.' Marius Petipa, who died in 1910, was a French ballet-master and choreographer and the developer of Russian classical ballet.

The audience gave the ballet an ovation. The theatrical director Gordon Craig was so overcome by it that he left after the interval in order to preserve its beauty in his mind. Chanel gave a ball, as she customarily did after premieres, and Diaghilev, buoyed up by the ballet's success, recovered much of his former enthusiasm.

Outside events rarely seemed to penetrate to the Ballets Russes. Would Diaghilev or the company have been aware, or cared, that 1928 saw the discovery of penicillin by Alexander Fleming; the first flight across the Atlantic by a woman, Amelia Earhart; the first picture transmitted by television; the first 'talkies'; and the emergence of Micky Mouse from the Disney Studios.

Later in June the company returned to Her Majesty's Theatre in London. The Duke of Connaught had replaced Rothermere as patron and Sir Thomas Beecham again offered financial help. The fashionable first night audience, glittering in tiaras and resplendent in tails, was particularly taken with *Apollon*, which Stravinsky conducted himself.

Although it was a busy season, Diaghilev insisted that a new ballet, based on Handel's music and orchestrated by Sir Thomas Beecham, was put together and rehearsed. Called *The Gods Go A-Begging*, it turned out a decided success, despite the company's belief that it was all too rushed.

Diaghilev's belief in his own ideas remained rock solid and he continued to prove that he retained his magic touch.

It was a time of ideas, of frontiers being pushed. That year, *Lady Chatterley's Lover* by D.H. Lawrence was privately printed in Florence; Virginia Woolf wrote *Orlando*, tracing the life of a beautiful youth through his male and female manifestations; and Edmund Blunden wrote *Undertones of War*, which emphasised the waste of war in its description of the double destruction of man and nature in Flanders.

After leaving London the company toured the provinces, visiting cities like Birmingham and Manchester, with Diaghilev allowing the eighteen-year-old Alicia Markova her chance to dance two classic pas-de-deux. The tour was considered by some critics a success, but Grigoriev complained that though the first nights were generally full, houses dwindled after that as the company was hardly known in the provinces. More worrying, King George V had double-pneumonia and his death would mean the tour being interrupted.

Massine left at the end of the season. Diaghilev was relatively unperturbed by this as Massine was dancing less and the last two ballets he had choreographed, *Le Pas d'Acier* and *Ode*, had not pleased Diaghilev. What upset him more was the news that Ida Rubinstein was setting up a ballet season in Paris, and successfully commandeering composers and painters who had originally worked for Diaghilev. Massine was one: others included Stravinsky, Benois and Nijinska.

Diaghilev went to the opening night, describing it acidly in a letter to Lifar: 'The house was full, but there was a good deal of paper [people with free seats] about, mostly her friends. Not one of us, however, were given seats, neither myself, Boris, Nouvel, Sert or Picasso ... we only just, just managed to get in. All our people were there, Misia [Sert], Juliet [Duff], [Cyril] Beaumont, [Princesse de] Polignac, Igor [Stravinsky] and other musicians ... the whole thing was astonishingly provincial, boring and long drawn-out, even the Ravel [*Bolero*] which took 14 minutes. It's a big company, but totally lacking in experience: they just made mistake after mistake, and seemed not to have the slightest notion of ensemble.' He slated Nicolaeva [Legat] who wore a 'slime-yellow dress, and pranced about in a classico-bacchanalian manner on her toes.'

He was highly amused, however, when the dancer Unger appeared on stage in an 'open pink shirt with blue trimmings and a short red velvet cloak, wearing a red wig and a bright green wreath on top of it, made up to look like the worst sort of coxcomb.'[5]

Diaghilev returned the following night and found a little more to praise. But the house was full and remained so and Diaghilev worried that the Rubinstein company would outstrip his own. 'We've got to prove to this bourgeois crowd how immeasurably superior we are, in spite of the fact that our sets weren't painted yesterday, that our costumes aren't quite so fresh,' he wrote to Lifar.[6]

Diaghilev's health then was not good, though exactly when he contracted diabetes isn't known. He suffered from some common symptoms of the illness: continual thirst, weight loss, weakness, wanting unusually large amounts of food at meals, vulnerability to infections and boils and frequent urination. Diabetes was known in the 18th century as 'the pissing evile.'

He had consulted a doctor in London in 1926 but spurned the Spartan dietary regime that was prescribed for diabetes, refusing to take saccharin rather than sugar or to cut out chocolate.

Indeed when in 1928 in Monte Carlo, dressed elegantly as usual in black coat and white silk scarf, he met Nicolas Nabokov, they repaired to a confiserie and ate chocolates and pastries and talked about dieting. Diaghilev pointed to his empty plate and said laughingly, 'This is my way to treat diabetes.' He did not seem to take the illness seriously.

A medical breakthrough had occurred that decade in treating diabetes. In 1921, Canadian doctors at the University of Toronto discovered the hormone insulin was a remedy for diabetes and the following year the first injection of insulin was successfully given to a young boy in Toronto. It saved his life.

Insulin needed to be taken in conjunction with diet and exercise and was not yet widely available. According to *The Lancet* in November 1922, it was still unobtainable then in Britain. However, by the following year it was being dispensed in European hospitals in countries like Austria, Germany and Switzerland. Some doctors still thought it too revolutionary and told diabetic patients to rely on a specific diet. There is no evidence that Diaghilev was contemplating the treatment.

But when he visited a Dr Dalimier in Paris in the spring of 1929 it was clear at that point to his friends, let alone his doctor, that his health had seriously deteriorated. He was much thinner, with bags under his eyes and sagging facial skin. His body was covered in boils which refused to heal. It made him slow-moving and lethargic. He could no longer, Boris Kochno noticed, even be bothered to dye his hair carefully ('l'artifice etait visible').

Dalimier, who saw Diaghilev twice at the end of July 1929, was seriously concerned by his condition, particularly the unhealing boils, and according to Chanel diagnosed Diaghilev as being in the last stages of diabetes. Diaghilev did not want to hear this truth, merely writing to Lifar to say that his wound was not yet healed and that 'Dalimier was dumbfounded at the sight, and says I've had a lucky escape'. He ended the letter laughingly saying, 'Be a good boy now you're turning six.'[7]

Dalimier tried to prevent Diaghilev from his plan of going to Germany, saying he needed to take a serious cure – presumably insulin – and was also against him going to Venice as the humidity there could exacerbate the boils. But though Dalimier told him to rest for the remainder of the summer, Diaghilev responded by immediately booking tickets for a European music tour.

The doctor also recommended that Diaghilev take more fresh air. Diaghilev's response was to dine with his friend Walter Nouvel at an outside table in the Bois de Boulogne. And when one of his anxious friends tried to stop him opening a bottle of champagne, he replied with surprise, 'Oh, but it's *Sunday*.'

Was he really unaware of how ill he had become? Sokolova was horrified at the way he now looked: 'His face was ashen, the flesh was loose round his cheeks, his eyes were sunken and his grey hair showed through the dye ... He looked as though he were suffering and spoke very little.'[8]

His look of suffering was hardly surprising as his body was covered in boils which he refused to allow a nurse to treat. Nicolas Nabokov noticed that his face 'was puffy with the glazed yellow quality of diabetics during or after an attack.'[9]

Had Diaghilev only taken insulin treatment at any number of European cities, his diabetes might have been successfully contained. it seems inconceivable he would not have embarked on such a relatively simple measure to save, or at least prolong, his life. However he may not have realised or accepted the seriousness of his condition, or ranked his fear of hypodermic needles as greater than his need for treatment.

20

'I Shall Not See You Again'

The company welcomed in the year 1929 with an exuberant party in Paris on New Year's Eve. Diaghilev was busy planning three new ballets and delighted with his new young discovery, the handsome and gifted sixteen-year-old Russian composer and pianist, Igor Markevich.

Markevich later married Nijinsky's elder daughter, Kyra, but Diaghilev was immediately enamoured on first seeing him. At the time Diaghilev was fifty-seven and ill with diabetes, so there may have been little sexual involvement. However, Markevich undoubtedly brought a new excitement and interest into Diaghilev's life.

When the company arrived in Monte Carlo in January, work began at once on the new ballets. One was *Le Bal* by the Italian composer, Vittorio Rieti. Diaghilev made so many changes in the score that Rieti finally sent him a last version saying he could do what he liked with it, but that he, Rieti, refused to make any further alterations.

Another ballet was Stravinsky's *Renard*. This had been produced seven years ago, but with long-forgotten choreography by Nijinska. As she was now working for Ida Rubinstein, the task of re-choreographing was given to Lifar.

The third ballet, *The Prodigal Son*, was by Prokofiev. Lifar was expecting to dance the main role in this ballet, but Diaghilev's involvement with him had waned, he no longer called for him at the end of rehearsals and relations between the two were now strained. Diaghilev was wary about Lifar being heavily involved in two of the ballets, so asked Anton Dolin to replace him in *The Prodigal Son* – an ironic decision, given he had once replaced Dolin by Lifar.

The Monte Carlo season began in April and *Le Bal* was a great success. Its attractive décor was by the Italian painter Giorgio de Chirico and in one scene the marbled walls were echoed by the material of the costumes. There were men in fluted top hats, with colourful spots and stripes, white wigs everywhere and a white rocking horse. It created a vivid sense of the supernatural.

Diaghilev was pleased with the production, but left for Paris before the season ended. He was unwell, still suffering from boils. His condition was not helped by news from Grigoriev that the casino authorities in Monte Carlo wanted the company's stored scenery removed as the storage charge of 6,000 francs a year was owing. The scenery would not be released until at least half the amount was paid.

In May, the company headed for the Sarah Bernhardt Theatre in Paris. Given Diaghilev's long association with Lord Rothermere, he had asked the editor of the European *Daily Mail* for free publicity. An earlier request had been rejected but this time he was lucky and the *Mail* agreed to publicise the ballet both in Paris and in the new season in London.

Rothermere also left instructions that Lady Juliet Duff be sent the sum of £500 towards Diaghilev's expenses in London – news she greeted with great thankfulness. She had been busily fund-raising, but had written to Diaghilev anxiously to ask if Rothermere would be contributing, as his money was indispensable.

She told Diaghilev she had had a lot of pledges, that the Courtaulds were giving £300 (though she added unkindly that 'she is sick and I can see clearly that she will be of no other use. She is a bird brain, and my God what a bore!'.) She admitted, however, that 'Emerald [Cunard] was marvellously kind, booking seats and giving them money and goodwill.' Her letter ended with 'a thousand friendships.'[1]

Rothermere expected a return for his £500, insisting that the money was dependent on 'Miss Nikitina' joining the Ballet early June, working with it during the London season, receiving a salary equal to that of the Premier Ballerina, and being given every chance in the principal parts.

The Paris season was going well. *The Prodigal Son* had a striking décor by Georges Rouault – Lifar's rose-red costume blended with the dusky red landscape and the scarlet swords – and *Le Renard*, a mixture of dance and acrobatics, was equally enthusiastically received by the first night audience.

Diaghilev had taken a chance with *Le Renard* and, alongside the dancers, used trained acrobats who could do feats beyond the dancers' capabilities. The older members of the audience were less pleased, complaining that choreography had descended into mere acrobatics.

Russian critics in Paris also attacked Diaghilev for departing from the classical tradition. In reply, Diaghilev wrote an article in a Russian magazine repudiating their arguments and stating that he found it essential to move on and not be content merely to repeat himself.

Despite his defiant stance, he was veering between enthusiasm and depression. He joined his circle of friends, however, at *Les Capucines* restaurant to drink to the Ballets Russes' 21st season in Paris: they included Lifar, Misia Sert, Coco Chanel, Picasso, Roualt, Stravinsky, Prokofiev, Cocteau and Kochno.

However, his magic circle of those working for him was diminishing. He considered Stravinsky, currently employed by Ida Rubinstein, to be a traitor – failing to understand that Stravinsky could no longer live on air; Picasso was unapproachably busy; and he had lost touch with really old friends like Alexandre Benois. Although Lifar was in the company and Diaghilev still sought the stimulus of the young and creative, he was turning increasingly to friends with whom he was comfortable and who understood him, like his long-term secretary, Boris Kochno.

Diaghilev also had regrets for a changing Paris: the tramways had gone, replaced by streets full of cars. Many of the old cafes and nightclubs had been replaced by brash new modernised ones, lacking charm. Montparnasse so beloved by its artists was now mainly abandoned by them.

However Diaghilev's current concern was with where the company could hold its London season. To his delight he was able to book The Royal Opera House, Covent Garden – the first time the company had danced there since 1920.

Interviewed by the *Observer* the day before the opening, Diaghilev referred to the Marchioness of Ripon, whose spirit he felt still pervaded the Opera House, and who was 'the first person in England to love and appreciate our work.' He then paid tribute to her daughter, Lady Juliet Duff, for being 'the principal patron of our present season' which he hoped would be as brilliant as the ones her mother patronised.[2]

Lady Juliet had worked extremely hard to raise sufficient funds to defray the expenses of the season. She had written to Diaghilev, as usual in French, on 12 June 1929 to say (translated): 'Dear Darling, even for you I could not do this again next year. One writes a hundred letters which are only answered at the end of several weeks and then one must write another hundred to touch silver. We have turned up £2,000.'[3]

She thought that would be enough to cover expenses at Covent Garden, but asked with irritation why his agent had asked for the money to be sent to him immediately as it was crucially needed for the London season. However, Diaghilev got his way. Was it merely coincidence that he needed to pay for 17 more rare books just delivered to him?

The first night was on 1 July. Dolin commented that 'Youth came back that night to Diaghilev. Dressed perfectly, with a white carnation in his buttonhole, opera hat and stick, he came and spoke to us all on stage and gave us his blessing as he always did before the beginning of an important season.'[4]

Diaghilev was sure the season would be a success. One advantage was that the popular Tamara Karsavina was to appear in *Petrushka*. When Karsavina saw Diaghilev again at Covent Garden, she ran to meet him as he walked slowly behind the backcloth 'leaning on the cane that he used to whirl round

Bakst's set for Petrushka *would be the backdrop for one of the Ballets Russes' most enduringly popular ballets*

in such a debonair way.' They walked, arm in arm, to her dressing room, where he sat down heavily. 'Gone was all the buoyancy, the peculiar lazy grace.' He told her that he had left his bed to come to her: 'Judge of my love.'[5]

He seemed unworried by his health, however, telling Karsavina about his new young protégé, Igor Markevitch, whom he intended to bring to the public's notice. He did indeed organise that he played concertos in between the ballets, but these failed to create much enthusiasm.

Aware that the farmyard fable *Le Renard*, with its acrobatic animal movements, would attract controversy, Diaghilev wrote to *The Times* to argue that the boundary between dancing and acrobatics was indefinable.

Harold Acton, who saw Diaghilev then, thought he was 'a shade of his former self and his ballets proceeded with a hectic flash, a trifle mechanically, as if they were affected by the weariness of the great impresario.' He dined with him and Lady Cunard at the Savoy and commented: 'The ageing magician was feverishly gay, but at moments I detected a resemblance to King Fuad [of Egypt]: he had the same tyrannical eyes ... the same air of Oriental opulence.'[6]

Grigoriev thought the Covent Garden season had been most successful, with all the new ballets being admired, even if the dazzling days had gone. However Sacheverell Sitwell, a loyal supporter, found he sometimes sat in a half empty theatre leading the applause. Times were changing: that year saw the Wall Street crash and the start of a world-wide economic depression. In Britain unemployed Glasgow workers took part in a Hunger March from Scotland to Trafalgar Square.

Towards the end of the season Dolin hosted a party in his Chelsea studio. The ballerina Lydia Sokolova, who had received excellent notices for her current performance in *Le Sacre du Printemps*, was there and upset at seeing Diaghilev's obvious ill-health. There was a hush as he appeared.

Beaumont, too, was shocked by the change in the impresario's appearance from the year before. 'His cheeks were of a strange leaden pallor and he appeared to be a very sick man' although he admitted 'the cynical glance, the familiar curl of the lip, were still there.'[7] Nevertheless he seemed reserved and uncommunicative.

Although he looked alarmingly ill, Diaghilev was known for his ability to transform himself. As Gordon Craig said 'He could look the oldest man in the town when you met him at noon and at eight, when the curtain was about to go up, he would look the youngest.'[8] Everyone assumed this rejuvention would continue.

At the end of the season in July the cast assembled on stage and Diaghilev, walking heavily and obviously in pain, quietly bade them farewell. 'You are leaving tomorrow,' he said, 'and I shall not see you again until the autumn. I wish you all to have a good rest and return to work refreshed and invigorated. We have a busy year before us. All my contracts are signed and for the first time in our whole career we have an uninterrupted series of engagements already fixed. I thank you for the excellent work you have done, which has been largely responsible for any success we may have had. Goodbye – and good luck!'[9]

Diaghilev implied he looked to the future with as much enthusiasm as he had ten years ago, shaking hands with everyone present, but Balanchine thought he looked terrible. 'His cheeks were as pale and lifeless as dough; his eyes, under which were dark circles, glittered feverishly. His massive head drooped and he moved with painful effort, as if his body were a burden too great for him to carry. When he spoke it was in a voice so low that one had to strain to hear him.'[10]

Diaghilev had run the Ballets Russes apparently effortlessly. Understandably it had taken its toll on his health: he had the constant strain of keeping up with new movements in art; finding new musicians, painters, choreographers and welding them together; and finally being financially responsible for some 50 or 60 people in war and in peace.

The strain was now only too evident. Nevertheless, Diaghilev was still working, still planning ballets with Strauss and Hindemith. And in his determined insistence to defy age he would stay up till early morning with his various young protégés. Rather than admit tiredness, he warded it off by surrounding himself with youth and beauty. Following this tradition, he left London with his new young protégé, Igor Markevich, anxious to educate him in the glories of European music and art.

Nabokov encountered Diaghilev at the Baden Baden music festival where he had come to hear a new work by Hindemith, his latest composer-collaborator. Diaghilev was with Markevich and his old friend the Princesse de Polignac and said he intended to take Markevich to visit Richard Strauss and to hear some Wagner or Mozart at the Munich Opera.

He seemed cheerful enough as he spoke about his plans for the forthcoming seasons, but old friends who saw him this year commented on his ill-health. Markevitch, on the other hand, found him buoyant, enthusiastic and planning for the future. Markevitch was young enough to be impressed by Diaghilev in his fur coat and monocle, looking 'more important than all the other people' and entering a restaurant or theatre 'like a ship entering a harbour with little, little ships around him, which were all of us.'[11]

He was impressed at how Diaghilev brought out the best in artists, which they may not have achieved on their own. That could lead to difficulties. Diaghilev would tell Markevitch, 'here you should compose like that, here you should put the piano, here the orchestra should play and not the piano.'[12] Sometimes Markevitch must have wondered just who was the composer.

In August Diaghilev saw Markevitch off to Vevey 'walking alongside the train, clasping his hand, crying a little and making the sign of the cross over him.'[13] Diaghilev then travelled to the Lido in Venice to stay at the Grand Hotel des Bains. In the past the Adriatic air had revived him and restored his health; but now his weakness increased. Lifar joined him in Venice early August.

At first glance, Lifar almost failed to recognise him: his pallor was waxen and he looked enfeebled and bedraggled. Diaghilev had always tended to leave ties, handkerchiefs and underwear behind in hotels and this time he had left virtually everything in Germany. He told Lifar he felt tired and extremely weak and had a terrible pain in his back.

At the time Misia Sert and Chanel were cruising around the Dalmatian coast on the Duke of Westminster's yacht. Misia received a radiogram from Diaghilev in Venice saying, 'Am sick; come quickly. Serge.' They went at once in apprehension.

They found Diaghilev in great pain, immensely haggard, and drenched in perspiration. He was tired, still had a sharp pain in his back, found his legs

too weak to carry him, couldn't sleep or eat and clutched his dinner jacket around him to keep warm despite the heat of the hotel.

He was delighted to see Misia and whispered that he loved her in white and asked her to promise him she would always wear it.

Misia sent for a local physician, who did not endorse Diaghilev's French doctor's diagnosis of diabetes. Instead he speculated it could be rheumatism, typhus, influenza or septicemia. Diaghilev neither revealed nor discussed what his French doctor had said.

His condition at one stage seemed to improve and Chanel left to resume her cruise. Misia Sert stayed on. The improvement did not last and his condition worsened over the next few days.

He talked about his homeland, his memories of his first journeys abroad which moulded him into the man he became, his early triumphant seasons in Paris. After 12 August he was not strong enough to leave his bed and his fever worsened to such a degree the doctors thought he may indeed have typhoid fever. Before too long he relapsed into delirium, speaking of himself in the past tense.

Misia Sert spent the day of 18 August with Diaghilev, but after leaving him was telephoned with the news that Diaghilev had gone into a coma. She returned to his bedside and asked a priest to carry out the last rites. She, Lifar and Kochno were with him when he died at dawn on 19 August 1929, aged fifty-seven.

The feelings of the two men, who had long been hostile and jealous of each other, exploded into a fury at the emotion of Diaghilev's death. 'Kochno threw himself on Lifar, who was kneeling at the other side of the bed. Shaken by rage, they rolled on the floor, tearing at each other's clothes, biting one another like wild animals: two mad dogs fighting over the body of their master.'[14] The nurse had to help Misia to separate them so the body could be laid out.

Sculptors were called in to make the death mask, shocking Lifar when, to remove the finished mask, they struck a heavy blow on Diaghilev's head.

There was insufficient money to pay the hotel, medical staff and the funeral ceremonies. Misia Sert was about to pawn her diamond necklace when Chanel returned and settled the debts and also paid for the funeral, which took place two days later.

A mass was held at the Greek Orthodox cathedral in Venice where a Russian priest and the choir of San Georgio del Greci chanted the Slavic funeral service.

Then Diaghilev's coffin covered in tuberroses, tea roses and carnations was placed in a black funeral gondola with its gilded winged angels ('a floating bed of honour' Chanel called it) before being rowed across the Venetian lagoon to the Russian cemetery on the small island of San Michele.

Kochno and Lifar, Sert and Chanel, all dressed in white, followed in another black gondola. The priests chanted and it was an impressive, theatrical sight, one which Diaghilev would have artistically appreciated.

Lifar found he could not cross the threshold of the church on the island, despite being supported by Misia Sert and Chanel, as an 'unknown force' prevented him. After several efforts he managed it, only to collapse, 'with a terrible scream' by the altar. Chanel recalled Lifar and Kochno demanding to go all the way to the tomb on their knees and snapping at them, 'Stop that nonsense, if you please.'[15]

The scenes at the graveside, amid the cypresses, continued to resemble an operatic thriller. The unknown force claimed Lifar once again and he was forced to hurl himself into the grave. Restrained from his Laertes-style behaviour, he was led from the cemetery. The mourners dropped flower petals onto the coffin.

Amid a flutter of unpaid bills the creditors moved in after his death, seizing the mortgaged sets and costumes and leaving his dancers stranded, alone with only their memories to support them.

For Diaghilev died as he had lived much of his life, 'in a hotel room, a homeless adventurer, an exile, and a prince of the arts.'[16]

His legend lives on. He left a dazzling heritage of colour and brilliance.

Epilogue

The death of Diaghilev was the death of the Ballets Russes. He was the maestro, the mainspring, the focal point of a whole artistic movement: without him, members of the company felt rudderless. He had bound them together: all had striven to please him.

The pianist Artur Rubinstein said that on the announcement of Diaghilev's death, 'the whole of artistic Paris was in mourning. The loss of this great magician of beauty bereaved our hearts; we were suddenly aware of our great debt to him for the years of unforgettable enchantment and excitement which this great man bestowed upon us so generously. Young composers became orphans and dancers cried at the news.'

No one in the company could believe they would never again see his familiar presence at first nights, with his top hat and tails, fur-lined coat, streak of white hair, monocle and stick; never again quail at his temper tantrums; or see him watching them through his tiny pair of opera glasses.

One dancer particularly affected by Diaghilev's death was the young Alicia Markova, currently being groomed to take some of the great roles like Giselle and Odette. Diaghilev had shaped her career and she felt unable to dance 'without his inspiration and outside the ideal setting he created for his artistes.'

The European newspapers expressed the general feeling of the end of an era: 'The puppet-master is gone; the puppets must be returned to their boxes'; and, later, 'Former Diaghilev dancers booked to appear in reviews and cabaret turns.'

At the time of Diaghilev's death the standard contract for the company at Monte Carlo remained open. It was taken over by the cultured head of dramatic theatre at Monte Carlo, Rene Blum, who booked in various ballet groups. Two years later he created his own Ballets Russes de Monte Carlo and asked Balenchine, who had worked for Diaghilev, to be choreographer.

Meanwhile, in England, a collection of people including Maynard Keynes and his wife, the ballerina Lydia Lopokova, Ninette de Valois, Marie Rambert, Constant Lambert and Arnold Haskell, formed the Carmago Society. This gave ballet performances on Sunday nights and eventually led to the formation of Marie Rambert's Ballet Club, the founding society of British ballet. In 1931 Ninette de Valois joined with Lilian Baylis of the Old Vic to form the Vic-Wells ballet, the national ballet of Britain. Meanwhile, from 1929, Serge Lifar directed the Paris Opera ballet.

Some 20 years after Diaghilev's death, the choreographer Balanchine wrote that contemporary choreographers were only just realising the enormous artistic debt they owed to him. He had the gift of not only seeing the potentialities of choreographers, composers, designers and dancers, but also what work, style and period best suited them best.

There has always been awareness of Diaghilev's legacy, of what was owed to him technically, of his vision in bringing the Russian ballet to Europe. He was the magnet that attracted the top talent – composers like Stravinsky, dancers like Nijinsky, painters like Picasso and choreographers like Fokine and Balanchine – and Diaghilev, the empire builder, had the talent to weave them all together, to fuse the arts. He brought about the renaissance of ballet for the generations who came after him.

His personal involvement with his own company was irreplaceable and his death made its members aware of their deep sense of loss. It was expressed by the ballerina Lydia Sokolova who, on hearing of his death, said: 'As the awful truth sank into my consciousness, my knees gave way and I lay on the sand, burying my face in my hands.'

Diaghilev had always called the company 'his children.' They now truly felt that they had lost their father.

Notes

1   The Boy from Perm

1. Alexandre Benois, *Memoirs*, vol 2, translated by Moura Budberg (Chatto & Windus, 1964), p.162
2. Serge Lifar, *Serge Diaghilev* (London: Putnam, 1940), p.29
3. Arnold Haskell, in collaboration with Walter Nouvel, *Diaghileff: His Artistic & Private Life* (London: Victor Gollancz, 1955), p.72
4. Victor Borovsky, *Chaliapin* (London: Hamish Hamilton, 1988) p.127
5. Cyril Beaumont, *The Diaghilev Ballet in London* (London: Putnam, 1940), p.231
6. Nicolas Nabokov, *Old Friends and New Music* (London: Hamish Hamilton, 1951), p.53
7. Bronislava Nijinska, *Early Memoirs*, translated and edited by Irina Nijinska and Jean Rawlinson (New York: Holt, Rinehart and Winston, 1981), p.253
8. Matthew Sturgis, *Aubrey Beardsley* (London: HarperCollins, 1998), p.358
9. Lynn Garafola and Nancy Van Norman Baer (eds), *The Ballets Russes and Its World* (London: Yale University Press, 1999), pp.51–52
10. Benois (vol 2), p.82–83
11. Prince Peter Lieven, *The Birth of Ballet-Russes* (Allen & Unwin, 1936), p.33
12. Haskell, p.87
13. Benois (vol 2), p.159

14. Lieven, p.38
15. Orlando Figes, *Natasha's Dance: a cultural history of Russia* (London: Allen Lane, 2002), p.269
16. Benois (vol 2), p.166
17. Rupert Hart-Davis (ed), *The Letters of Oscar Wilde* (London: Rupert Hart-Davis, 1962), p.734
18. Haskell, p.119

2 Gentlemen's Mischief

1. Dan Healey, 'Masculine Purity and "Gentlemen's Mischief": sexual exchange and prostitution between Russian men 1861–1941' (*Slavic Review*, vol 60, No.2, Summer 2001), p.234
2. Healey, p.247
3. Simon Karlinsky, *The Sexual Labyrinth of Nicolai Gogol* (London: Harvard University Press, 1976), p.275
4. Karlinsky, p.279
5. Neil Miller, *Out of the Past* (London: Vintage Books, 1995), p.199
6. Leo Lerman: *The Grand Surprise: the Journals of Leo* Lerman (New York: Alfred A. Knopf, 2007), p.52
7. Lerman, p.52
8. Haskell, p.138
9. Benois, vol 2, p.205
10. Haskell, p.72
11. Miller, p.86
12. Shari Benstock, *Women of the Left Bank* (London: Virago, 1986), p.47
13. Francis Steegmuller, *Cocteau* (Boston: Little, Brown, 1970), p.23
14. Martha Hanna, 'Natalism, Homosexuality, and the Controversy over *Corydon*' in (eds) Jeffrey Merrick and Bryant T. Ragan, *Homosexuality in Modern France* (London: Oxford University Press, 1996), p.203
15. Colette, *Earthly Paradise* (London: Penguin, 1974), p.302
16. Steegmuller, p.34
17. Merrick and Ragan (eds), p.203
18. John Drummond, *Speaking of Diaghilev* (faber and faber, 1997) p.300

3 'Tactless but Talented'

1. Haskell, p.137

2. Coryne Hall, *Imperial Dancer: Matilde Kschessingska and the Romanovs* (London: Sutton Publishing, 2005), p.64

3. Tamara Karsavina, *Theatre Street* (London: Heinemann, 1930), p.224

4. Haskell, p.121

5. Haskell, p.125

6. Karsavina, p.157

7. W.A. Propert, *The Russian Ballet 1921–1929* (London: John Lane The Bodley Head, 1931), p.ix

8. Anthony Parton, *Mikhail Larionov* (New Jersey: Princeton University Press, 1993), p.4

9. Karsavina, p.157

10. *Petersburg Gazette*, 1 January 1904

11. Fredrika Blair, *Isadora* (London: Thorsons, 1987), p.116

12. Ellen Terry, *The Russian Ballet* (London: Sidgwick, 1913), p.14

13. Nabokov, p.95

14. Nabokov, p.94

15. Garafola, p.69

4   Goodbye to St Petersburg

1. W.A. Propert, *The Russian Ballet in Western Europe, 1909–1920* (London: John Lane The Bodley Head, 1921), p.12

2. Katherine Wright (ed) *Chaliapin: Pages From My Life,* vol 1 (New York: Harpers, 1927), p.174

3. Denis Babley, *The Theatre of Edward Gordon Craig* (London: Eyre Methuen, 1981), p.94

4. Benois, *Reminiscences*, p.287

5. Alexandre Benois, *Reminiscences of Diaghilev* in collection 'Serge Diaghilev and Russian Art', vol 2 (Moscow, 1982), p.243

6. Colette, p.309

7. Arthur Gold and Robert Fizdale, *Misia* (London: Papermac, 1982), p.130

8. Serge Lifar, *Serge Diaghilev* (London: Putnam, 1940), p.175

9. Gold and Fizdale, *Misia*, p. 132

10. Lifar, *Diaghilev*, p.177

11. Igor Stravinsky, *Chronicle of My Life* (London: Gollancz, 1936), p.251

12. Vitale Fokine (trans) *Fokine: Memoirs of a Ballet Master* (Toronto: Little, Brown, 1961), p.138

13. Garafola, p.213

14. Fokine, p.149
15. Cyril Beaumont, *The Diaghilev Ballet in London* (London: Putnam, 1940), p.238
16. S.L. Grigoriev, *The Diaghilev Ballet 1909–1929* (London: Penguin, 1960), p.15
17. Beaumont, pp.238–9
18. Edmonde Charles-Roux, *Chanel* (London: Jonathan Cape, 1976), p.232
19. Figes, p.275

5   Soaring Talent

1. Alexandre Benois, *Reminiscences of the Russian Ballet* (London: Putnam, 1941), p.167
2. I.S. Silberstein and A.N. Savinov, *Alexander Benois Reflects* (Moscow, 1968), p.501
3. Propert, 1909–1929, p.4
4. Wallace Fowlie (ed), *The Journals of Jean Cocteau* (Museum Press, 1957), p.218
5. Fowlie, p.55
6. Charles Castle, *Folies Bergere* (London: Methuen, 1982), p.76
7. Castle, p.76
8. Karsavina, p.238
9. Karsavina, p.235
10. Ellen Terry, p.21
11. Ethel Mannin, *Confessions and Impressions* (London: Jarrolds, 1930), p.255
12. Fitzroy Maclean, *Holy Russia* (London: Weidenfeld and Nicolson, 1978), p.205
13. Lynn Garafola and Nancy Van Norman Baer (eds), *The Ballets Russes and Its World* (London: Yale University Pres, 1999), p.5
14. Haskell, p.70
15. Haskell, p.90
16. Karsavina, p.177
17. Lydia Sokolova, *Dancing for Diaghilev* (London: Columbus Bjooks, 1989), p.38
18. Fowlie, p.53
19. Nijinska, p.375
20. Stephen Walsh, *Igor Stravinsky* (Jonathan Cape, 2000), p.127

21. Serge Lifar, *Ma Vie* (London: Hutchinson, 1970), p.30

6   Splashing all Paris with Colours

1. Lieven, p.125
2. Nijinska, p.294
3. Walsh, p.138
4. Nijinska, p.318
5. Michael Powell, *A Life in Movies* (Faber and Faber, 1986), p.97
6. Steegmuller, p.84
7. Miranda Seymour, *Ottoline Morrell* (London: Hodder & Stoughton, 1992), p.137
8. Karsavina, p.259

7   London: 'Exciting to be Alive'

1. Robert Skidelsky, *John Maynard Keynes*, vol 1 (London: Macmillan, 1983), p.251
2. Virginia Nicholson, *Among the Bohemians* (London: Penguin, 2003), p.226
3. E.F. Benson, *As We Were* (London: Longman, 1971), p.180
4. Benson, p.181
5. Benson, p.183
6. Neil Tierney, *The Unknown Country: A Life of Igor Stravinsky* (London: Robert Hale, 1977), p.39
7. Beaumont, p.232
8. Ellen Terry, p.32
9. Daphne Fielding, *Esmerald and Nancy: Lady Cunard and Her Daughter* (London: Eyre & Spottiswoode, 1968), p.42
10. Sir Thomas Beecham, *A Mingled Chime: Leaves From an Autobiography* (London: Hutchinson, 1944), p.198
11. Nijinska, p.347
12. Nijinska, p.393

8   Crash Crash Cling Clang Bing Bang Bing

1. Count Harry Kessler, *The Diaries of a Cosmopolitan, 1918–1937* (London: Weidenfeld & Nicolson, 1971), p.202
2. Nijinska, p.456

3. Grigoriev, p.76

4. Fokine, p.203

5. Steegmuller, p.77

6. Richard Buckle, *Nijinsky* (London: Phoenix, 1998), p.284

7. *Le Figaro*, 30 May 1912

8. Walsh, p.243

9. Richard Buckle, *Diaghilev* (London: Weidenfeld and Nicolson), p.300

10. Seymour, p.165

11. Robert Gaythorne-Hardy (ed), *Ottoline* (Faber and Faber, 1963), p.227

12. Buckle, *Nijinsky*, p.302

13. Harold Acton, *Memoirs of an Aesthete* (London: Methuen, 1948), p.129

14. Blanche, p.258

15. Buckle, *Nijinsky*, p.307

16. Marie Rambert, *Quicksilver* (London: Macmillan, 1972), pp.58–59

17. James Gardiner, *Gaby Deslys* (London: Sidgwick and Jackson, 1986), p. 78

18. Sokolova, p.19

19. Maxim Gorky, *Chaliapin* (London: Hamish Hamilton, 1988), p.102

20. Victor Borovsky, *Chaliapin* (London: Hamish Hamilton, 1988), p.68

21. Sergey Prokofiev, *Sergey Prokofiev Diaries*, trans: Anthony Philips (London: Faber and Faber, 2006) p.428

22. Chanel, p.126

23. Gertrude Stein, *Autobiography of Alice B. Toklas* (London: John Lane The Bodley Head, 1933), p.149

24. Jacques-Emile Blanche, *Portraits of a Lifetime* (London: J.M. Dent, 1937), p.259

25. Walsh, p.204

26. Laird McLeod Easton, *The Red Count: The Life and Times of Harry Kessler* (California: University of Californian Press, 2002), p.207

9   Nijinsky's 'Treachery'

1. Propert, 1909–1929, p.31

2. *The Times*, 12 July 1913

3. *The Morning Post*, 12 July 1913

4. Sokolova, p.47

5. Alan Jefferson, *Sir Thomas Beecham* (London: Macdonald and Janes, 1979), p.128

6. Carol Rosen, *The Goossens* (London: Andre Deutsch, 1993), p.41

7. Count Harry Kessler, p.207
8. Romola Nijinsky, *Nijinsky* (London: Gollancz, 1933), pp.191–192
9. Sokolova, p.49
10. Sokolova, p.49
11. Romola Nijinsky, p.202
12. Gold and Fizdale, p.160
13. Gold and Fizdale, p.160
14. Walsh, p.220
15. Count Harry Kessler, p.208
16. Grigoriev, p.100
17. Mss, Musee de l'Opera
18. Romola Nijinsky, *Nijinsky*, p.210
19. Seymour, p.189
20. Nijinska, p.489
21. Anthony Parton, *Mikhail Larionov* (New Jersey: Princeton University Press, 1993), p.74
22. Parton, p.4
23. Skidelsky, p.284
24. Gold and Fizdale, p.161
25. Grigoriev, p.105
26. Grigoriev, p.106
27. Powell, p.642
28. Leonide Massine, *My Life in Ballet* (London: Macmilan, 1968), p.48
29. Benois, *Reminiscences*, p.378
30. Propert, 1909–1929, p.39
31. Beecham, p.120–121
32. Prokofiev, p.585
33. Prokofiev, p.705

10 America to the Rescue

1. Acton, p.37
2. Colette, p.242
3. Sylvester, p.27
4. Mss Musee de l'Opera
5. Beaumont, p.133
6. Walsh, p.244
7. Nabokov, p.68
8. Colette, pp.243–244

9. Garafola, pp.261–262
10. Grigoriev, p.116
11. Lieven, pp.354–354
12. Charles Chaplin, *My Autobiography* (London: The Bodley Head, 1964), p.205
13. Chaplin, p207
14. Steegmuller, p.180
15. Walsh, p.268
16. Acton, p.57
17. William Wiser, *The Crazy Years: Paris in the Twenties* (London: Thames and Hudson, 1990), p. 83
18. Arthur Rubinstein, *My Many Years* (London: Jonathan Cape, 1980), p.104
19. Patrick O'Brian, *Picasso* (London: HarperCollins, 2000), p.218
20. Jean-Paul Crespelle, *Picasso and His Women* (London: Hodder and Stoughton, 1969), p.118
21. O'Brian, p.219
22. Steegmuller, p.177
23. John Richardson, *A Life of Picasso: The Triumphant Years, 1917–1932* (London: Jonathan Cape, 2007), p.15
24. Richardson, p.67
25. Richardson, p.68
26. Wiser, p.139
27. O'Brian, p.225

11   Nijinsky: the Final Split

1. Walsh, p.241
2. Osbert Sitwell, *Laughter in the Next Room*, vol 4 of *Left Hand, Right Hand* (London: Macmillan, 1949), p.110
3. Massine, p.123
4. Count Harry Kessler, p.273
5. Crespelle, p.12
6. Wendy Baron, *Miss Ethel Sands and Her Circle* (London: Peter Owen, 1977), p.154
7. Sitwell, p.16
8. Beaumont, p.113
9. Seymour, p.300
10. Sitwell, p.18

11. Sitwell, pp.21–22
12. Sitwell, p.23
13. Vera Brittain, *Testament of Youth* (London: Fontana/Virago, 1979), p.462

12 Picking Up the Pieces

1. Leonard Woolf, *An Autobiography:2 1911–1969* (London: Oxford University Press, 1980), p.191
2. Brittain, p.469
3. Walsh, p.292
4. Sitwell, p.145
5. Sitwell, p.144
6. Royal School of Ballet scrapbooks
7. Noel Riley Fitch, *Sylvia Beach and the Lost Generation* (London: Souvenir Press, 1984), p.42
8. Steegmuller, p.237

13 The Lord of the Dance Brought Down

1. Romola Nijinsky, *Nijinsky*
2. Buckle, *Nijinsky*, p.499
3. Buckle, *Nijinsky*, p.503
4. Count Harry Kessler, *The Diaries of a Cosmopolitan* (London: Weidenfeld and Nicolson), p.355
5. Karsavina, p.295

14 The Vogue for Vogue

1. Taper, p.95
2. Acton, p.86
3. Jonathan Croall, *Gielgud* (London: Methuen, 2000), p.22
4. Massine, p.133
5. Massine, p.132–133
6. Propert, 1909–1929, p.52
7. Clive Bell, *Old Friends* (London: Chatto & Windus, 1956), pp.187–188
8. Charles Ricketts, *Self-Portrait* (London: Peter Davies, 1939), p.301
9. Walsh, p.302
10. Seymour, p.301

11. Royal School of Ballet scrapbooks
12. Crespelle, p.241
13. Grigoriev, p.165
14. Sokolova, p.156
15. Chanel, p.228

15 Exit Leonide Massine

1. Propert, 1921–29, p.1
2. Richardson, p.8
3. John Drummond, *Speaking of Diaghilev* (faber and faber, 1997), p.71
4. Drummond, p.300
5. Julie Kavanagh, *Secret Muses: the life of Frederick Ashton* (New York: Pantheon Books, 1996), p.217
6. Walsh, p.326
7. Drummond, p.27
8. Drummond, p.75
9. Charles Cochran, *The Secrets of a Showman* (London: Heinemann, 1925), p.367
10. Larionov, p.186
11. John Gielgud, *Backward Glances* (London: Hodder and Stoughton, 1989), p.202
12. Ninette de Valois, *Come Dance with Me* (London: Hamish Hamilton, 1957), p.48

16 Paris In the Twenties

1. Fitch, p.59
2. Ronald Hayman, *Proust* (London: Heinemann, 1990), p.483
3. Richard Davenport-Hines, *A Night at the Majestic: Proust and the Great Modernist Dinner Party of 1922* (London: faber and faber, 2006), p.6
4. Davenport-Hines, p.13
5. *The Times*, 8 May 1922
6. Richardson, p.204
7. Kendall Taylor, *Sometimes Madness is Wisdom: Zelda and Scott Fitzgerald* (New York: Ballantine Books, 2001), p.101
8. Taylor, p.201
9. Garafola, p. 261

10. Wiser, p.154
11. Billy Kluver and Julie Martin, *Ki Ki's Paris: Artists and Lovers 1910–1930* (New York: Harry N. Abrams, 1989), p.134
12. *The Observer*, January 29, 1922
13. *The Observer*, January 29, 1922
14. O'Brian, p.264

17 Enter Serge Lifar

1. Serge Lifar, *Serge Diaghilev* (London: Putnam, 1940), p.258
2. Serge Lifar, *Ma Vie* (London: Hutchinson, 1970), p.33
3. Beaumont, p.289
4. Cyril Connolly, 'A Tyrant of Taste' in *The Condemned Playground* (London: Routledge, 1945), p.223
5. Drummond, p.75
6. Lifar, pp.122–123
7. Sidney Buckland (ed), Francis Poulenc: *Selected Correspondence, 1915–1963* (London: Gollancz, 1991), p.302
8. Easton, p.273
9. Buckland, p.80
10. Buckland, p.60
11. Kavanagh, p.62
12. Kavanagh, p.76
13. Haskell, p.27
14. Alex Danchev, *Georges Braque* (London: Hamish Hamilton, 2006), p.161
15. Sokolova, p.219
16. Drummond, p.46
17. Chanel, p.231
18. Garafola, pp. 266–267
19. Chanel, p.229
20. Boris Kochno, *Diaghilev and the Ballets Russes* (London: Allen Lane the Penguin Press, 1971), p.216
21. Kavanagh, p.307
22. Nabokov, p.147
23. Lifar, p.36
24. Borovosky, p.26
25. Lifar, p.49
26. Lifar, p.41

27. Drummond, p.62

18   New Passions for Old

1. Rosen, p.113
2. Grigoriev, p.214
3. Mss, Centre for Performing Arts, Lincoln Centre, New York
4. Lifar, p.49
5. Sokolova, p.246
6. Beaumont, p.255
7. Propert, 1921–1929, p.38
8. Propert, 1921–1929, p.42
9. Mss, Centre for Performing Arts, Lincoln Centre, New York
10. Hugo Vickers, *Cecil Beaton* (London: Weidenfeld and Nicolson, 1985), pp.75–76
11. Sarah Bradford, *Sacheverell Sitwell: Splendours and Miseries* (London: Sinclair Stevenson, 1993), p.162
12. Grigoriev, p.240
13. Propert, 1921–1929, pp.56–57
14. Beaumont, p.274
15. Janet Flanner, *Paris was Yesterday: 1925–1939* (London: Angus and Robertson, 1973), pp.55–56
16. Grigoriev, p.246

19   The Shadow of Diabetes

1. Taper, p.100
2. Nabokov, p.157
3. Nabokov, p.158
4. Nabokov, p.158
5. Serge Lifar, *Diaghilev*, p.474
6. Lifar, *Diaghilev*, p.479
7. Lifar, *Diaghilev*, p.509
8. Sokolova, pp.278–279
9. Nabokov, p.159

20   'I Shall Not See You Again'

1. Mss, Centre for Performing Arts, Lincoln Centre, New York

2. *The Observer*, 30 June 1929

3. Mss, Centre for Performing Arts, Lincoln Centre, New York

4. Dolin, p.205

5. Karsavina, p.352

6. Acton, pp.221–222

7. Beaumont, p.296

8. Taper, p.110

9. Grigoriev, p.264

10. Taper, p.109

11. Drummond, p.283

12. Drummond, p.283

13. Buckle, *Diaghilev*, p.538

14. Gold and Fizdale, p.261

15. Chanel, p.261

16. Nabokov, p.160

Bibliography

Acton, Harold, *Memoirs of an Aesthete* (London: Methuen, 1948)

Babley, Denis, *The Theatre of Edward Gordon Craig* (London: Eyre Methuen, 1981)

Baron, Wendy, *Miss Ethel Sands and Her Circle* (London: Peter Owen, 1977)

Beaumont, Cyril W., *The Diaghilev Ballet in London* (London: Putnam, 1940)

Beecham, Thomas, *A Mingled Chime: Leaves from an Autobiography* (London: Hutchinson, 1944)

Bell, Clive, *Old Friends* (London: Chatto & Windus, 1956)

Benois, Alexandre, *Memoirs*, vol 2, trans Moura Budberg (London: Chatto & Windus, 1964)

Benois, Alexandre, *Reminiscences of the Russian Ballet*, trans by Mary Britnieva (London: Putnam, 1942)

Benson, E.F., *As We Were* (London: Longman, 1971)

Benstock, Shari, *Women of the Left Bank* (London: Virago, 1986)

Blair, Fredrika, *Isadora* (London: Thorsons, 1987)

Blanche, Jacques-Emile, *Portraits of a Lifetime* (London: J.M. Dent, 1937)

Borovsky, Victor, *Chaliapin* (London: Hamish Hamilton, 1988)

Bradford, Sarah, *Sacheverell Sitwell: Splendours and Miseries* (London: Sinclair-Stevenson, 1993)

Brittain, Vera, *Testament of Youth* (London: Fontana/Virago, 1979)

Buckland, Sidney (ed), *Francis Poulenc: Selected Correspondence 1915–1963* (London: Gollancz, 1991)

Buckle, Richard, *Diaghilev* (London: Weidenfeld and Nicolson, 1979)

Buckle, Richard, *Nijinsky* (London: Phoenix, 1998)

Castle, Charles, *Folies Bergere* (London: Methuen, 1982)

Chaplin, Charles, *My Autobiography* (London: The Bodley Head, 1964)

Charles-Roux, Edmonde, *Chanel* (London: Jonathan Cape, 1976)

Cochran, Charles, *The Secrets of a Showman* (London: Heinemann, 1925)

Colette, *Earthly Paradise* (London: Penguin, 1974)

Connolly, Cyril, *The Condemned Playground* (London: Routledge, 1945)

Crespelle, Jean-Paul, *Picasso and His Women*, trans Robert Baldick (London: Hodder and Stoughton, 1969)

Croall, Jonathan, *Gielgud* (London: Methuen, 2000)

Danchev, Alex, *Georges Braque* (London: Hamish Hamilton, 2006)

Davenport-Hines, Richard, *A Night at the Majestic: Proust and the Great Modernist Dinner Party of 1922* (London, faber and faber, 2006)

Drummond, John, *Speaking of Diaghilev* (London: faber and faber, 1997)

De Valois, Ninette, *Come Dance with Me* (London: Hamish Hamilton, 1957)

Easton, Laird McLeod, *The Life and Times of Harry Kessler* (California: University of California Press, 2002)

Fielding, Daphne, *Esmerald and Nancy: Lady Cunard and Her Daughter* (London: Eyre and Spottiswoode, 1968)

Figes, Orlando, *Natasha's Dance: a cultural history of Russia* (London: Allen Lane, 2002)

Fitch, Noel Riley, *Sylvia Beach and the Lost Generation* (London: Souvenir Press, 1984)

Flanner, Janet, *Paris Was Yesterday 1925–1939* (London: Angus and Robertson, 1973)

Fokine, Vitale (trans), *Fokine: Memoirs of a Ballet Master* (Toronto: Little, Brown, 1961)

Fowlie, Wallace (ed) *The Journals of Jean Cocteau* (Museum Press, 1957)

Garafola, Lynn and Baer, Nancy Van Norman (eds), *The Ballets Russes and Its World* (London: Yale University Press, 1999)

Gardiner, James, *Gaby Deslys* (London: Sidgwick and Jackson, 1986)

Gaythorne-Hardy, Robert (ed), *Ottoline* (London: faber and faber, 1963)

Gielgud, John, *Backward Glances* (London: Hodder and Stoughton, 1989)

Gold, Arthur and Fizdale, Robert, *Misia: The Life of Misia Sert* (London: Papermac, 1980)

Gorky, Maxim, *Chaliapin* (London: Hamish Hamilton, 1988)

Grigoriev, S.L., *The Diaghilev Ballet 1909–1929* (London: Penguin, 1960)

Hall, Coryne, *Imperial Dancer* (London: Sutton, 2005)

Hart-Davis, Rupert (ed), *The Letters of Oscar Wilde* (London: Rupert Hart-Davis, 1962)

Haskell, Arnold, *Diaghileff: His Artistic and Private Life* (London: Gollancz, 1935)

Hayman, Ronald, *Proust* (London: Heinemann, 1990)

Jefferson, Alan, *Sir Thomas Beecham* (London: Macdonald and Janes, 1979)

Karlinsky, Simon, *The Sexual Labyrinth of Nicolai Gogol* (London: Harvard University Press, 1976)

Karsavina, Tamara, *Theatre Street* (London: Heinemann, 1930)

Kavanagh, Julie, *Secret Muses: The Life of Frederick Ashton* (London: Random House, 1996)

Kessler, Count Harry, *The Diaries of a Cosmopolitan, 1918–1937* (London: Weidenfeld and Nicolson, 1971)

Kluver, Billy and Martin, Julie, *Ki Ki's Paris: Artists and Lovers 1910–1930* (New York: Harry N. Abrams, 1989)

Kochno, Boris (trans: Adrienne Foulke), *Diaghilev and the Ballets Russes* (London: Allen Lane, 1971)

Lerman, Leo, *The Grand Surprise: the Journals of Leo Lerman* (New York: Alfred A.Knopf, 2007)

Lieven, Prince Peter, *The Birth of Ballets Russes* (London: Allen & Unwin, 1936)

Lifar, Serge, *Ma Vie from Kiev to Kiev*, trans James Holman Mason (London: Hutchinson, 1976)

Lifar, Serge, *Serge Diaghilev* (London: Putnam, 1940)

Maclean, Fitzroy, *Holy Russia* (London: Weidenfeld and Nicolson, 1978)

Mannin Ethel, *Confessions and Impressions* (London: Jarrolds, 1930)

Massine, Leonide, *My Life in Ballet* (London: Macmillan, 1968)

Merrick, Jeffrey and Ragan, Bryant T., *Homosexuality in Modern France* (London: Oxford University Pess, 1996)

Miller, Neil, *Out of the Past* (London: Vintage Books, 1995)

Nabokov, Nicolas, *Old Friends and New Music* (London: Hamish Hamilton, 1951)

Nicholson, Virginia, *Among the Bohemians* (London: Penguin Books, 2003)

Nijinska, Bronislava, *Early Memoirs*, ed and trans by Irina Nijinska and Jean Rawlinson (New York: Holt, Rinehart and Winston, 1981)

Nijinsky, Romola, *Nijinsky* (London: Gollancz, 1933)

O'Brian, Patrick, *Picasso* (London: HarperCollins, 2003)

Parton, Anthony, *Mikhail Larionov* (New Jersey: Princeton University Press, 1993)

Powell, Michael, *A Life in Movies* (faber and faber, 1986)

Prokofiev, Sergey, trans Anthony Philips, *Sergey Prokofiev Diaries* (faber and faber, 2006)

Propert, W.A., *The Russian Ballet, 1921–1929* (London: John Lane The Bodley Head, 1931)

Propert, W.A., *The Russian Ballet in Western Europe, 1909–1920* (London: John Lane The Bodley Head, 1921)

Rambert, *Quicksilver* (London: Macmillan, 1972)

Richardson, John, *A Life of Picasso: The Triumphant Years, 1917–1932* (London: Jonathan Cape, 2007)

Ricketts, Charles, *Self-Portrait* (London: Peter Davies, 1939)

Rosen, Carol, *The Goossens* (London: Andre Deutsch, 1993)

Rubinstein, *My Many Years* (London: Jonathan Cape, 1980)

Seymour, Miranda, *Ottoline Morrell* (London: Hodder and Stoughton, 1992)

Silberstein, I.S. and Savinov, A.N., *Alexander Benois Reflects* (Moscow, 1968)

Sitwell, Osbert, *Laughter in the Next Room*, vol 4 of *Left Hand, Right Hand* (London: Macmillan, 1949)

Skidelsky, Robert, *John Maynard Keynes vol 1: Hopes Betrayed 1883–1920* (London: Macmillan, 1983)

Sokolova, Lydia, *Dancing for Diaghilev* (London: Columbus Books, 1989)

Steegmuller, Francis, *Cocteau* (Boston: Atlantic Monthly/Little Brown, 1970)

Stein, Gertrude, *Autobiography of Alice B. Toklas* (London: John Lane The Bodley Head, 1933)

Stravinsky, Igor, *Chronicle of My Life* (London: Gollancz, 1936)

Sturgis, Matthew, *Aubrey Beardsley* (London: HarperCollins, 1998)

Sylvester, David, *London Recordings* (Chatto and Windus, 2003)

Taper, Bernard, *Balanchine* (London: Collins, 1964)

Taylor, Kendall, *Sometimes Madness is Wisdom: Zelda and Scott Fitzgerald* (New York: Ballantine, 2001)

Terry, Ellen, *The Russian Ballet* (London: Sidgwick, 1913)

Tierney, Neil, *The Unknown Country: A Life of Igor Stravinsky* (London: Robert Hale, 1977)

Vickers, Hugo, *Cecil Beaton* (London: Weidenfeld and Nicolson, 1985)

Walsh, Stephen, *Igor Stravinsky* (London: Jonathan Cape, 2000)

Wiser, William, *The Crazy Years: Paris in the Twenties* (London: Thames and Hudson, 1990)

Woolf, Leonard, *An Autobiography:2 1911–1969* (London: Oxford Universitry Press, 1980)

Wright, Katherine (ed), *Chaliapin: Pages From My Life* (New York: Harpers, 1927)

Picture Sources

The author and publishers wish to express their thanks to the following sources of illustrative material and /or permission to reproduce it. Acknowledgements will be made in future editions in the event that any omissions have been made.

akg-images London, Getty Images, The Harvard Theatre Collection, The National Portrait Gallery, The Lebrecht Photo Library, Topham Picturepoint, RAI Novosti, Roger Viollet,

Acknowledgements

So many people helped me with their time and advice that I am unable to list them all individually, but I am particularly grateful to Anna Meadmore at the Royal Ballet School and Stephen Walsh. Above all my thanks go to Sally Juniper for her invaluable help with research.

I would like to thank the following publishers for permission to reprint from their publications: The Random House Group for permission to reprint from Stephen Walsh, *Igor Stravinsky*, Jonathan Cape, 2000; and Andre Benois, *Memoirs*, vol 2, translated by Moura Budberg, Chatto and Windus, 1964; and John Richardson, *A life of Picasso: the triumphant years 1917–1932*, Jonathan Cape 2008; to Pan Macmillan for *Misia* by Arthur Gold and Robert Fizdale, Papermac, 1980; to David Higham Associates for *Theatre Street* by Tamara Karsavina, Heinemann, 1931; to Yale University Press for the *Ballets Russes and its World* edited by Lynn Garafola and Nancy Van Norman Baer, 1999; to Orion Publishing Group for *Nijinsky* by Richard Buckle, Weidenfeld and Nicholson, 1979 and for *Diaghilev: His Artistic and Private life* by Arnold Haskell, Victor Gollancz, 1935; to Harper Collins for Patrick O'Brian, *Picasso*, 2003; to Faber and Faber for *Speaking of Diaghilev* by John Drummond, 1997.

I am also indebted to the following organisations: The Victoria and Albert Theatre Collections; The New York Public Library (Performing Arts Center); The London Library; Senate House Library; British Library; The Harvard Theatre Collection; The Wellcome Library; and The Ellen Terry Memorial Museum.

Index

38, 49, 63; and Paris exhibition, 48; and Ballets Russes, 67, 70, 77, 81, 85, 87, 89, 99, 102, 107, 111, 115, 146, 165; paints Nijinsky, 79; and *The Firebird*, 81, 89; and outbreak of war, 142; appearance and manner, 151; and *La Boutique Fantasque*, 181–2; and *Sleeping Princess*, 195–6; illness and death, 199, 205

Balanchine, George, 32, 180, 224–5, 233, 236, 240, 249, 254

Balfour, A.J., 42

ballet costume, 6, 43, 146

Ballets Russes: foundation, 6, 57–64; and homosexuality, 30, 33; and Diaghilev's name, 65; Paris debut, 65–70; and art, 68; budget, 69, 78–9; and star system, 70, 150; and male dancers, 73, 150; becomes permanent company, 90; London debut, 95–6, 98–9; intellectual origins, 109; and outbreak of war, 140; impact in America, 145–50; celebrates thousandth performance, 169; post-war popularity, 172–3, 180–1; and modernism, 180; role of women, 215; twenty-first season, 246; ending of, 253–4

Ballets Russes de Monte Carlo, 254

Barcelona, 156, 160–3, 178, 224–5

Barnes, Djuna, 207

bath-houses, 22

Battleship Potemkin, 46

Baylis, Lilian, 254

Beach, Sylvia, 200–1, 207

Beardsley, Aubrey, 12, 15, 20, 43, 119

Beaton, Cecil, 212, 232

Beaumont, Cyril, 8, 98, 110, 113, 142, 165, 211, 229, 235, 241, 248

Beecham, Sir Joseph, 101, 121

Beecham, Thomas, 101, 121, 123, 133, 240

Beethoven, Ludwig van, 104, 202

Beggarstaff Brothers, 226

Belfast, 14, 174

Belgium, 210

Bell, Clive, 137, 167, 172, 182

Bell, Vanessa, 30

Benois, Alexandre, 36, 45–6, 48–53, 55, 123, 132, 236, 246; and St Petersburg circle, 1–2, 4–6, 11, 13–17, 32; and Vassili Zulkov, 20; and St Petersburg theatres, 34, 38, 60; and Diaghilev's fear of illness, 49–50, 202; and Ballets Russes, 65, 67, 77, 83–5, 87, 90–2; and *The Firebird*, 83; parting with Diaghilev, 109, 111, 134; and Bolshevik revolution, 152; criticism of Diaghilev, 218; and Rubinstein, 241

Benois, Camille, 2

Benois, Nikolai, 2

Benson, E.F., 95

Berlin, 4, 20, 32, 103, 105, 112, 120, 136, 138, 227

Berners, Lord, 232

Bernhardt, Sarah, 12, 30

Biarritz, 164

Birie, Charles, 14

Birmingham, 189, 240

Blanche, Jacques-Emile, 12, 39, 110–11

210, 212–13, 216–17, 228, 244;
and split with Diaghilev, 123,
127; and Nijinsky's illness, 178;
rejoins Ballets Russes, 195; and
'new modernism', 212; marriage,
222; leaves Ballets Russes,
223–4; and Rubinstein, 241,
244

Nijinska, Kyra, 244

Nijinsky, Romola, 105, 112, 121, 140,
147, 160–1; marriage, 123–7;
and Nijinsky's illness, 161,
174–8

Nijinsky, Vaslav, vi, 11, 39, 145, 221,
254; and Diaghilev, 30, 33, 52,
74–5, 78, 84, 111; ballet debut,
51–2; and Ballets Russes, 65,
67, 70, 72–5, 77, 87, 89–91, 93,
99; appearance and manner,
75, 122; contracts typhoid,
77–8; and Isadora Duncan,
79; breach of etiquette, 89–90;
and military service, 102; and
choreography, 103, 105, 107,
112–13, 115, 117–19, 123, 138,
188; and Romola de Pulszky,
104–5, 112, 121, 123–7; sits
for Rodin, 109; and Strachey,
109–10; row with Karsavina,
115; and Little Tich, 122–3;
split with Diaghilev, 123–7;
marriage, 123–7; dismissed
from Ballets Russes, 125–6, 130;
and outbreak of war, 140, 143;
and American tour, 143, 145,
147–50, 160; lack of empathy,
147–8; last appearances, 160–2;
mental illness and death, 161,
174–9

Nikitina, Alice, 229, 235, 239, 245
Nikolai Mikhailovich, Grand
Duke, 44–5
Normandy, 111
Norway, 141
Nourok, Alfred, 14, 16
Nouvel, Valechka (Walter), 4, 6, 11,
14–16, 38, 121, 192, 241, 243
Novgorod, 2
Novosti, 14
Noyes, Alfred, 169
Nutcracker, The, 6, 36, 224

O

Ode, 238–9, 241
Oedipus Rex, 233, 235
Ostend, 203, 232
Owen, Wilfred, 30, 172

P

Padua, 221
Paes, Sidonio, 162
Panaeva, Elena Valerionovna, 2
Pankhurst, Emmeline, 43
Parade, 153–9, 174, 181, 186, 190,
227
Paris: and Diaghilev's
European travels, 4, 20; and
homosexuality, 32; Russian
exhibition, 38; Russian art
exhibition, 46–9; Russian
operas in, 49, 52–3, 55;
Ballets Russes debut, 65–70;
reception of *L'Après-Midi*,
107, 109; reception of *Rite of
Spring*, 116–19; primitive art
exhibitions, 120; wartime,
138–40, 144, 153; reception
of *Parade*, 157–9; post-war,